STUDIES IN THE HISTORY
OF CHRISTIAN MISSIONS

R. E. Frykenberg
Brian Stanley
General Editors

STUDIES IN THE HISTORY
OF CHRISTIAN MISSIONS

Robert Eric Frykenberg

Christians and Missionaries in India:
Cross-Cultural Communication since 1500

Susan Billington Harper

In the Shadow of the Mahatma: Bishop V. S. Azariah
and the Travails of Christianity in British India

D. Dennis Hudson

Protestant Origins in India:
Tamil Evangelical Christians, 1706-1835

Jon Miller

Missionary Zeal and Institutional Control:
Organizational Contradictions in the Basel Mission
on the Gold Coast, 1828-1917

Brian Stanley, *Editor*

Christian Missions and the Enlightenment

Kevin Ward and Brian Stanley, *Editors*

The Church Mission Society and World Christianity, 1799-1999

Missionary Zeal
and
Institutional Control

*Organizational Contradictions
in the Basel Mission on the
Gold Coast, 1828-1917*

Jon Miller

WILLIAM B. EERDMANS PUBLISHING COMPANY
GRAND RAPIDS, MICHIGAN / CAMBRIDGE, U.K.

ROUTLEDGECURZON
LONDON

Published jointly 2003 by
Wm. B. Eerdmans Publishing Co.
255 Jefferson Ave. S.E., Grand Rapids, Michigan 49503 /
P.O. Box 163, Cambridge CB3 9PU U.K.
www.eerdmans.com
and by
RoutledgeCurzon
11 New Fetter Lane, London EC4P 4EE
RoutledgeCurzon is an imprint of the Taylor & Francis Group

Printed in the United States of America

07 06 05 04 03   7 6 5 4 3 2 1

Library of Congress Cataloging-in-Publication Data

Miller, Jon, 1940-
Missionary zeal and institutional control : organizational contradictions in
the Basel Mission on the Gold Coast, 1828-1917 / Jon Miller.
p.   cm. — (Studies in the history of Christian missions)
Rev. ed. of: The social control of religious zeal.
Includes bibliographical references (p.) and index.
ISBN 0-8028-6085-0 (pbk.)
1. Evangelische Missionsgesellschaft in Basel — History.
2. Missions, Swiss — Ghana — History. 3. Missions, German —
Ghana — History. 4. Ghana — Church history.   I. Miller, Jon, 1940-
Social control of religious zeal.   II. Title.   III. Series.
BV3625.G6 M55   2002
306.6′660234940667 — dc21

2002029659

British Library Cataloguing-in-Publication Data

A catalogue for this book is available fron the British Library.
RoutledgeCurzon ISBN 0-7007-1763-3

Contents

CONTENTS

Contents

Foreword

For a long time scholars tended to regard Christian missions merely as an epiphenomenon of European imperialism and missionaries as the unconscious agents of economic and class interests. In recent years this outlook has changed considerably, and mission topics now have become subjects for serious investigation in their own right. Included are such matters as the motivations of people for missionary service, the institutional development of mission agencies, the role of missionaries in the social and political development of the indigenous peoples among whom they worked, the impact of missions on the sending churches in the metropolitan countries, and the contribution of missions to the ecumenical and global consciousness of the Christian community. Mission themes are finding their way into the programs of scholarly conferences and the pages of scientific journals, and books and essay collections on the topic are listed in the catalogues of scholarly and trade presses alike.

Jon Miller's study is a welcome addition to this growing body of material. His work is of particular note because of its focus on a *Continental*, specifically German and Swiss, sending agency, the Evangelical Missionary Society at Basel, or as it is more commonly known, the Basel Mission. The overwhelming majority of the scholarly literature on missions focuses on British and North American enterprises; far less attention is paid to the activities of Europeans to carry the Christian faith to the distant parts of the world. This is especially the case with the story of Protestant missionary effort, partly because it began two centuries after the European-based Roman Catholic religious orders had set out to evangelize the world, and partly because most Protestant missionaries originated from English-speaking areas. However,

European Protestants did engage in mission work, albeit at a numerically lower level. Some missionaries came from the smaller countries, such as the Netherlands, Sweden, Denmark, and Norway, while others went out from places with a minority Protestant community, like the Paris Evangelical Missionary Society whose constituency was in France and the French-speaking Swiss cantons. However, the main source of Continental Protestant missionaries was the diverse collection of German-speaking entities in central Europe. This was not so noticeable at first because individual workers tended to identify more with particular states and regions than with Germany as a whole, and the situation changed only gradually after the formation of the German Empire in 1871.

Although there were some scattered individualized efforts earlier, it is generally accepted that the modern Protestant missionary movement began in the eighteenth century in Germany. August Hermann Francke and his remarkable charitable institution in Halle was one crucial factor. Schooled here was the first Protestant missionary to India, Bartholomäus Ziegenbalg, who went out in 1706, and during the course of the century over fifty others from Halle labored in the subcontinent, including such noteworthy figures as C. F. Schwartz, J. P. Fabricius, and John Z. Kiernander. Another contingent of Christian workers went to North America, beginning with Henry Melchior Muhlenberg in 1742. The other important element was the Moravian (Unitas Fratrum, or United Brethren) enterprise of Count Nikolaus von Zinzendorf in Saxony, which in 1732 dispatched its first missionaries to Greenland and the Danish West Indies. Their workers went to a variety of places during the course of the century, including the American colonies, Surinam, South Africa, and Estonia. By 1782 some 175 Moravian missionaries were serving in twenty-seven different places.

Moreover, the predominantly Congregationalist (London Missionary Society [LMS]) and Anglican (Church Missionary Society [CMS]) mission agencies founded in Britain during the 1790s recruited substantially in their early years from two training institutions in Germany. One was the school of Pastor Johannes Jänicke in Berlin (which existed from 1800 to 1849), and the other was the seminary of the Basel Mission, which opened in 1815. In fact, seventeen of the first twenty-four missionaries commissioned by the CMS came from the Berlin seminary (the most important being Carl T. E. Rhenius, who labored in South India). In 1833 approximately thirty workers trained at Basel were serving under the CMS, and over the passage of time the latter school supplied over a hundred missionaries to various British and Dutch societies. Until 1858 the CMS regularly subsidized the education of appointees at Basel. Among the outstanding figures schooled there were Samuel Gobat (Palestine), Karl Pfander (North India), Johann Krapf and Johann Rebmann (East Africa), and the linguist Sigismund Koelle (East Africa).[1]

German workers thus played a central role in the early Protestant missionary movement, and they had extensive ties with the British endeavors, both the earlier Society for Promoting Christian Knowledge (founded by 1699) and Society for the Propagation of the Gospel (1701) and the later LMS and CMS. However, during the course of the nineteenth century the Germans were numerically left behind as British and American missionaries poured on to the fields. By 1911 German workers constituted only 6.7 percent of the total Protestant missionary force. Nonetheless, in particular areas, as was the case with the Basel Mission on the Gold Coast, German-speaking missionaries exercised a disproportionate influence.

Although both the German and British movements were rooted in eighteenth-century Pietism and the concomitant evangelical revival, the cultural differences between the two movements were deep-seated. As the Germans became increasingly outnumbered, their resentments grew. They felt that Anglo-American writers and mission theorists completely overlooked or at best were giving little attention to the distinctively German contributions, and in effect were treating them as little more than stepchildren. They were especially dismayed by the optimistic, mainly postmillennialist, triumphalism that prevailed in Anglo-American circles, as exemplified by such catchwords as "advance," "expansion," "diffusion," and "the evangelization of the world in this generation." They insisted the mission emphasis should be to go into the world to teach all nations and build national churches within the cultural matrix of the receptor peoples, not ushering in the kingdom of God. They regarded the latter as the linkage of evangelization and civilization, whose goal would be the conversion of the peoples of the world to an Anglo-American style of Christian civilization and religion.

This fundamental difference in missiological outlook contributed to the cleavage between the Germans and Anglo-Americans, many of whom felt the Germans had drunk too deeply at the fount of *völkisch* romanticism. This was especially the case during the 1930s and 1940s when some writers accused the missions theorists of promoting a proto-Nazi *Blut und Boden* (blood and soil) doctrine of forming a *Volkskirche* (folk church) among an indigenous populace that was based on what some called "primordial" or "organic" cultural and social ties. Recent missiologists, such as Timothy Yates and those in the church growth school, have viewed the German idea of indigenization

---

1. See Jenkins, "Church Missionary Society."

much more favorably.[2] They insist that the emphasis on the corporate approach to missionary strategy can be just as effective, and in some situations even more so, as a shallower, individualistic approach of evangelizing as many people as possible over a short period of time.

An important feature of the German Protestant experience was the establishment of voluntary societies to carry out missionary work, of which the Basel Mission, founded in 1815, was one of the most dynamic examples. The reason for this is that churches in Germany were established on a territorial rather than a national basis, as were, for example, the Church of England, Church of Scotland, or Church of Sweden. This reflects the historical development of Protestantism in the country, in that during the Reformation era the churches were organized on the territorial principle (Landeskirche), whereby the prince or ruler of a state in the then-existing Holy Roman Empire determined the confession of his subjects. In many places the head of state not only mandated uniformity of belief but also exercised a dominant role in the church itself, issuing edicts on ecclesiastic matters and controlling the work of consistories and clerics alike.

The existence of over thirty territorial churches in nineteenth-century Germany meant that organized missionary activity would have to take place on a different basis than if a church per se were doing so. In no way did these churches conceive of themselves as denominations in an American fashion, and thus they did not create "boards" to carry out missions. The voluntary societies that developed for this purpose had no organic connection with a specific Landeskirche. Rather they saw themselves as the free outgrowth of the spirit of missions in the church as a whole. Thus a local organization formed a society and sought support from nearby congregations. That is why so many of the societies took their names from the city where the seat of the organization was, such as the Basel Mission. Then they set out to enlist backing from congregations elsewhere, regardless of what territorial church jurisdictions they might be located in, and by this means they built a broader constituency that was tied together through their publications and itinerating missions speakers. For Basel this meant drawing support from Basel and other Protestant German-speaking cantons in Switzerland and the south German state of Württemberg, a major center of Pietism and its successor movement, the early nineteenth-century revival, or Erweckung. Like the other societies, Basel believed that if it could instill the biblical idea of missions within local congregations, it eventually would come to permeate the entire church. Thus funds were raised not from the Landeskirche treasuries but through freewill

2. Yates, *Christian Mission*, pp. 34-56; Saayman, "Christian Keysser Revisited."

offerings by local congregations and individual benefactors. Then, too, it co-operated with the other groups in regional conferences and joined the Standing Committee of German Protestant Missions formed in 1885 that sought to coordinate the efforts to propagate a missionary vision throughout Germany. Being an independent corporate entity rather than the program board of a church, a characteristic that it shared with the other German missions, Basel tended to utilize personnel trained in its own special missions seminary rather than individuals who were theologically educated in the universities. Although this had the effect of accentuating differences between the society and the churches in whose territory it operated, the feeling was that whoever God had called (and, more important, the committee accepted) should be sent out to the foreign fields. Since the universities were essentially the province of the upper and middle classes, relying on this traditional means of training pastors would have meant excluding that proportion of the population skilled in working with its hands from the possibility of overseas service. Since the *Erweckung* had sunk deep roots in the masses, it would have been impossible to secure their support for and participation in missions unless people of humble standing would be allowed to serve abroad.

There were three basic types of mission societies in Germany — the ecumenical, the Lutheran confessionalist, and the faith missions (modeled on Hudson Taylor's China Inland Mission). Basel belonged to the first category. This meant that it tended to downplay confessional differences between Lutheran and Reformed and welcomed support from any congregation. Also it cooperated with other societies, even those in different countries, such as the British Church Missionary Society. That was possible because Basel ordained its workers, although that did not please those in the Church of England who from the 1830s placed increasing emphasis on the doctrine of apostolic succession. Differences over ordination thus led to the gradual estrangement of the Basel Mission from the CMS, and to a closer association with the Presbyterians, a relationship that proved to be significant for the future of the Basel work and the growth of the Presbyterian church in West Africa after the Basel missionaries were removed from the Gold Coast and Cameroon during World War I.

In sum, the voluntary principle was a characteristic of Basel, as it was of all the German Protestant missionary endeavors. It is an open question whether the societies were "parachurch" in the contemporary use of the term, or whether they were actually at their core "church" enterprises as some missiologists, particularly Gustav Warneck, the major figure in the scientific study of missions in Germany, claimed. I am not convinced that the societies were an integral part of the church.

A distinctive feature of Basel, one that was not shared by most of the other societies, was its emphasis on practical "industries." It sought to create autonomous communities where indigenous Christians would maintain an independent economic existence apart from the dominant colonial economy. This was best exemplified by the introduction of cocoa culture into the Gold Coast, and by the Basel industries in South India, especially the tile factory. The Basel missionaries created a trading company that contributed to the economic well-being of its communities and the development of the territories in which they labored. As Miller shows, they took what essentially was a south German agrarian ideal for the mission because of the intrinsic Christian virtues they associated with it. Whether it was doing the right thing for the wrong reasons, readers will have to decide for themselves.

In his analysis of the organizational tensions and social structures within the Basel Mission, Miller has provided rich insights into the functioning of a major German mission agency. He provides us with much food for thought about missions as agents of change and resistance in the colonial world, and he helps us to see that the German contributions to church building have had a lasting impact in the postcolonial world in Africa. They are indeed deserving of careful study, and he has led us into a field where future examinations will certainly bear rich fruit.

RICHARD V. PIERARD

Preface

The modern Christian missionary movement gathered strength in Europe in the late eighteenth and early nineteenth centuries, paralleling the drive toward overseas commercial and political expansion. In the two hundred years that have passed since that beginning, virtually every part of the world has been touched by the religious organizations that participated in those movements. The part that the evangelizing and institution-building efforts of missionaries played in the history of colonialism is of obvious significance, but my more immediate concern here is the internal properties of evangelical organizations. How they draw energy from the convictions of their members and then channel that energy toward their collective goals is of considerable intrinsic interest for the study of organizations and the sociology of religion. This historical case study of the Evangelical Missionary Society of Basel, Switzerland, is my contribution to the understanding of those dynamics.

The Basel Mission, as it is more commonly known, was identified with the religious movement called Pietism, a development that has provided grist for generations of social theorists, from the early work of Max Weber and Ernst Troeltsch to Robert Merton and, most recently, Mary Fulbrook and George Becker. In the nineteenth century the Baslers had missionary stations dispersed widely around the colonial world. Today they remain active in developing areas of Asia, Latin America, and Africa. I have used the Mission's archive in Basel to reconstruct much of its organizational history, drawing material first from the documentary record of the formative years between 1780 and 1815 in Switzerland, and then from the repository covering the group's activities on the Gold Coast of West Africa (present-day Ghana) from 1828 to World War I. I have focused primarily on this African venue and not others because of the extraordinary quality of the archival documentation for the Ghanaian enterprise. The outline of the investigation is set by three key concerns.

1. How did the members' subjective beliefs, material interests, and historical circumstances condition their involvement in the Mission? In trying to understand the attraction the organization held for its diverse members, I have been guided by the Weberian idea of "elective affinity." Participation in the Pietist movement was connected in intricate ways to the larger class structures of Switzerland and Germany. Shared religious convictions allowed the movement's members to bridge the deep class divisions that separated them and engage in a productive collaboration that lasted for a very long time. For the leadership, participation provided personal religious gratification and reinforced their already prominent social positions. For the ordinary missionaries, joining "the cause" provided a measure of social honor and opened up a possibility of social mobility that they and their progeny could not otherwise have expected. The accumulation of their social gains across several generations dramatically transformed their families' "life chances in the marketplace" and had interesting implications for change in the class structure from which they came.

2. What were the members willing to accept in the organization's structure of authority, and what were the sources of internal stress and contradiction in that structure? When it came to matters of social control, Pietist discipline pulled together charismatic, traditional, and bureaucratic modes of authority in a way that concentrated extraordinary power in the elite group at the center. But participation in this complicated apparatus was also empowering for the ordinary missionaries; as a good case in point, the religious and secular impact of their work on the Ghanaian social structure has been, and continues to be, quite substantial. Many of these effects can be attributed to the preoccupation with discipline that was embedded in the Pietist worldview and to the consensus on basic values and social vision that prevailed among the members of the Mission community. But paradoxically, serious long-term organizational trouble also issued from that same discipline and that same consensus. Much of the theoretical interest of this study lies in accounting for these contradictions.

3. In the face of the Mission's troubles, how were the members able to persist in their common evangelical activities and how did they manage to sustain the structure of the enterprise over the long term? For reasons that can be found in the social psychology of Pietist belief, the contradictions in the organization, no matter how much personal pain and interpersonal stress they caused, remained bearable for the members. As a result, I will argue, the trou-

bles did not directly undermine authority or create a demand for fundamental structural change in the organization, and the members held on to the patience and strength they needed to carry their projects forward.

During its nearly two centuries in Ghana the Basel Mission has had both detractors and defenders. Present-day members of the Mission community itself, including both Africans and Europeans, can be found on either side of the debate about its long-term impact on that country. Like other nineteenth-century missions, the Baslers took as their calling "bringing the gospel" to the "world of the heathen." This aim was deceptively modest. Underlying it were complicated assumptions about human nature and about the proper model for Christian society. These presuppositions justified interventions by the missionaries that, taken together, could mean the complete restructuring of "native" lives.

My purpose is not to serve up a partisan judgment of these interventions, and none should be inferred from my account. Sociologically, however, it is appropriate to ask how closely the Mission's actual history approximated the intentions of those who founded and led it and the men and women who provided the energy and action that actually sustained it. In my opinion, both the "authority wielders" and the "authority yielders" would take the Mission's eventual impact on the Gold Coast and its survival and acceptance in Ghana today as validation of the Pietist model of discipline that was the centerpiece of their undertaking.

A Note on the Revised Edition

This book originally appeared in 1994 as part of the Rose Monograph Series of the American Sociological Association, with the title *The Social Control of Religious Zeal: A Study of Organizational Contradictions*. This new version leaves the original framework essentially intact but incorporates many small and a few more significant changes in various parts of the analysis. Of particular note, additional information brought to my attention by Peter Haenger has enabled me to extend the discussion of Catherine Mulgrave, one of the more important women in the Mission's history. I have also augmented the text with visual representations of missionary activities drawn from the Mission's splendid collection of photographs. The new foreword provided by Richard Pierard locates the Basel Mission in the context of the larger Continental missionary movement of the nineteenth century; the afterword contributed by Paul Jenkins traces what has happened in the organization in the eighty-odd years since the story that I tell breaks off. These changes and additions will, I believe, make the narrative more accessible to the large and multidisciplinary community of scholars who share our fascination with the organizational features of missions.

What I offer here is an intensive case history of a single, albeit particularly interesting, missionary enterprise, and some of what I have reported may well be peculiar to this one organization. But more of what I have learned should resonate with the experiences of other missions and other religious undertakings, past and present. All missions by their very nature have to struggle with the tension between religious enthusiasm and organizational discipline, and the new title of the book, *Missionary Zeal and Institutional Control*, is meant to point more boldly to this common, even ubiquitous dialectic. *Missionary Zeal* refers to the motive energy that flowed from the deepest religious convictions of the members of missionary organizations; *Institutional Control* refers to the need to bring discipline to that energy in the interest of orderly accomplishment. The enthusiasm was indispensable but could undermine the discipline, and the discipline, equally indispensable, could crush as well as guide the enthusiasm. I expect that these contradictions, so visible in the Basel organization, are common in the experiences of many other missionary undertakings. This is a proposition that I wish to put into the larger conversation about mission history, in the hope that other researchers will either validate or challenge it by what they observe in their own work.

Acknowledgments

With their generosity, deep knowledge of the record, and commitment to careful scholarship, Paul Jenkins and Waltraud Haas-Lill made the Basel Mission Archive accessible to me, and they deserve a large share of the credit for the appearance of this volume, both in its original and in its revised versions. But I will allow them no share of the blame for any fugitive inaccuracies, weaknesses, or oversights that surely remain in the book. That accountability rests with me alone.

Historical research claims an inordinate amount of time. The various stages of this project claimed my energy for several years, during which I thoroughly enjoyed the work and appreciated the critical assistance of many of my colleagues. Close to me at the University of Southern California when I worked my way through the first edition were Linda Fuller, Michael Messner, Carol Warren, and Bill Staples. Farther away but no less generous with their counsel when asked to read this or that part of the analysis were George Becker, Barbara Laslett, Dietrich Rueschemeyer, Richard Lachmann, Norbert Wiley, and George Thomas. As this new version began to take shape, I benefited from the generous evaluations of the book by Mark Chavez and Adam Seligman.

Brian Stanley and Robert Frykenberg welcomed me into the community of scholars who participated in the many rich conferences of the North Atlantic Missiology Project, and then later encouraged and guided my efforts to revise this book for Studies in the History of Christian Missions. Thanks to their patience, this work will now be available to a wider audience, and for that I am deeply grateful. Finally, I am much indebted to Richard Pierard and Paul Jenkins (again!) for providing the thoughtful bookends (the foreword and afterword) that now frame the book and help it to stand erect.

At the very beginning, this research was supported by a grant from the University of Southern California's Faculty Research and Innovation Fund, an absolutely vital source of support for new scholarly initiatives. Subsequent support came (however unwittingly) from the taxpayers of the United States by way of National Science Foundation (NSF) grants SES-8308952 and 8520752. Joanne Miller, the director of the sociology program at NSF when I applied for support, has my gratitude for her assistance and, especially, for her ecumenical approach to methodology. Her successor, Mark Abrahamson, was similarly generous with his advice and counsel when I returned to the NSF well for additional support.

CHAPTER 1
_____

Evangelical Missions and Social Change

In order to prove whether a [seminarian] is of God or whether he can be a missionary or not . . . it is necessary to smash him down mercilessly in order to determine conclusively whether he is capable of bearing the discipline. . . . Just as was the case with the traitor Judas, whom the Lord had to bear for a long time, so must it sooner or later come to the same point of decision [for the individual seminarians].[1]

Brother Schiedt [is] guilty of unbearable scoundrelry . . . deliberate animosity, lying, and obvious cheating. There at home you could hardly imagine how far a person can go, once they have abandoned all honesty and strayed from the path of the Lord.[2]

Is this the way we follow the law of brotherly love?[3]

Zeal is an extraordinary human resource but a volatile one. What is most interesting about it sociologically is how different organizations manage to channel

---

1. Statement by the Basel Mission Inspector Joseph Josenhans, quoted by Hesse, *Joseph Josenhans,* pp. 212ff. Here and throughout the monograph, translations from the original German of published and archival documents are my own.

2. Basel Mission Archive (BMA), Report of the Conference on the Suspension of Brother Schiedt, Akropong, December 4, 1848; D-1,2, no. 23a.

3. BMA, Letter from the Missionary Hermann Halleur to the Inspector, November 1, 1843 (D-1,2, 1842-1848, no. 10).

it, or just as often fail to channel it, into coherent and sustainable social action. This is a case history of how that challenge was confronted by one remarkable enterprise, the Evangelical Missionary Society of Basel, Switzerland (Evangelische Missionsgesellschaft zu Basel). During the nineteenth century the Basel Mission was active in many areas around the world, including the Caucasus, Persia, India, China, and Cameroon, but I have concentrated primarily on the record of its presence on the Gold Coast of West Africa, today called Ghana, from the 1820s to World War I. The section of the Mission's archive that covers that venture is extraordinarily complete; I have described that repository in the appendix. Thanks to the availability of that resource, I have been able to trace the social backgrounds of the participants with considerable accuracy; I have isolated the beliefs, resources, and control hierarchies that brought both coherence and discord to their activities; and I have examined some of the events that severely tested their ability to endure as an organization.

Important clues to the Basel Mission's experience are contained in the three passages from the archive that appear in the epigraphs. The first captures a fierce premise that inspired many in the leadership in their approach to discipline in the organization. The second, a judgment of one man's behavior written by a committee of his colleagues after they had endured years of conflict with him, is emblematic of the interpersonal stress that complicated the work of those in the field. The third is a grievance voiced by a missionary on the brink of resignation; it signals the personal anguish of many of those who witnessed and lived with this stress in their daily lives. A central goal of this research has been to trace the connection between the premise visible in the first quotation and the interpersonal alienation and personal distress revealed by the other two. How were the organizational choices made by those in positions of power — and justified by them in almost biblical terms — implicated in the social disharmony experienced by the ordinary missionaries? That question makes this a study of organizational contradictions. It is equally a study of institutional persistence, not failure, in the face of such contradictions. Deep-seated personal and interpersonal struggles were in evidence throughout the period covered by my investigation (and in the years beyond it), but the Basel Mission is now well past the 175th anniversary of its founding.

This is a sociological study, and in assembling the Mission's story I have followed Max Weber's counsel in asking historically grounded questions about the ways in which shared beliefs and meanings bring sense to social action and about the interplay of individual agency and social constraint in that process.[4]

---

4. Weber, *Methodology;* see also Dawe, "Theories of Social Action," and Giddens, *The Constitution of Society,* pp. 5ff.

Weber's methodological strategy strongly prefigures what is called the "new institutionalism" in contemporary organizational sociology, a much discussed but loosely defined framework that reflects a welcome renewal of interest in the role of culture in the shaping of organizations. Like Weber, those identified with this approach pay attention to both symbolic and material determinants of organizational persistence, failure, and legitimacy; they are alert to the causes and consequences of institutional contradiction and conflict; and they recognize the significance of time and place.[5] All these concerns are present in my investigation, and I make frequent reference to that growing body of work in my discussions.

I have also taken Weber's view that any particular course of action or institutional arrangement reflects the "elective affinities" *(Wahlverwandtschaften)* that weave together the personal beliefs, vested interests, and historical circumstances of the participants.[6] That phrase, "beliefs, interests, and circumstances," is a leitmotif to which I will return frequently in the pages that follow. The sharpest illustration of this approach can be seen in *The Protestant Ethic and the Spirit of Capitalism,* in which Weber argued that the convergence of the religious convictions, emerging political and economic concerns, and changing social situations of diverse groups brought them together in that medley of activities we recognize as contemporary capitalism. Many of the details of his historical argument remain controversial, but Weber's general conception of social change and his strategy for approaching an understanding of it provide the central focus for this study. Because his approach has decisively influenced my investigation both theoretically and methodologically, it calls for some elaboration.

Weber insisted that shared ideas (in the present context, Württemberg Pietism) may act as the "switching mechanism" that sets a general direction for a course of action, but the developments in that action also depend upon the material resources and cultural situations of the actors.[7] The concept of

---

5. See Powell and DiMaggio, eds., *New Institutionalism.* Useful summaries of the approach appear in Meyer and Scott, eds., *Organizational Environments,* and Zucker, "Institutional Theories of Organization." Arthur Stinchcombe's attention to the historical dimension appeared earlier and influenced the development of the institutional perspective. See "Bureaucratic and Craft Administration" and "Social Structure and Organizations." In the sociology of religion, an analogue to this general approach can be seen in the work of Robert Wuthnow (see, for example, "International Realities").

6. *From Max Weber,* pp. 63-65. It was clearly Weber's conception that inspired C. Wright Mills's argument (in *The Sociological Imagination,* chap. 1) for focusing on the intersection of biography and history in sociological analysis.

7. *From Max Weber,* p. 280; Bendix, *Max Weber,* pp. 64ff.

"elective affinity" is useful for describing both the manner in which different categories of actors are initially drawn together into a common activity (the emergence or founding phase) and the ways their shared action is shaped and sustained after they have become an established organization (the phase of institutionalization or consolidation). The first of these usages frames my discussion of the Basel Mission's origins, which I trace to the opportune convergence and collaboration in a common religious cause by individuals who were widely separated in their experiences and backgrounds. The second meaning of elective affinity is more in evidence in my discussion of the internal organizational structure created and reproduced by the Mission's participants. In both usages — emergence and institutionalization — it is recognized that a particular "collision" of actors, events, or collective actions may be the result of a "historical accident" of the sort that often shapes the course of social change.[8] In this regard it is relevant to note that the Basel Mission was driven by Pietist, Calvinist, and Lutheran beliefs in the period of transition from traditional to modern rational-legal social structures in Europe, and that Mission participants were challenged (threatened is perhaps a better word) in immediate ways by the philosophical skepticism of the Enlightenment and the still reverberating political example of the French Revolution. These are all factors that figured prominently in Weber's analysis of the tangled evolutions of religion, ideology, and social structure, and the analysis I offer will contribute some fine-grained detail to that larger picture. For me it added a dimension of interest to the investigation to know that the historical events, cultural concerns, and real choices facing the Mission's participants were the same social issues that, on the level of society as a whole, captured the attention of the founders of the modern social sciences.

"Elective affinity" and "historical accident" are contingent notions of change. They do not encourage a search for deterministic connections or invariant sequences of organizational development. Yet the fascination of the Basel Mission does not depend upon the claim that its structure was "inevitable" or that its experiences were "typical" of a large class of organizations. More to the point is to ask how, against all probabilities, it has survived for the better part of two centuries with its identity and many of its original reasons for existence intact. The members of the Mission community were conscious agents of change when they set about devising a structure that not only met their practical needs but also directly expressed their religious intensity

---

8. This view is developed at length in Weber, *Economy and Society*, 1:264ff. See also Bendix, *Max Weber*, pp. 63-64; Schluchter, *Western Rationalism*, pp. 139-48; Collins, *Max Weber*, pp. 94ff.; and Giddens, *The Constitution of Society*, p. xxviiiff.

and provided, they thought, an institutional model for the cultures abroad in which they were about to invest their energies. In creating such a new religious force in the world, however, they had to remain alert to the limits imposed by their social surroundings. It is open to question how long the organization could have survived if the community centered around Basel had been strongly unreceptive, culturally, to the Pietist cause or if powerful groups had been determined to resist and expel, rather than tolerate and even encourage, the evangelical movement that it represented; I will show that avoiding such potential local opposition in the early days was Mission leadership's first strategic victory. Nor could the Mission have sustained itself without the resources to carry the effort forward, any more than it could have prospered if the leaders and the rank-and-file members had not had a shared inspiration and a common occasion to place the evangelical organization at the focal point of their lives. There is much to be learned from how the members navigated the turbulent stream of opportunities and limitations in which they found themselves.

An interpretive case history is the method of choice for an investigation like this one. I have tried to determine the ways in which religious beliefs were translated into organizational structures and how the decisions shaped by those structures were tied to recognizable social consequences. In pursuing such questions I have made use of many kinds of information, and have been alert to unintended as well as intended outcomes, to contradictions, and to the passage of time and changing circumstances. These are the basic necessities of the analytic approach that sociologists call "interpretive," and the ability to address them is the defining virtue of the case study method.[9] The investigation has been opportunistic in the sense that I have embraced serendipity and followed fugitive clues into unanticipated areas, but at the same time I have tried to keep the focus on clear analytic questions and explicit research procedures so that the plausibility of what I have to report can be evaluated and any provocative questions that are generated can be followed up in future investigations.[10] In the end, what must be judged is the extent to which the logics and the contradictions at work in the Basel Mission provide not templates but clues to life in other organizations and other move-

9. The recent collection of papers edited by Joe Feagin et al. *(A Case for the Case Study)* offers the most comprehensive discussion of the strengths and weaknesses of this approach.

10. It is this kind of "spin-off," rather than strict "replicability," that has been the chief contribution of the classic case studies in organizational sociology, among them Philip Selznick's *TVA and the Grass Roots*, Peter Blau's *The Dynamics of Bureaucracy*, and Alvin Gouldner's *Patterns of Industrial Bureaucracy*.

ments. Only investigations that are explicitly comparative will answer that question with any certainty,[11] but looking ahead with such a larger inquiry in mind, it is useful to speculate about how far the implications of this one portrayal might extend.

To characterize it very broadly, the Basel Mission is in that category of "enthusiastic" collectivities that must *exploit* and at the same time *contain* individual zeal in the pursuit of larger collective purposes. Such enterprises carry a variety of labels, each calling attention to a different aspect of their reality. They fall under the rubric that Amitai Etzioni called "normative," where participation based on personal commitment intersects with discipline based on shared moral values.[12] Nanette Davis and Bo Anderson have preferred the term "value drenched" to describe projects that are propelled by their members' strongly held beliefs,[13] while James Wood has used "value-fostering" to describe such groups that are specifically religious and oriented to the protection and implementation of their own core values.[14] Further parallels could be drawn to the communitarian organizations studied by Rosabeth Kanter and Benjamin Zablocki, or to the ideologically driven "alternative" organizations described by Joyce Rothschild and Allen Whitt.[15] Finally, many of the questions I have asked about the "management of zeal" in the Mission parallel those asked about recruitment, consensus formation, and mobilization in social movements, as this area has been defined by John McCarthy and Mayer Zald and others.[16] The forms of social organization called to mind by these diverse terms do not form a homogeneous family, but they are cognates and do share with each other, with the Basel Mission, and quite probably with most missions the need to strike a balance between individual fervor and organizational discipline. It is also likely that the many organizations covered by these terms will share the Mission's potential for internal contradictions and strategic problems in carrying out their activities. To the extent that this is true, the experiences of the Mission may provide useful insight into their survival or demise.

11. Ragin, *The Comparative Method*, chap. 3.

12. Etzioni, *Comparative Analysis*.

13. Davis and Anderson, *Social Control*.

14. Wood, *Leadership in Voluntary Organizations*. This category has been enriched recently by Mary Jo Neitz *(Charisma and Community)*, Susan Rose ("Women Warriors"), and Stephen Warner *(New Wine)*.

15. Kanter, *Communes*; Zablocki, *The Joyful Community* and *Alienation and Charisma*; Rothschild and Whitt, *The Cooperative Workplace*.

16. See Zald and McCarthy, eds., *Dynamics of Social Movements*; Klandermans, "Mobilization and Participation"; Snow et al., "Frame Alignment Processes"; and McAdam et al., "Social Movements."

Overview of the Investigation

The Participants

Chapter 2 concerns motivation and the balance between religious commitment and personal gain that exists for individuals. This discussion will stress the fact that the social origins of the controlling elite in the Mission, that is, those who founded and guided the organization, were very different from those of the ordinary members who carried its work abroad. Nevertheless, there was an unforced alliance between the two groups that lasted for generations. Recognizing the intrinsic spiritual satisfaction that this uncommon alliance offered to all its members, I have characterized it as a kind of *class collaboration for the sake of religion.* In many ways the relationship between the leaders and the rank and file both reflected and buttressed the existing traditional order that surrounded the Mission. Participation in the movement enhanced the social honor of the founders; moreover, the control by this group over the direction of the movement replicated their power and privilege in the larger society, and immersion in the Mission's daily affairs provided individuals with an arena for interaction — a place for networking, to use contemporary jargon — in which their enduring secular and economic ties to others like themselves were regularly reinforced.

For the ordinary missionaries the situation was not the same. In the short term their subordination to the leadership circle inside the Mission mirrored their subordinate place in traditional village society. In the long term, however, their objective circumstances were profoundly altered by their participation in the movement. However conservative their social and religious attitudes may have been when they approached the Mission, the changes they experienced in their family lives after joining it removed them from an old, familiar social context and contributed to the inexorable alteration of the class and status structure from which they had come. They saw most of these transforming effects on their lives as positive. By joining the Mission and becoming ordained members of the clergy, the male missionaries accumulated cultural capital and experienced significant upward social mobility (the women in the movement, as we will see, are a different story). The offspring of the missionaries consolidated the gains of their fathers and within a generation became firmly anchored in the emerging professional classes of Germany and Switzerland. What is more, these profound secular effects of activities that were religiously and ideologically conservative in origin were not confined to Europe. This mission, like many others, also played an important, if again largely unintended, role in the emergence of a new division of labor

7

and the beginnings of a modern class structure in West Africa. As Weber made clear in his essay on the Protestant ethic, the synergy created by the interpenetration of religious and secular structures and the merging of religious and secular energies affects the course of social change in complicated and often unanticipated ways.[17] How the changing opportunity structure affected the flow of members to the missionary movement has often been asked, but there is equal reason to ask about the reciprocal effects of that missionary movement on subsequent developments in the class structure.

Enthusiasm and Discipline

Chapter 3 concentrates on matters of authority. On one level the hierarchy that the leadership created for the Mission was a management device, instrumental in origin and aimed at the efficient fulfillment of organizational goals, and can be evaluated for its effectiveness from that perspective. But an analysis that stopped there would be dangerously superficial, because that structure was not only an instrument for conveying the evangelical message, it was actually part of the substance of that message. In offering a theory of legitimacy in religious organizations, sociologist James Wood points out that in churches the core values commonly function as part of the action mandate entrusted to the leadership.[18] In the Basel Mission, I will argue, there was even more to it than that. The complex structure that evolved was itself a direct expression of Pietist beliefs about the proper way to organize life. Those beliefs contained elements of religious charisma, social tradition, and bureaucratic rational-legalism. It is clear from the way the members of the Mission's governing committee described their own roles, for example, that they relied upon a kind of charismatic justification to authenticate the goals they set for the organization. A familiar refrain was, "The will of God is recognizable in the will of the Committee." But they also took advantage of their privileged location in the structures of traditional authority outside the Mission to give force to their directives inside the organization ("Obey your social superiors"), and they drew heavily on bureaucratic mechanisms and legal-contractual rationales to give a coherent outline to the Mission's structure of control ("Above all, there must be order!").

Attention is often directed to the incompatibilities among these three forms of imperative control because each, in Weber's view, is attuned to a

17. Weber, *Protestant Ethic.*
18. Wood, *Leadership in Voluntary Organizations,* chap. 6.

particular configuration of historical circumstances and cultural rationales. Where there are shared beliefs that bridge across their potential incompatibilities, however, they can coexist and reinforce each other in any number of combinations, especially in periods of social transition.[19] With this premise as the guideline, I will offer an interpretive account of the coexistence of these three forms of control within the Mission and go on to describe the consequences of that coexistence in the lives and actions of the missionaries. When the Mission founders drew upon their rich vocabulary of control, they struck responsive chords in the lives of those who volunteered to serve as ordinary missionaries. The recruits had beliefs about divine will and revealed wisdom that ratified the governors' claims to institutional charismatic legitimacy; a reinforcing message about the need for compliance came to the rank and file from the traditional expectations that accompanied their relatively modest status origins in village society; and the urge to obedience was further underlined by their practical experiences in the increasingly rationalized economy that people in their social situation were beginning to face. By accepting the premises that knit together the diverse elements of the Mission's complex regime, and by participating directly in the socialization of the new members who followed after them, the ordinary missionaries ensured the continuation of the very structure of authority that had assumed the initiative over their own lives.

Contradictions

The religious enthusiasm implicit in Pietism was effectively contained and shaped by the hierarchy I have described, but a narrative that stopped with the emergence of that triangulated structure would only begin to tell the story. There was, to be sure, a substantial consensus about the structure's various legitimating principles; nevertheless, discipline in the Mission displayed more than one fundamental contradiction. In chapter 4, I make the point that, ideologically and emotionally, the subordinate members accepted the strictures of Pietist hierarchical discipline. If they followed those strictures to the letter in the field, however, they were left with little guidance as to how to address the uncertainties in their work in creative and effective ways. To be responsive to the demands they faced in their new surroundings, they sometimes needed to move outside prescribed organizational procedures. Those

19. Weber, *Economy and Society*, 2:1133; see also Schluchter, *Western Rationalism*, pp. 128ff., and Willer, "Weber's Missing Authority Type."

who seized the initiative in that way became rule-breakers, almost by definition, and therefore made themselves candidates for harsh organizational discipline ("smash them down mercilessly"). I look closely at the actions of three
individuals who were prepared to take this drastic step and whose extraordinary personal force, or charisma as individuals, directly tested the institutional charisma of the formal leadership. The behavior of these innovators
was unscripted, and the liberties they took with established procedures had
mixed and unpredictable outcomes. Some were good for the organization;
others bordered on disaster. If these individuals are seen through the lens of
the Mission's religious concern for order and conformity, they were among
the organization's most troublesome members. At the same time, the vigor
and direction they contributed to the organization were indispensable to its
work, and they were often treated as mission heroes. For this reason I have
called them "strategic deviants," a term I have coined to highlight the paradox
of strategically welcome outcomes produced by forbidden action. I suspect
that this pattern is quite common in missionary organizations.

The situation in the field was further complicated by a second contradiction, caused by a policy called "mutual watching," common in many religious
organizations, that required the missionaries to scrutinize each other's behavior constantly and report any shortcomings they observed to superiors. Being
willing to exercise this surveillance over their peers was considered a sign of
Pietist strength, but approbation for this "virtue" could only be earned by exposing the weaknesses of colleagues, even friends. As an organizational imperative the policy accomplished its primary objective: it brought the informal social control of equals by equals into the service of official hierarchical
policy. It was no surprise, however, either to participants or to detached observers at the time, that the practice also eroded mutual trust and deflected
the missionaries' religious energy and idealism into unproductive and divisive interpersonal conflict precisely at the time their unfamiliar and threatening new environment required them to rely upon and support each other.

Persistence

These two dilemmas colored the experiences of the Mission throughout the
period covered by my investigation: creativity was coupled to deviance, and
mutual surveillance went hand in hand with mutual distrust. It is perhaps the
Mission's most remarkable feature, however, that it survived these troubles.
Armed only with present-day notions of organizational effectiveness, few
who witnessed the Mission's formative years on the Gold Coast would have

judged its chances of long-term survival, let alone success, to be very high. Yet the organization endured decade after decade without a fundamental alteration in its structure, and this in circumstances characterized by its own leaders — with a certain irony, to be sure — as "permanently extraordinary."[20]

In the fifth and final chapter I ask how this endurance was possible. I find some answers in the importance the Mission attached to its special Pietist identity and in the social psychology of religious belief. The Pietist ethos, I believe, could "institutionalize" the contradictions that beset the Mission and paradoxically turn the liabilities they created into new sources of collective resolve. The trials of the missionary life were rationalized (in the sense, not of being excused, but of being made to seem reasonable) by defining them as the "cross to be borne." In this way troubles were taken for granted and enclosed within the members' emotional and ideological zone of forbearance. Individuals caught in the snares of contradictory organizational expectations were anesthetized against the pain caused by those policies and often responded by investing even more energy in their evangelical duties. At the same time, organizational decision makers were shielded from accountability for decisions they made (had to make, in their view) that were clearly implicated causally in the Mission's problems. Difficulties they created by their decisions and/or could never decisively resolve were prevented from undermining their legitimacy or that of the organizational regime over which they presided.

Historical and Cultural Context

The evangelical missions of the nineteenth century were able to summon an array of biblical injunctions, assumptions about human nature, and conceptions of the ideal society to justify their intervention in other cultures. Equally diverse were the practical strategies they used in pursuit of their objectives. What they had in common, in abstract terms, was their determination to influence the course of social change beyond the boundaries of their own societies; shaping the cultures of others could be said to be their defining organizational goal. Sometimes their intervention called for the complete transformation of indigenous lives and social institutions; at other times there was a consonance between missionary and native beliefs that motivated missionaries to work for the preservation of some aboriginal forms at the same time they were striving to supplant others.[21] In either case,

20. Cited by Waldburger, *Missionare und Moslem*, p. 74.
21. Michael Coleman's *Presbyterian Missionary Attitudes toward American Indians,*

whenever they succeeded in sweeping away the old, missions immediately faced the task of consolidating the new, and for this reason they found themselves committed to both change and continuity. They varied widely in their influence and freedom of action, but in many cases they were important and relatively autonomous agents of social change in the colonial world.[22]

Yet despite their simultaneously transformative and conservative nature, missions are not often the central subject of a sociological investigation. David Heise made a compelling case for their claim on our attention thirty years ago, but how little the situation has changed since then can be seen in the renewal of his appeal in several of the selections in Wade Clark Roof's more recent collection on religion and the social order.[23] In that volume Lamin Sanneh puts the issue this way: "Anyone surveying the scene today will be struck by how the subject of Christian missions has been comprehensively banished from nearly all respectable academic syllabi and from mainstream religious scholarship."[24] A particular oddity is the near absence of interest in missions in comparative and historical studies of political economy and social change.[25] The missionary movement was extremely popular for generations, both in North America and in Europe, with a fascination and a claim on resources and personal commitments that cut across class and status lines.[26] The agents of overseas missions were sent throughout the world and therefore were present as (often prescient) observers and participants in virtually every phase of the emergence of the modern world system. A wealth of information about that global process resides in their archives, in their collective memories, and in the traces their activities have left and continue to leave behind them. It is a wealth that remains largely unexploited. Outside the circle of mission scholars, the Basel Mission in particular is not widely known,[27] and many of the events I describe took

1837-1893 offers clear examples of the attempt at cultural eradication; Richard Gray's recent book, *Black Christians and White Missionaries,* offers a provocative discussion of the inevitable amalgamation of native and European beliefs.

22. Miller, "Missions, Social Change"; Miller, "Politics, Economics"; Maduro, "New Marxist Approaches."

23. Heise, "Prefatory Findings"; Roof, ed., *World Order and Religion.*

24. Sanneh, "Yogi and the Commissar," p. 175.

25. Three notable exceptions are Beidelman, *Colonial Evangelism;* Burns, "The Missionary Syndrome"; and Langer and Jackson, "Colonial and Republican Missions."

26. Moorhouse, *The Missionaries.*

27. But see Baëta, ed., *Christianity in Tropical Africa;* Brokensha, *Social Change at Larteh;* Eiselin, "Zur Erziehung"; F. H. Fischer, *Der Missionsarzt Rudolf Fisch;* R. Fischer, *Basler Missionsindustrie in Indien, 1850-1913;* Gründer, *Christliche Mission und Deutscher Imperialismus;* Hallden, *Culture Policy;* Jenkins, "Villagers as Missionaries"; Jenkins, "Class Analysis"; Jenkins, "Sozialer Hintergrund und Mission"; Middleton, "One Hundred and

place in that organization well over a century ago. For this reason it will be helpful to locate the Mission more precisely in its time and place.

Origins of the Basel Mission

The Pietist movement with which the Basel Mission was identified was active in Europe as early as the seventeenth century and remained visible and energetic in some areas well into the nineteenth century.[28] Doctrinally its adherents stayed close to the heart of dominant Protestant beliefs. In the main they did not spin free as some sects had done from the established Lutheran and Calvinist churches. Yet Pietism was an emotionally intense set of beliefs and practices that placed especially strong emphasis on spiritual rebirth, close individual reading of Scripture, personal asceticism, discipline, and — apart from occasional expressions of millenarianism — social conservatism. In its various forms it played an important part in the institutional changes and reactions to change that shaped the modern industrial world.

The version of the Pietist movement that was most influential in the churches of southern Germany and Switzerland in the late eighteenth and early nineteenth centuries is called Württemberg Pietism, after the region in which it found its strongest expression.[29] Shared Pietist devotion and belief brought the actors in our story together across the social class, geographical, and confessional differences that otherwise divided them, and Pietism's tenets gave distinctive shape to the activities they pursued together. These beliefs included a strong commitment to missionary evangelism,[30] and the

---

Fifty Years"; Miller, "Class Collaboration"; Miller, "Institutionalized Contradictions"; Miller, "Missions, Social Change"; Odamtten, *Missionary Factor;* Osafo, *Beitrag der Basler Mission;* Prodolliet, *Wider die Schamlosigkeit;* Tufuoh, "Relations"; Vogelsanger, *Pietismus und Afrikanische Kultur;* and Waldburger, *Missionare und Moslem.*

28. I have not attempted in this book to provide a comprehensive characterization of Pietism. I have relied heavily on other authors for my understanding of the movement, most notable among them Troeltsch, *Social Teaching,* vol. 2; Ritschl, *Three Essays;* Beyreuther, *Geschichte des Pietismus;* Weber, *Protestant Ethic,* pp. 128ff.; Merton, "Puritanism, Pietism, and Science" (in *Social Theory,* pp. 628-60); Merton, "Fallacy"; Becker, "Pietism and Science"; Becker, "Fallacy"; Becker, "Pietism's Confrontation"; Fulbrook, *Piety and Politics;* Scharfe, *Die Religion des Volkes;* and Walker et al., *History.*

29. Some call Württemberg Pietism "late" Pietism, and Erich Beyreuther (*Geschichte des Pietismus,* chap. 7) calls it the "fourth generation" of Pietism, to distinguish it from the earlier expressions of the movement dating from the seventeenth century.

30. Walker et al., *History,* pp. 590ff.; Beyreuther, *Geschichte des Pietismus,* pp. 343ff.; Forell, *Christian Social Teachings,* p. 257.

Basel organization played a visible and important part in the overseas missionary movement that accompanied the economic and cultural expansionism of nineteenth-century Europe.

The Mission's early history was linked directly to that of a group called the German Society for Christianity (Deutsche Christentumsgesellschaft).[31] The society was created in Basel in 1780 as a Bible study and discussion group, bringing together prominent Swiss and German clergymen, community leaders, business owners, and academic theologians who identified themselves with the Pietist movement and wanted to give visible, outward expression to their religious beliefs. Because of the increasingly strong missionary element in their thinking, the members founded the Basel Mission in 1815 as a seminary for the education of overseas evangelists. The first cohort of young recruits who completed the course of study in the new seminary were not sent out as Basel missionaries per se, but were seconded to older, established evangelical organizations based in Holland (the Dutch Missionary Society), Germany (the North German Mission Society), and England (the Church Missionary Society). By 1821, however, the founders decided that the Mission must establish religious outposts abroad in its own name in order to bring the distinctive Pietist worldview to regions that were still laboring in "unchristian darkness."

This operation began with the sending of Basel missionaries to Russia to evangelize among the Jews, Tartars, and Armenians there.[32] A mission to Liberia was attempted in 1826 but did not succeed in establishing a foothold.[33] Two years later, at the invitation of the Danish Crown and the Danish Lutheran Church, the first team of four Basel missionaries arrived in the colonial fort at Christiansborg on the Gold Coast of West Africa. That arrival, in December of 1828, marks the beginning of the effort that is our primary focus here. There had been Portuguese missions in the West African region as early as the fifteenth century, so the Baslers were by no means the first missionaries to the Gold Coast.[34] They may well have been the most persistent, however.

31. More formally, it was known as Deutsche Gesellschaft zur Beförderung Reiner Lehre und Wahrer Gottseligkeit (German Society for the Promotion of Pure Instruction and True Piety). For basic chronological facts and events here and elsewhere, I have relied frequently, but not exclusively, on Schlatter, *Geschichte der Basler Mission*, vols. 1-4, and Witschi, *Geschichte der Basler Mission*, vol. 5. These are internal histories written for the Mission, however, and I have maintained some professional distance from their authors' interpretations of events.

32. These efforts are well described by Waldburger, *Missionare und Moslem*.

33. Schlatter, *Geschichte der Basler Mission*, 3:9ff.

34. Reindorf, *History*; Neill, *History of Christian Missions*, 1st ed., p. 118; Clarke, *West Africa and Christianity*, p. 10.

Their arrival marked the start of an endeavor that, though at times stretched very thin, was able to continue essentially uninterrupted until World War I.

That 1914-1918 European conflict complicated the colonial politics of Africa in ways that made the Mission's position on the Gold Coast temporarily untenable.[35] After the Danes (in 1850) and the Dutch (in 1872) left the region, Britain took over control of their territories, and because many of the Basel missionaries were German nationals, they were thought to be a threat to the British colonial position. Many were detained soon after the war began, and in 1917 the U-boat sinking of a British ship off the coast of Africa prompted the colonial authorities to arrest those Baslers who remained in West Africa. Those men were interned on the Isle of Man for the duration of the war, and as a measure of the threat the missionaries were thought to pose, the British ordered the burning of the history books they had been using in their schools (because of a perceived pro-German bias). The Mission's entire (by now quite extensive) institutional infrastructure of villages, farms, churches, schools, trading stores, and workshops was turned over to the United Free Church of Scotland. The Baslers were not allowed to return to the Gold Coast in any significant role until 1926. They have maintained a continuous presence there since that time, and today are involved in a "partnership" (the term currently preferred to "mission") with the autonomous Presbyterian Church of Ghana, which, not incidentally, identifies its own founding with the arrival in 1828 of the first Baslers. Together, the Mission and the now fully indigenous Presbyterian church pursue a variety of religious, medical, technological, and educational projects.

In the beginning the Mission's claim to legitimacy in West Africa was based on its desire to create and sustain a Pietist Christian presence and to bear witness against the ravages of the European slave trade and the economic exploitation that accompanied and followed that trade. Three strategies aimed at the moral and social reconstruction of African society were paramount in the Mission's pursuit of its evangelical goals:

First, *preaching the gospel in the local vernacular* was essential; here the Mission followed the belief, traceable to Luther and common to many Protestant missions, that an individual's mother tongue is the only proper medium for the insight that produces conversion and salvation.

Second, the Mission considered *education, especially Bible education,* to be vital (see plates 1-4). This instruction, too, had to proceed in the indigenous language, and for the same reason: individuals had to be able to experience

35. An important source for my summary of this period is Agyemang, *We Presbyterians.*

15

the Word directly for themselves in the language of their birth. From the mid–nineteenth century, English was also taught in the Mission's schools (a concession to the colonial realities of the region), and in general language study and the promotion of literacy ranked high on the list of missionary projects and accomplishments. Several members of the Mission gained wide recognition for their expertise as translators and linguists.[36]

Third, *the teaching of modern husbandry and craft skills* was thought to be the best way to create the material basis for strongly organized and self-suffi-cient Christian villages, or "Salems" as they came to be called in Ghana. West Africa's indigenous, that is, precolonial, cultures and economic systems have been described as stable and rational adaptations to the environment and re-source base of the geographic region.[37] Well before the early 1800s, however, these structures had been massively disrupted by earlier European incur-sions, particularly those caused by the slave trade.[38] In the nineteenth cen-tury, colonial administrations promoted foreign-controlled plantation econ-omies that destroyed communal life and reduced many Africans to landless and often itinerant agrarian proletarians.[39] For this reason the Basel Mission strongly opposed those policies.[40] True to the Lutheran influence on their beliefs, the Baslers were convinced that only autonomous villages patterned on a European, and especially an idealized south German, agrarian model (see plate 5) would support the vital institutional web of family, church, edu-cation, and stable vocation that was necessary for a truly pious life.[41] In their view these villages were certainly to be preferred to "spoiled" and "heathen" native settlements and the emerging administrative/commercial towns asso-ciated with colonialism. Christiansborg, for example, was often referred to as a place of decadence and temptation, and moving the Mission's evangelism

36. Groves, *Planting of Christianity*, 2:228; Neill, *History of Christian Missions*, 1st ed., p. 260; Mobley, *Ghanaian's Image*, p. 22; Clarke, *West Africa and Christianity*, p. 59. S. K. Odamtten's comment (see Odamtten, *Missionary Factor*, pp. 116-17) on the contrasting at-titude toward serious indigenous language studies of British missionaries is interesting: "It appears that . . . the missionaries who came from Victorian England shared the prevailing view that English was the Heaven-sent medium of religion and civilisation."

37. Hopkins, *Economic History*.

38. Hopkins, *Economic History*; Reindorf, *History*.

39. See Hallden, *Culture Policy*; Cohen, "From Peasants"; Magubane, "Evolution."

40. This period is described in detail in Hallden, *Culture Policy*; see also Scharfe, *Die Religion des Volkes*; and Gründer, *Christliche Mission und Deutscher Imperialismus*. For similar episodes in other missions, see Langer and Jackson, "Colonial and Republican Mis-sions"; and Miller, "Missions, Social Change."

41. Jenkins, "Villagers as Missionaries"; Lehmann, *Pietismus und Weltliche Ordnung*; Troeltsch, *Social Teaching*, vol. 2, chap. 2.

away from that seat of colonial administration was a breakthrough accomplishment. It was ethnocentric of the Baslers, to be sure, to think that the proper African community could only be based on what was most desirable and familiar to Europeans. Paradoxically, though, to the extent that the model they promoted for African Christians stressed economic independence from the dominant colonial economy, it could sometimes put the missionaries directly at odds with powerful European colonial interests. In the hands of some missionaries, that model also provided space for the survival of some indigenous but "surprisingly Christian" social forms, a point to which I will return in chapter 4.

My account of the Mission's organizational history is not uncritical, but in writing it I have not assumed any brief either to censure or to validate the motives that propelled its work in West Africa. Objectively, its mere endurance in exceptionally difficult circumstances indicates that it was not, *in its own terms,* an organizational failure. It did, and still does, sustain a Christian presence in Ghana, and it did, and still does, bear strong and consistent witness to its beliefs about the dangers of economic dependency. In short, it did far more than simply endure as a token of Pietist fortitude. The fervor, resources, and missionary lives it invested did not always lead to precisely the outcomes it intended. Nevertheless, in the end it came to have a profound impact on the culture and social structure of Ghana. For this reason alone, the history of its survival would be worth mining for the insight it might provide about other value-driven organizations, active in other difficult social settings.

A missionary who was active in Ghana from the 1950s to the 1980s put the matter of the Mission's impact well in a casual conversation with me after he retired. The marks left on Ghanaian culture by the Basel Mission, he said, "go as deep as the grain in a block of wood, capable of resisting every attempt to sand them away." To that impact on West Africa must be added the results of the Mission's efforts elsewhere in the colonial world.[42] And yet, even knowing about its perdurability and the strong impression it made as an agent of social change, it is difficult to read through the record of its troubled experiences in

---

42. The Gold Coast was not the only field in which the Mission's accomplishments were noteworthy. Jonas Dah ("Basel Mission in Cameroon") describes its influence on the social structure of another part of Africa. Kenneth Latourette (*Christian Missions in China*) describes its educational impact in China, and William Faunce (*Social Aspects*) says its economic and technical contributions in India were considerable. See also Rudolf Fischer (*Basler Missionsindustrie in Indien, 1850-1913*) concerning the Mission's industrial projects in India; and Andreas Waldburger (*Missionare und Moslem*) on the Mission's work in Islamic areas.

the nineteenth century and not be surprised that it could survive that period at all. The search for the reasons for this persistence leads deeply into the values of the participants and into the structure of the organization they created; these will provide the chief topics for discussion in the chapters that follow. In order to set the context for that search, it is useful first to preview the kinds of organizational trouble the Mission faced and then relate in a little more detail some of the evidence for its lasting effect on Ghana.

Organizational Trouble

Missionary organizations were present wherever European colonial influence spread in the search for resources, markets, and labor. In Africa in particular, the history of missionary activity has been a long one. Portuguese missions were established at Elmina on the Gold Coast in 1482 and in the Congo in 1490 as part of the exploration set in motion by Henry the Navigator.[43] Five hundred years later foreign missions remain active in Namibia, the most recent African nation to emerge from white domination.[44] The missionary movement and colonialism came out of the same cultural background, but the former was first of all religious in origin while the latter was driven at its core by economic and geopolitical interests. There was never a complete convergence of interests between them. The degree of collusion versus tension varied with the specific mission and changed with time and place, but seen broadly, it is clear that the relationship was essentially symbiotic. Stated simply, church people could be useful to empire builders by preparing "natives" for entry into the system of colonial hegemony, and colonial adventures could benefit missions — in fact, often made such enterprises possible — by opening the so-called heathen world to Christian evangelizing and by protecting missionaries to some extent from the opposition that could come from com-

43. Clarke, *West Africa and Christianity,* chap. 1; Neill, *History of Christian Missions,* 1st ed., p. 118.

44. I refer here only to European missions dating from the beginning of the colonial era. There were missionary movements in earlier times, and there are surviving Christian communities in Africa whose origins predate Christianity in Europe. Christianity in Ethiopia, for example, dates from the fourth century (Neill, *History of Christian Missions,* 1st ed., pp. 46-47), and there were Christian communities in North Africa even earlier than that (pp. 32ff.). Some Basel missionaries whose roles I describe in later chapters believed that the features of indigenous culture that were able to survive contact with Europeans in the 1800s were actually derived from those very early East African and North African Christian influences. This perception was a key factor in their attempts to defend those structures when Mission policies threatened to erase them.

mercial traders, indigenous tribal leaders, and individual Africans who resented their incursions.[45]

It is important to note in this connection that Switzerland was not a colonial power and could not provide the Basel Mission with a "captive" field for its evangelizing efforts in the way it can fairly be said that Britain did for such powerfully connected organizations as the (Anglican) Church Missionary Society (CMS) or that Germany did for some of the Protestant and Catholic missions based in that country. Because of the Baslers' marginality in the political-economic scheme of things abroad, it was in their interest to try to stay in the good graces of colonial administrations in different regions and to adjust to the changes that accompanied the shifting of control from one such power to another. At the same time, lest it lose its identity and autonomy, themselves values of considerable religious importance for Pietists, the Mission could not allow itself to become too dependent or permit its program to be reduced to an adjunct of colonial political and commercial interests. Reflecting this delicate balance, it at times relied on colonial authorities to protect and advance its interests,[46] and at other times found itself in open opposition to those authorities.[47] Most of the time, however, it worked in the middle region between those extremes of dependency and opposition. In no small part the Mission's ability to create a strategic and tolerated, even appreciated, position for itself can be traced to the care that was taken to avoid complications and geopolitical entanglements.

45. Jonas Dah's description (in "Basel Mission in Cameroon") of a complex three-way symbiosis among the Basel Mission, the colonial government, and tribal leaders in Cameroon is a particularly apt illustration: African leaders used Christianity to get an education for some of their constituents, or subjects; missionaries used the education they offered to get converts; and the government saw the African Christians trained in the Mission's schools as the source of a disciplined civil workforce.

46. When the British announced in 1865 that they were giving up the Gold Coast, the Basel missionary Elias Schrenk wrote an influential pamphlet ("What Is to Become of the Gold Coast?") that, together with his testimony before the British Parliament, was instrumental in persuading them to stay. It is clear from Schrenk's arguments that he feared that the survival of the Basel Mission on the Gold Coast would be in jeopardy if the British were to leave. This incident is also discussed by Fred Agyemang, *We Presbyterians*, pp. 57-58. David Brokensha, in *Social Change at Larteh*, pp. 15ff., has offered yet another description of the different ways in which the Mission relied on colonial authorities to protect its freedom of action.

47. This was more the case in German-controlled areas of West Africa than in the regions under British control. See Gründer, *Christliche Mission und Deutscher Imperialismus*, and Hallden, *Culture Policy*. In British-controlled areas the Mission was careful to protect its independent identity, but before World War I began it did not find itself in open opposition to British policies or British colonial administrations.

By the early 1800s Catholics, Anglicans, and Methodists already had missionaries in Africa. The region of West Africa then called the Gold Coast was controlled by the Danes, with Christiansborg as their administrative center, and it was for reasons of their own that representatives of the Danish Crown and the Danish Lutheran Church encouraged the Basel Mission to send its agents there.[48] Because Pietism had followers in more than one established confession, the Mission remained officially nondenominational, but before its early representatives to the Gold Coast could be posted they had to be formally ordained as Lutheran clergy, either in Denmark or, later, in Württemberg.[49] To "tread carefully" with established church and colonial interests seems to have been the watchword. The first four missionaries sent to Christiansborg were admonished to obey their own Mission leadership and the Danish Crown implicitly, do nothing to interfere with colonial arrangements or dispute the authority of the (Danish Lutheran) church, stay out of denominational disputes, and avoid trade and local politics at all costs. "You are not bourgeois tradespeople," they were told, "you are not servants of the State; you are not ministers of any particular church; you are not teachers and not employees of the government; rather, you are messengers of Jesus Christ in the Heathen World."[50] Seventy years later missionaries were similarly instructed to avoid being identified too closely with the British colonial authorities. When the missionary Fritz Ramseyer, for example, was posted to the Gold Coast in 1901, he was told to stay clear of the government and to do so in a way that made it abundantly clear to Africans that the Mission and the government were not part of the same organizational effort.[51]

The Danes and later the British were, of course, free to invite the Mission to work in the areas of West Africa under their colonial control, but they could not guarantee the missionaries a welcome reception or, for that matter, provide a supportive environment in which the Mission could pursue its evangelical work.[52] The early Basel missionaries complained that neither the

48. Schlatter, *Geschichte der Basler Mission*, 3:19ff.

49. Schlatter, *Geschichte der Basler Mission*, 1:23-24.

50. These instructions can be located in BMA D-10,3,3, Afrika, 1828. At about the same time, the Wesleyans active on the Gold Coast were being told to follow the motto "Fear God and honour the King," and that "your only business is to promote the moral and religious improvement of the persons to whom you may have access, without in the least degree, in public or private, interfering with their civil condition." Wesleyan Methodist Missionary Society, *WMMS Reports, 1838-1840*, pp. xi, xii-xiii.

51. This direction appears in Ramseyer's posting order, in BMA *Instruktionen*, October 2, 1901. Essentially the same message urging circumspection went to missionaries bound for Cameroon, India, and China.

52. Clarke, *West Africa and Christianity*, p. 41.

European (and nominally Christian) colonials nor the Africans attracted to the colonial center showed much interest in religion in general or in them in particular. The missionary Johannes Henke, a member of the first team of four young men sent to the region, wrote a series of letters on such matters in 1830 and 1831. In one letter he wrote to the Committee that the Europeans he had encountered were "so rotten" that he refused them the Lord's Supper,[53] and in another he wrote at length about the Africans' lack of interest in his efforts to share the gospel with them.[54]

To compound the trials of the missionaries, tropical medicine was almost nonexistent in the 1820s, and Europeans were shockingly vulnerable to the illnesses endemic to the West African region. All three of Henke's colleagues who went out with him in 1828 died from tropical diseases within weeks or months of their arrival in Christiansborg.[55] Henke himself survived somewhat longer, but for all the sacrifices he made, including within two years his own life, he could claim little impact, either on the native Africans or on the European colonials with whom he lived and among whom he worked. It captures the situation perfectly to point out that the first Basel Mission doctor, Christian Heinze, who was posted to the region in 1832 to try to improve the health of the other missionaries, died from tropical fever within weeks of his arrival.[56]

This bleak story of death among the missionaries and disinterest or hostility from the intended objects of their ministry characterized the Mission's experience in West Africa for many years to follow. The numbers are telling. The archive's central personnel record, the *Brüderverzeichnis*, shows that six of the first ten missionaries sent out in the fifteen-year interval between 1828 and 1843 died within one year of their posting. Two more of the ten died before they finished three years of service. To put that information another way, the three-year survival rate for missionaries in those early years was 20 percent. The Mission marked the end of its first quarter-century on the Gold Coast in 1853; the same records show that by that year twenty-six agents had been sent there, and eleven of them had died from illnesses contracted in Africa before they finished their fifth year of work for the organization. Many, like Dr. Heinze, were

53. BMA, letter of May 20, 1830, D-1,2, Christiansborg, 1830, no. 2.

54. BMA, letter of January 30, 1831, D-1,2, Christiansborg, 1831, no. 5. I. Tufuoh (in "Relations") examined the missionaries' early letters from the Gold Coast and reached the same conclusion about the lack of receptiveness among the Europeans there.

55. The Basel Mission's contribution to the development of tropical medicine is treated in detail in F. H. Fischer, *Der Missionsarzt Rudolf Fisch.*

56. Schlatter, *Geschichte der Basler Mission,* 3:27-28; F. H. Fischer, *Der Missionsarzt Rudolf Fisch,* pp. 27-40.

dead within weeks or months of their arrival in Christiansborg. Another six of the twenty-six resigned in bitterness and disappointment, quit under intense interpersonal pressure from colleagues and supervisors, or were "defrocked," that is, dismissed outright *(entlassen)* for breaches of discipline. I will have more to say about some of these cases in chapter 4.

Adding together all the causes for attrition in the first twenty-five years (including death, resignation, and dismissal), two-thirds of the Mission's agents on the Gold Coast (seventeen of the twenty-six posted) were lost.[57] Necessarily, those who remained in the organization were caught up in the tragedies and conflicts that swept away their colleagues, and the effectiveness of their work was seriously eroded as a consequence. Imagine, for example, the despair that must have followed Dr. Heinze's death before he could have any beneficial effect on the survival chances of the others. In purely practical terms, the loss of the Mission's investment in the training and material support of those who died, resigned, or were dismissed was a significant drain on its resources.[58] In time the organization protected itself against some of this loss by suggesting that missionaries were responsible for repaying the costs of their education if they failed to serve in the ways expected of them.[59]

During the period that the Mission was experiencing high attrition among its agents, the number of Africans who were religiously drawn to the Pietist version of Christianity remained very small, if we are to judge from the numbers the Mission itself considered accurate. Although it was certainly not for want of effort on his part, the man in charge of the Basel Mission's Ghana

---

57. The Basel organization was not alone in suffering such a rate of loss. For the general picture consult Bartels, *Roots of Ghana Methodism,* or Clarke, *West Africa and Christianity.* When the Wesleyans wrote the early history of their Gold Coast mission, they said this: "Our first worker . . . landed at Elmina on New Year's Day, 1835. In less than six months he was dead, and for over a year the work was suspended. The next [two] workers . . . landed September, 1836. Within fourteen months both were dead. That same year (1837) Rev. Peter and Mrs. Harrop reached Cape Coast. Neither of them lived a month." Wesleyan Methodist Missionary Society, *WMMS Reports,* 1913-1914, p. 163. About the CMS in Sierra Leone, Jocelyn Murray (*Proclaim the Good News,* p. 23) says, "In 1826, it is recorded that of seventy-nine persons sent out (including wives) in twenty-two years, only fourteen remained, most of the others having died." Geoffrey Moorhouse (*The Missionaries,* pp. 321ff.) reports that in central Africa the London Missionary Society lost twenty missionaries in fourteen years.

58. Over the entire 1828-1914 period covered by my research, one hundred missionaries died on the Gold Coast, fifty-five of them before they had been there three years. Forty-nine of the wives died during the same interval; among these, twenty-seven lived less than three years.

59. See the Basel Mission *Hausordnung* of 1860, p. 15, paras. 14-15 (BMA reference Q-9,31,11).

outpost in 1840, Andreas Riis, could take credit for no true converts at that time, although he had by then been in Africa for eight years.[60] In some situations, Peter Clarke reports, European colonials were as likely to be converted to African religions as Africans were to be drawn to Christianity.[61]

To be sure, from the beginning some Africans were attracted to the Mission's schools and villages or sent their children there for the material advantages they saw in a European education. Yet by the Baslers' own assessment, the first baptisms of truly "converted" adult Africans did not take place until nearly twenty years after the beginning of the Gold Coast effort.[62] According to anthropologist John Middleton, those drawn to the Mission in its first few years fell into three principal categories: princes (sons of kings and chiefs who, in matrilineal systems, had no hope of becoming rulers and whose fathers wanted them to have the advantage of a European education); ex-slaves (who could sometimes break their bonds when the Mission "bought them free" and who found a supportive reception in the Christian community that they could not expect elsewhere); and widows and others (such as deserted women, orphans, children with birth anomalies, and outcasts) who were often denied any legitimate role or form of support in their native communities.[63] Beyond these marginal groups, the "harvest of souls" was very small.

In 1851, twenty-three years after the Baslers' efforts began, only forty-six black Christians could be counted in the Mission community. In a practice that was common among British missions of the time, twenty-five of those forty-six were West Indian volunteers (the Mission called them "repatriates") who had been brought as a group from Jamaica to the Gold Coast to form the nucleus of the Mission's village-building effort. They were accepted for this experiment because they were *already Christian* and therefore could not, strictly speaking, be counted as "converts" for the Mission.[64] (Catherine Mulgrave, whose important place in the Mission's history is described in chapter 4, was in this group of voluntary immigrants.) Intertribal conflicts among native Africans sometimes complicated the work of the missionaries and added to this already discouraging picture.[65] Relations with colonial governments and the politically and economically motivated groups that clustered around them could be further sources of uncertainty and controversy.

60. Mobley, *Ghanaian's Image*, p. 22; Groves, *Planting of Christianity*, 1:301; Neill, *History of Christian Missions*, 2nd ed., p. 260.
61. Clarke, *West Africa and Christianity*, p. 14.
62. Schlatter, *Geschichte der Basler Mission*, 3:43.
63. Middleton, "One Hundred and Fifty Years," p. 4.
64. Schlatter, *Geschichte der Basler Mission*, 3:49.
65. Schlatter, *Geschichte der Basler Mission*, 3:100-107.

I will discuss many of these difficulties in more detail in later chapters. Here I only wish to make the point that they were an integral part of the environment in which the Mission worked. Of equal interest are the severe internal, interpersonal problems, largely of the Mission's own making, that were no less important in determining the organizational climate. Of particular significance was a disciplinary regime (described in chaps. 3 and 4) that conformed closely to Pietist values and for that reason crushed initiative and creativity and eroded the missionaries' bonds of interpersonal trust, badly needed in the turbulent conditions they faced in Africa. There was scarcely a time that the Mission was not racked by this "social pain," the name I have given to the recurrent and apparently inescapable interpersonal friction that compromised the missionaries' best efforts in the field.

By most standards of organizational success and longevity, it could be argued that the Mission's Gold Coast venture should have collapsed long before the century was over. The environment was always dangerous and uncertain; native reactions were often indifferent, sometimes hostile; the missionaries' beliefs and the official organizational policies that were set for them in Basel took little account of the conditions of life in Africa and therefore restricted their ability to respond to the difficulties they faced; and for over a quarter-century only the most meager evidence of religious success (defining success narrowly and quantitatively as the number of truly "reborn" converts) was forthcoming. There were times when in the face of all these complications the leadership discussed the wisdom of abandoning the Gold Coast effort altogether.[66] Yet they never actually took this drastic step. The missionaries marked for service there insisted on the continuation of that effort despite the danger and distress they knew they faced. In the long run the endeavor did not fail; instead it persisted, and by midcentury it had developed the ability to survive its predicaments, if not ever decisively to overcome them. From that point forward the Mission's African membership gradually increased;[67] it expanded its reach into new areas of the Gold Coast; and by the end of the period I have chosen to study it had rooted itself very deeply and, apparently, permanently in the culture and social structure of that region of West Africa. Understanding that intuitively improbable record of survival is the compelling puzzle that captured and has held my interest as a sociologist.

66. Schlatter, *Geschichte der Basler Mission*, 3:32, 41-42.
67. Schlatter, *Geschichte der Basler Mission*, 3:49.

The Lasting Impact of the Mission

The traces of the Basel Mission's influence on Ghana are to be found both in the system of beliefs it promoted and in the organizational template that served as the means of conveyance for those beliefs. In the nine decades that passed between the posting of the first missionaries in 1828 and the forced interruption of its work during World War I, the *Brüderverzeichnis* shows that over 400 of the Mission's agents had gone to the Gold Coast. Included in this number were some 250 ordained missionaries, a number of single women hired as schoolteachers, and a sizable contingent of nonordained (but seminary-trained) representatives of various skilled crafts working under contract for the Mission. Included also were a company of Mission-trained traders (*Vertragskaufmänner*), whose task was to provide a Christian commercial alternative (the Basel Mission Trading Company) to the ordinary colonial traders who, the Mission leadership believed, often exploited and corrupted the people of the area (plates 6 and 7).[68] Not numbered among these ordained and unordained male representatives of the Mission were the wives who joined the men once they had been allowed to marry. The labor of these women in the Mission community was at least equal to that of the men, and in the view of some was even more crucial to the success of the organization (see plates 1, 3, and 8).[69] They worked with native women and children once it had been recognized that a new Christian community could not be built if the Mission's evangelizing activity focused primarily on adult males; they were instrumental in cementing the family relations that were emerging in African Christian families; they were the primary conveyors of domestic

68. For a discussion of this concern on the Mission's part, see Schlatter, *Geschichte der Basler Mission*, 3:390. S. K. Odamtten says that in 1883, 40 percent of the German trade to West Africa was liquor (*Missionary Factor*, p. 215). I do not know the basis for his estimate, which he offers as an index of the corruption brought to Africa by Europeans, and I have not seen similar estimates for other areas of colonial Africa.

69. See, for example, Haas-Lill, "Missionsgeschichte aus der Sicht der Frau"; Konrad, *Missionsbräute*; and Agyemang, *We Presbyterians*, pp. 31ff. The Mission acknowledged the importance of the work of women in the way it bound the missionaries' wives contractually to the organization and spelled out their critical place in the division of labor in the field. I will say more about this in chapter 2. For examples of these contractual arrangements, see "Verordnungen über die Persönliche Stellung der Missionare Revidiert 1886" (Regulations concerning the personal position of the missionaries, revision of 1886) (BMA Q-9,21,7: Section V). See also "Bedingungen für die in den Dienst der Basler Missionsgesellschaft Auszusendenden Bräute" (Conditions for the brides to be sent out in the service of the Basel Mission Society) (BMA Q-9,21,18, February 1889, and Q-9,26,40, n.d.).

training and education for female children of convert families; and they played a vital role in the health care, indeed the daily well-being, of the entire Mission community.[70]

Although there were other religious groups that operated on a larger scale in Africa,[71] the details of the Basel Mission's long-term effect on the Gold Coast place it among the more influential missionary undertakings that have been described in the literature. Native Ghanaian observers from the nineteenth century to the present have documented the Mission's impact as an agent of social change in their country. An early example can be seen in the history written by the native pastor Carl Reindorf, and more recent commentaries have been offered by C. G. Baëta, Ernest Osafo, Fred Agyemang, and S. K. Odamtten.[72] Harris W. Mobley has assembled a revealing collection of native Ghanaian reactions to Christian missionaries, approving and critical alike, from the early 1800s to the 1960s.[73] I will say more about such assessments in the next chapter, but for now the general conclusion that can be drawn from them is that the Mission was indeed an important factor in the emergence of modern Ghanaian society.

Church officials in Ghana and "in-house" Basel Mission chroniclers have also attested to the Mission's influence on the Gold Coast, as have a number of academic historians and other social scientists. For my purposes, an especially revealing assessment was compiled during World War I by the Presbyterians of the United Free Church of Scotland. It will be recalled that in 1917 British colonial authorities asked this group to take over the Mission's activities, at least for the duration of the European war.[74] In preparation for this takeover, the Scots reviewed the Baslers' accomplishments in detail and completed a survey of the Mission's institutional resources. They described an organization that was quite robust, given its precarious beginnings. The mis-

70. For a critical view of the activities of the Basel Mission women, one that sees them primarily as contributing to the development of a dependent workforce for colonial capitalism, see Prodolliet, *Wider die Schamlosigkeit.* For a response to this criticism, see Haas-Lill, "Missionsgeschichte aus der Sicht der Frau."

71. For a listing of the missions active in Africa by the middle of the nineteenth century, see Newcomb, *Cyclopedia of Missions.* For more recent accounts of the nineteenth-century missions working in parts of Africa other than the Gold Coast, see Groves, *Planting of Christianity;* Gründer, *Christliche Mission und Deutscher Imperialismus;* Oliver, *Missionary Factor;* Neill, *History of Christian Missions,* 1st ed.; and Beidelman, *Colonial Evangelism.*

72. Reindorf, *History;* Baëta, ed., *Christianity in Tropical Africa;* Osafo, "Beitrag der Basler Mission"; Agyemang, *We Presbyterians;* and Odamtten, *Missionary Factor.*

73. Mobley, *Ghanaian's Image.*

74. See Wilkie, "An Attempt"; Falk, *Growth.*

sionaries were resident in eleven major stations, around which were scattered at varying distances a large number of smaller settlements, called "outstations." The Scots estimated the size of the overall Mission community in 1917 at thirty thousand members, of whom twelve thousand were judged to be "committed," that is, authentically "converted" or "reborn" Christians. As many as ten thousand pupils, boys and girls alike, were being taught in an extensive network of about 180 schools and seminaries.[75] This network has since come to constitute a vital part of the educational system of Ghana.[76] David Brokensha has reported that in some communities "Basel" has survived into contemporary usage as the colloquial word for "school," and John Middleton has credited that educational system with the generation of relative prosperity and the prospect of upward social mobility for those in the privileged circle of mission Christians.[77]

Seminaries built by the Mission gave training to teachers, catechists, preachers, and theologians. Toward the end of the century, the introduction of modern European medicine, sometimes in collaboration and at other times in competition with native healing practices, became an integral part of the Pietist Christian strategy.[78] Strong support was given to European crafts and agricultural technologies, and crops were introduced that were considered well suited both to the native culture and to the independent villages that were envisioned for the Christian Africans. The Mission's technical schools produced carpenters, locksmiths, cartwrights, watch repairers, masons, tailors, bookbinders, printers, blacksmiths, furniture makers, sawyers,

---

75. Clarke, *West Africa and Christianity,* pp. 96-97. The Mission's own reckoning of the numbers in their region of influence was somewhat more conservative. The yearly report *(Hundertundzweiter Jahresbericht der Evangelischen Missions-Gesellschaft auf 1. Juli 1917)* estimated the overall population of the area in which the Mission was active at 560,000. They put the number of Mission community members at 27,338, indicating that they considered about 5 percent of the indigenous population to be within their circle of influence. Among those in the community, 13,115 (just under half) were counted as converted and eligible for communion *(Abendmahlsberechtigt).* The number of new Christians baptized during 1916 was 915, and the number of pupils in Mission schools was put at 9,138. Regardless of whether the estimates of the Baslers or those of the Scots are accepted as more accurate, this situation is clearly vastly different from the situation of the Mission fifty years earlier. For a comparison with another organization, in 1913 the Wesleyans working near the Baslers claimed 16,333 "Full Members" (undefined) in an "Adult Baptized Community" of 62,983. Wesleyan Methodist Missionary Society, *WMMS Reports, 1913-1914.*

76. Wallerstein, *The Road to Independence,* pp. 137ff.

77. Brokensha, *Social Change at Larteh,* p. 23; Middleton, "One Hundred and Fifty Years."

78. F. H. Fischer, *Der Missionsarzt Rudolf Fisch.*

and shingle makers (see plates 8-14).[79] Cocoa was introduced and encouraged as a cash crop (see plates 15 and 16).[80] There were some misgivings about this commodity because of the distraction caused by the wealth it generated, but it continues today as a leading export and source of foreign exchange for the region.[81] Other crops introduced into the Mission community and cultivated for use and export included mangoes, cocoyam, breadfruit, coffee, sugarcane, avocado pears, oranges, bananas, beans, cotton, rubber, and arrowroot.[82]

In another vein, Brokensha has provided an interesting index of the Mission's importance in one local Ghanaian community, the town of Larteh.[83] In 1880 Christians there constructed, at their own expense, a chapel "measuring eighty-five feet by thirty-two feet, [seating] 800 and [with] coloured-glass windows and a sixty-five-foot tower with an iron cross" (p. 20). This was followed in 1908 by a building large enough for 1,800 worshipers, which is still in use (see plate 17). In general, Brokensha reported, churches and schools built by the Mission are among the largest buildings to be seen in most of the villages and towns in the region of its Gold Coast activities (p. 18).

Under the direction of the Scots, who took over from the Baslers, the Presbyterian Church of Ghana grew to institutional independence out of the structures and communities established by the Basel Mission. In 1926, after a nine-year absence, the Baslers themselves were allowed to return and resume their work. Their presence in Ghana today is witness to how securely anchored the Mission has become since that return. It has been over a century and a half since the first Basler arrived in Christiansborg, more than seventy years since the British suspended the Mission's activities during World War I, and a third of a century since the country emerged from colonial rule, pledging itself under Kwame Nkrumah to struggle free of both the symbols and the realities of foreign cultural domination. The mission historian Stephen Neill uses strong language in assessing the Mission's accumulated impact prior to Ghanaian independence: "The missionaries found Ghana divided, poor, ignorant, and racked by the slave trade. It was in no small measure due to their

79. Agyemang, *We Presbyterians*, pp. 21-23.
80. Middleton, "One Hundred and Fifty Years," p. 6; Neill, *History of Christian Missions*, 1st ed., p. 260.
81. Brokensha, *Social Change at Larteh*, pp. 16ff. Less obvious at the time of the introduction of cocoa farming was the connection between it and the spread of hookworm disease brought about by the movement around the countryside of large numbers of unattached laborers. On this point, see F. H. Fischer, *Der Missionsarzt Rudolf Fisch*, pp. 398ff.
82. Agyemang, *We Presbyterians*, pp. 21-22.
83. Brokensha, *Social Change at Larteh*, pp. 20-21. Parenthetical numbers in this paragraph are from this work.

efforts that in 1957, when Ghana, first of the peoples of tropical Africa to emerge from colonial to national status, attained to full independence, it was united, rich, educated, and able to hold its own in the competitive world of western civilization."[84]

Neill's assessment, now somewhat dated, is that of a European and might be expected to overstate the influence of European-inspired changes. As counterpoint, in the Ghanaian Fred Agyemang's history of the Presbyterian Church of Ghana (successor church to the original Basel Mission), the effects of the educational infrastructure established by the Mission are described in a similar way. After independence, he writes,

> [W]e [Presbyterians] produced the first Speaker in the nation's parliament, five university vice-chancellors, one President of our Republic, one of the two first District Commissioners, the first government hospital nurse, the first scholarship awarded . . . for overseas study, the first two Ghanaian secretaries to Cabinet, the first Ghanaian commercial airpilot, the first woman lawyer and judge, two deans of the medical school, the first woman religious minister, the first commissioner of police, the first army officers, the first inspector-general of police, the first woman veterinary surgeon, [and] the first head student of the University of the Gold Coast.[85]

Of course, not every observer shares these expansive assessments of the Mission's impact. In his account of the period leading up to independence in Ghana, Immanuel Wallerstein dismisses, or more accurately, essentially ignores, the impact of the missions, noting only that Christianity was embraced by no more than 10 percent of the population as the country approached its separation from Britain.[86] For a student of social change in Africa, however, Wallerstein seemed in this work to be curiously unaware of how far the importance of the Christians exceeded their numbers. He cited a remark by Ako Adjei, one of Nkrumah's closest associates in the nationalist movement, to the effect that missionary work was a form of "spiritual aggression or spiritual imperialism,"[87] but he neglected to point out that Adjei was himself educated in Basel Mission schools, remained a lifelong Christian, and argued forcefully for the inclusion in African nationalism of an element of "tolerant Christian hu-

---

84. Neill, *History of Christian Missions,* 2nd ed., p. 260.
85. Agyemang, *We Presbyterians,* p. 8.
86. Wallerstein, *The Road to Independence,* p. 17.
87. Wallerstein, *The Road to Independence,* p. 20.

manism," which he believed recognized the intrinsic value of all indigenous cultures.[88] Nor did Wallerstein point out that Nkrumah, who was educated by Catholic missionaries, described himself as a radical nationalist, Marxian socialist, and nondenominational Christian, in that order.[89] In the year of Ghana's independence, Nkrumah addressed the delegates to the International Missionary Council, which was then meeting in his country, in this way:

> Ghana is proud to pay its tribute to the great work of missionaries in West Africa. If you have time to visit more widely in this country, you will often find as you travel along the roads, little cemeteries lost in the bush where lie buried the brave men and women who, in bringing the Christian faith to this country, gave "the last full measure of their devotion." They knew that they faced the certainty of loneliness and imminent risk of death. Yellow fever decimated them and their families. But still they came. They belong to the martyrs of Christianity.[90]

Peter Kodjo, a participant from Ghana at a recent workshop on mission history held in Basel in 1992, described how the *organizational* example of the Mission in particular has replicated itself, like a genetic code, in virtually all the institutions of that emerging nation.[91] Confirmation of his assessment and a suggestion of one way in which that replication has occurred can be found in the July 1986 edition of the *Christian Messenger*, a newspaper published by the Presbyterian Church of Ghana. Prominently featured in that issue were reports of speeches given by two functionaries of the government headed by Flight Lieutenant Jerry Rawlings. This government, like Nkrumah's at an earlier time, worked to present itself as independent, progressive, and iconoclastic, and it is of interest that both speeches summarized by the *Messenger* call to mind the language used by Nkrumah thirty years earlier. The first address, given by a regional party secretary to a church celebration, was reported as follows: "[The Secretary] minced no words when he said that it was ... the rigid

88. Mobley, *Ghanaian's Image*, pp. 59ff.

89. Mobley, *Ghanaian's Image*, pp. 59 n, 96-97.

90. Cited by Mobley, *Ghanaian's Image*, p. 24.

91. Kodjo was a discussant in the conference based on my research, titled "Herren und Brüder: Struktur und Glaube, Gehorsam und Initiative in der alten Basler Mission." 7. Workshop zur Geschichte der Basler Mission und Ihrer Partnerkirchen. 28-29. November, 1992, im Basler Missionshaus ("Masters and brethren: structure and belief, obedience and initiative in the historical Basel Mission." Seventh workshop on the history of the Basel Mission and its partner churches. November 28-29, 1992, in the Mission House in Basel, Switzerland).

Presbyterian training [in] respect, humility, obedience and truth that placed many sons and daughters into leadership positions. . . . [He] reminded the congregants that no nation however rich her resources could progress if her citizens were undisciplined [and that] the moral transformation of the society was not only the responsibility of the [government] but for all especially the churches."

An accompanying article summarized the comments of a district party secretary who was on hand when a government-sponsored health clinic was turned over to the church:

[The district secretary] said he has respect for the impeccable discipline of the Presbyterian Church, and appealed to the church to bring back those qualities to raise the moral standard of pupils and students. "We want to train our children to be God-fearing, respectful, obedient, humble, honest and patriotic and we rely on you for this change. . . . The Presbyterian Church is noted for her discipline, rectitude and humility and I appeal to the authorities not to relent in their efforts in intensifying this teaching."

Crucially, this representative of a radical government continued: "I also appeal to the Ghana Educational Service to contact the Presbyterian Church of Ghana for the curriculum which the missionaries used to train us."

The response by the Presbyterian leadership to the image of close church-state relations suggested by these officials was wary, but at the same time its confident tone underscores the lasting institutional impact on that society of the Basel Mission and the indigenous church that it fostered: "The moderator of the Presbyterian Church of Ghana has said that both the church and state are inseparable institutions, which must unite to seek peace, progress and welfare of the people. . . . Any act of divisionism, ill feeling and distrust [between church and state] . . . would not be in the interest of the nation. [Furthermore,] as children of God it is the bounden duty of those in responsible positions in secular and sacred institutions to realise that they are servants and are accountable to the people."[92]

As these examples are meant to show, there is little doubt of the impact of missionary Christianity as an agent of social change in Africa. In the interest of balance, however, Richard Gray has cautioned that the relationship between European and African beliefs was far from one-sided.[93] One key to the

---

92. *Christian Messenger* (July 1986).
93. Gray, *Black Christians*, pp. 2-6; see also Clarke, *West Africa and Christianity*, p. 4.

nature of their encounter, Gray argues, lies in the conviction common to many indigenous African religions that the influence of evil in the world can be eradicated or countered if certain forms and practices are properly followed. Rulers and ruled alike are bound to those formal necessities, and as long as religious functionaries participate in the assessment of compliance with them, they are in a position to say whether nonreligious authorities represent evil or its antithesis. This is a potent responsibility. Secular authorities who have been judged by religious leaders to be out of step with ritual requirements can find their legitimacy and therefore their power being undermined in a very real way.[94] In its natural context, then, indigenous religion could be a threat to the established order as easily as it could support the status quo. In either mode, it is a far from insignificant or derivative factor in social continuity and change.

Christianity in Africa did not displace these indigenous notions, according to Gray, but rather fused with and was altered by them in such a way that the resulting synthesis of beliefs about ritual propriety contains the same potentially critical dialectic today.[95] Depending on what they saw (and see) happening around them at any given time, African Christians might embrace, reject, or seek to change the African status quo, and they were (and are) similarly capable of embracing, rejecting, or introducing change to an emerging mission, colonial, or postcolonial regime. The Rawlings government, though legally elected for the first time in 1992, has for years been an authoritarian military regime with progressive-to-radical leanings; its receptivity to church practice and the willingness of Christian religious functionaries in turn to express judgments about the "bounden duty of those in responsible positions" indicate that this critical dynamic is as alive today as it was in the colonial past. In a more general way, this two-way influence between indigenous and imported religion also cautions against the assumption that the Basel Mission or any other Western organization had an unanswered impact on African culture.

Connections

Organizations like the Basel Mission draw on resources and pursue goals that set them apart from the administration and production enterprises that have

---

94. This argument can be seen as a variation on a theme developed by Jürgen Habermas in *Legitimation Crisis.*

95. Gray, *Black Christians,* p. 6.

occupied most of the attention of organizational sociologists. This relative neglect of missions is itself a reason, but not the only one, for focusing attention on them. They did not stand free of larger political and economic forces; but their influence as agents of change was substantial, as was the synergy created by the merging of European and African beliefs. These effects belie the notion that missions in general, and the Basel Mission in particular, were peripheral players whose traces in the colonial drama will be faint compared with those left by more "fundamental" economic and political forces.

The quality of the Basel Mission's archival record makes it an excellent place to ask how such organizations attract participants and hold their memberships together, how they marshal their material and human resources in the causes they pursue, and how they survive their institutional adversities, including the ones they generate for themselves. If the Mission is viewed as much as possible without abstraction or ideological filters, it can be seen just how unusual it was and how improbable its ambitions were. It was a collection of German and Swiss farmers and craftsmen and their essentially middle-class spouses who, at the behest of the social elites in their own communities, went off to persuade the people of the Gold Coast that the Pietist version of Christianity was their best hope for the construction of a morally and materially better life. Described in this stark way, the biggest surprise is that the efforts of the first missionaries did not simply shatter, never to resume, on their initial contact with African reality. After over a century and a half in Ghana, the present-day members of the organization are heirs to the institutional record and collective memory of those early missionaries, and they still pursue a strong afterimage of the original Pietist vision. The ethnocentrism and theological absolutism that took them to Africa in the beginning have receded, but the commitment to the promotion of economic independence and indigenous development in Ghana (and in other emerging nations) continues.[96] It is ironic that this emphasis on collective self-reliance places the Mission today among the more progressive overseas missions; in the 1800s it looked backward to the preindustrial period for its social and economic inspiration and regarded itself without apology as reactionary. The Mission was seen in the same way by some other contemporary missionary groups and by colonial interests who regarded themselves as more "modern," "realistic," and "forward-looking" than the Baslers.

96. The financial accounting for the Mission in the yearly report for 1992 (*Evangelische Missionsgesellschaft* 1992) showed a budget of 13.7 million Swiss francs to support the work of eighty-two mission representatives and cooperative projects in thirteen countries in Asia, Africa (including Ghana), and Latin America.

The early Mission was a study in contrasts, a striking mixture of enthusiasm and practicality, opportunism and restraint, sacrifice and hubris. Regardless of how its early activities are judged today, it is clear that long before its work was interrupted in 1917 a niche had opened up and the Mission had settled firmly into it. The Mission needed Christian converts and a field in which to labor, and both Africans and the British colonials who ruled their land were interested in developing channels through which natives could move into productive positions in the growing state apparatus and market economy. There were clear affinities among these diverse sets of interests. The full reasons for the emergence of this niche must be traced to economic and geopolitical factors that lie, for the most part, outside the scope of this investigation.[97] I will concentrate instead on how the Mission endured through very precarious times and therefore came to be strategically poised to occupy that niche when it did open up. It is true that the organizational skills and the training given the missionaries became more sophisticated over the years and the physical danger they faced from tropical illnesses diminished. But seen from the inside, they never put the painful interpersonal crises and organizational contradictions that I will describe decisively behind them, and the environment surrounding the Mission remained turbulent. Knowing why the organization did not collapse under the weight of these difficulties is the key to understanding why it was still in place and able to take on the important role that changing circumstances eventually created for it.

97. This is the task carved out for itself by the "natural selection" approach defined in Hannan and Freeman, "Population Ecology of Organizations."

CHAPTER 2

The Participants

To understand the Basel Mission it is necessary to understand its membership. I have traced the social origins of the leadership and the ordinary missionaries, and I have asked what the members of each category gained, personally and collectively, from their commitment to the evangelical movement. The Mission was far from egalitarian, but it is evident that both groups were empowered by their participation, though in quite different ways. It is also clear that the experiences of many of the members went well beyond the purely religious goals of the organization. Special attention is focused on the social mobility of the missionaries and the consolidation of those gains by their offspring. Other parts of the discussion concern the participation of women in the organization, the rules and realities of marriage, the importance of status consciousness and invidious class distinctions among the participants, and the possible effects of the missionary movement on class structures in Africa and Europe. Studies of similar topics in other missions provide points of comparison.

Class Collaboration for the Sake of Religion

As Max Weber pointed out, class and status barriers in "enthusiastic" movements often yield to "fraternization and exuberant community sentiments," and indeed, the missionary movement enjoyed social approval and financial support across many levels of European society.[1] The actual mode of participation in the movement by people from different classes, however, was quite

1. *From Max Weber*, p. 52; Moorhouse, *The Missionaries.*

variable. As a general rule, persons from privileged and influential back-grounds provided leadership while those who provided labor, that is, who carried on the day-to-day work of evangelism in the field, were from more modest origins. The Pietist movement, whose strong missionary impulse led to the creation of the Basel Mission, is a good case in point. In the Würt-temberg region Pietism did not claim a majority of the members of any class as adherents,[2] but it appealed to some individuals in all social categories.[3] The widely dispersed support and fund-raising groups (called *Hilfsvereine*) that provided the financial underpinning of the Basel Mission reflected the entire range of this social diversity. Inside the Mission, however, it was essentially the poles of the diversity that were reflected in the organization's active mem-bership; the members of the elite founding and governing circle were sharply separated, socially and economically, from the men and women who were ex-pected to carry the evangelical message abroad.

"Fraternization" (Weber's term) is not the best description of the relation-ship between the leadership and the missionaries, but common religious val-ues and beliefs certainly knit together their divergent reasons for joining "the cause." The Mission provided both the instrument and the legitimacy each group needed to translate their evangelical beliefs into social action. Yet while their shared commitment to Pietism brought them together in a joint project, it did not mean that they shared the initiative in shaping and directing that project, any more than they enjoyed equal privileges or opportunities outside it. I will show in chapter 3 that the governing group's firm monopoly of con-trol in the Mission was a mirror image of their economic and political influ-ence and their social prestige in the larger society.

Although the two main groups who participated in the Mission were not equal in any material respect, it must also be pointed out that neither group was compelled to join the missionary movement, and neither entirely lacked alternative outlets for its religious energies and resources. Their meeting in the Mission can therefore be characterized as a mutually rewarding and es-sentially voluntary collaboration that developed, significantly, at a time when modern class antagonisms were becoming more sharply drawn in other social arenas. The period that saw the origin and growth of the major European missions was also marked by increasing working-class conscious-ness and conflict, both of which took visible form in the revolutions of 1848, in the emergence of large-scale labor organizations, and in the growth of a broad array of radical, or at least populist, working-class political move-

2. Fulbrook, *Piety and Politics*, p. 41.
3. Fulbrook, *Piety and Politics*, pp. 36-37, 39ff.; Scharfe, *Die Religion des Volkes*, p. 136.

ments.[4] The opportunity to participate in the missionary movement might have been one instrumental factor in keeping young people from the villages and from the land from being pulled into that growing class polarization.

I use "shared commitment" and "collaboration" in a cautious way to describe the relationship between decision makers and decision followers in the Mission. I do not suggest that there was a complete identity of interests or expectations between the two; I agree with Ed Young's observation that expressions of commitment to shared values can mask deep divisions of interests or even be used as the medium through which such divisions come to be expressed as overt conflict.[5] What is clear, however, is that there were opportune points of complementarity — or in the present context, "elective affinities" — in the religious beliefs, material interests, and historical circumstances of the Mission's participants. The meshing of their worldviews was sufficient to bring the different groups together and keep them together for over a century of shared effort.

The Membership

In the 1840s an Anglican bishop could describe in these words the separation between leaders and followers in the Church Missionary Society (CMS), the powerful evangelical Anglican society based in London: "It has been the custom to think of missionaries as an inferior set of men, sent out, paid and governed by a superior set of men formed into a committee in London. Of course then you must have examiners and secretaries and an office to see that the inferior men are not too inferior; and you must have a set of cheap colleges in which the inferior men may get an inferior education and you must provide an inferior sort of ordination which will not enable them to compete in England with the superior men."[6]

Such frank language is not often encountered in the primary mission literature,[7] but the social separation and class protectiveness that the passage alludes to, if not the uncharitable underlying attitude suggested by its language, are reflected in the divide between leaders and followers in a great many religious organizations. The Basel Mission provides a particularly sharp example.

4. Hobsbawm, *The Age of Revolution,* esp. chaps. 11-13; Calhoun, *Question of Class Struggle;* Burawoy, *Manufacturing Consent.*
5. Young, "Naming of the Rose."
6. Quoted by Oliver, *Missionary Factor,* p. 12 n.
7. A less loaded statement of the same facts concerning class differences in the CMS is offered by Murray, *Proclaim the Good News,* pp. 17-18.

The Leadership

After its creation by the German Society for Christianity in 1815, the Mission's leadership was lodged in a self-perpetuating circle of men, called "the Committee," that usually had about twelve life members, sometimes fewer. Only one woman, Juliane von Krüdener, who came from an aristocratic Russian family and was a confidante and spiritual adviser to Czar Alexander I, was intimately involved in the founding and early financial support of the Mission. Von Krüdener was an important participant in the Society for Christianity and, beyond that, appears to have been a charismatic and effective evangelist among the higher social circles in Europe.[8] The records of the Committee's earliest meetings reveal that the men who comprised that body spoke of Frau von Krüdener among themselves with respect and acknowledged her extraordinary success in attracting adherents and financial contributions to the Mission. Her presentation of a collection of jewelry, for example, which she was able to entice as gifts from wealthy Pietist women of the region, was seen as a pivotal event in the founding of the Mission.[9] Albert Ostertag, himself a Committee member from 1848 to 1871, wrote an intimate account of the Mission's earliest days in which he credited von Krüdener with bringing a number of influential people to the cause of the Mission, including some who became members of its controlling elite.[10]

The men in the early Mission leadership used the term "patriarchy" to describe themselves, reflecting what they thought was a biblically sanctioned rule of decision making, but this did not lead them to exclude this resourceful woman from open and meaningful participation in the formative stages of the Mission. In the end, however, Juliane von Krüdener's very effectiveness alarmed those of the civil and clerical authorities of Basel who were not involved in the Mission. To these men she was enigmatic and controversial, a peripatetic outsider, and it worried them that a powerful and potentially sep-

8. Stähelin, *Christentumsgesellschaft,* pp. 8-10, 92. Von Krüdener was a socially prominent member of the Russian nobility. Married to a diplomat, she was visible in intellectual circles in Paris, especially after the appearance of a sensational autobiographical novel *(Valérie),* supposedly inspired by her separation from her husband. She came to Basel and became involved in religious circles there after her conversion to Moravian Pietism. When she left Basel in 1815, she joined the intimate circle around Tsar Alexander I and claimed credit for his decision to create the "Holy Alliance" among Russia, Austria, and Prussia. I have written at greater length about von Krüdener elsewhere; see Predelli and Miller, "Piety and Patriarchy."

9. See Basel Mission Archive (BMA) *Komiteeprotokolle* (Committee Minutes) 1, p. 52, for the meeting of May 27, 1815. Committee Minutes are hereafter abbreviated *KP.*

10. Ostertag, *Entstehungsgeschichte,* pp. 255-56.

aratist religious movement like Pietism should number in its vanguard a person who was not of their own familiar social network. They were especially concerned that such a movement might come to be dominated by a woman. Those authorities pressed von Krüdener to sever her ties to the German Society for Christianity and the Basel Mission and leave the city. In the face of this opposition she returned eventually to Russia. Joining her when she left Basel were some men who were among the important early Mission enthusiasts, including one member of the Committee.[11] After her departure, no woman entered the tight policy-making circle of the Basel Mission for the next hundred years.

Because of their eminence, the social origins, economic fortunes, community involvements, and marital alliances of the men who maintained control of the Mission are generally well known.[12] Earlier studies by Wilhelm Schlatter, Renate Vogelsanger, and Andreas Waldburger have described many aspects of the Committee's role and assembled some of the details of its membership.[13] In addition, the Mission archive contains a file on each Committee member, as well as, in many cases, their biographies and obituaries. Still other information on family backgrounds was gleaned from the eight-volume biographical registry for Switzerland, the *Historisch-biographisches Lexicon der Schweiz*.[14] Finally, useful details on individuals' occupations, civic and clerical offices, family trees, and marriage alliances were retrieved from the Archive of the City of Basel *(Staatsarchiv)*. When this information on the Committee members is pieced together, it is apparent that the Mission's leaders were drawn with few exceptions from the higher levels of bourgeois society in Switzerland and southern Germany.

The Swiss members of the inner circle, whose lives are more extensively documented than the Germans', often described themselves and were described by others as "aristocratic Baslers."[15] The choice of labels is revealing. There is in a strict sense no hereditary aristocracy in Switzerland, which has had a series of confederal and federal republican forms of governance since 1291.[16] Frau von Krüdener was probably the only one of the founders who

11. Ostertag, *Entstehungsgeschichte*, pp. 337ff.; Schlatter, *Geschichte der Basler Mission,* 1:16ff.

12. Waltraud Haas-Lill, who worked closely with me throughout this research, assembled much of the basic documentation for this part of the analysis.

13. Schlatter, *Geschichte der Basler Mission,* vol. 1; Vogelsanger, *Pietismus und Afrikanische Kultur;* and Waldburger, *Missionare und Moslem.*

14. Türler et al., *Historisch-biographisches Lexikon der Schweiz.*

15. Schlatter, *Geschichte der Basler Mission,* 1:133.

16. Schmid, *Conflict and Consensus,* chap. 1.

could rightly wear the label of aristocrat. Nevertheless, the frequent use of the term says something important about the leaders' self-conception, and it reflects their enduring prominence in the life of the community. When Ernst Troeltsch wrote about these individuals, he identified them with "Swiss industrialism and Basel wealth" and aptly called them a "republican aristocracy."[17] Many of their family names and fortunes can be documented as far back as the fifteenth century, and the records indicate that some were descended from refugees from the Counter-Reformation elsewhere in Europe, Huguenots in particular, who migrated to Basel in the sixteenth and seventeenth centuries. As a group, these families — committed, energetic, and entrepreneurial — could easily have posed for Max Weber's portrait of the early European capitalists.[18]

The German members of this leadership were always fewer in number than the Swiss. Some of them, like the Swiss, were from relatively privileged backgrounds. One such was Johann Georg Kellner, *Oberpostmeister* in Braunschweig. According to Ostertag's account, Kellner had considered himself an "enlightened" student of Voltaire and Rousseau, but found himself in difficulty with the government imposed on his homeland by Napoleon.[19] He was asked to use his access to the mails to gather information on his countrymen, but rather than do this he went to prison. During his incarceration he came to be a strong opponent of the "liberating" trends unleashed by the Enlightenment and the French Revolution. He became a fervent Bible student, moved to Basel to participate in the German Society for Christianity, and was part of the group from that society that founded the Mission. It was also in Basel that he came under the influence of Frau von Krüdener; he left the Mission after only one year on the governing Committee and followed her when she and her retinue resettled in Russia.

More typically the German members of the Mission leadership gained distinction for their theological training rather than for their social or economic prominence. Most of them had studied and later taught at Tübingen University,[20] which by the time of the Mission's founding had become an important seat of Pietist learning.[21] In a strict sense their social standing was intermediate between the Swiss "aristocrats" and the ordinary missionaries; they shared the education, social visibility, and attitudes of the leadership

---

17. Troeltsch, *Social Teaching*, 2:687.

18. Weber, *Protestant Ethic*.

19. Ostertag, *Entstehungsgeschichte*, pp. 272ff.

20. Schlatter, *Geschichte der Basler Mission*, 1:5.

21. Beyreuther, *Geschichte des Pietismus;* Fulbrook, *Piety and Politics*.

group, but their national and cultural origins were somewhat closer to those of the rank and file.[22]

The general pattern of leadership that has persisted throughout the Mission's history emerged during the formative years between 1815 and 1821. During those six years the Committee clarified its duties and expanded its roster from seven to eleven members. In all, fifteen men served during that period, including replacements for four who died or withdrew. Uncharacteristically, no reliable background information survives for one member. The backgrounds of the other fourteen are as follows.

- The Mission's principal founder, the son of a Lutheran minister from Württemberg, was a longtime activist in Pietist causes and, in addition to the Basel Mission, was cofounder of several other religious organizations.
- The Mission's first "inspector" (the title of the person who served as executive director), the son of a shoemaker, was a theologian and pastor from Württemberg, educated at Tübingen University.
- Two local pastors came from prominent Basel families, whose members included merchants, politicians, engineers, and guild masters.
- A pastor who taught in the Mission seminary came from a Basel family originally known as coppersmiths and plumbers but who by the time of the Mission's founding had achieved recognition as theologians and academics.
- A professor of theology at Basel University (also associated with Marburg, Tübingen, and Heidelberg) came from a Swiss family whose members included prominent bankers, merchants, theologians, and political notables.
- A Basel University professor of philosophy and mathematics was a member of a traditional Basel family that included the owners of a firm of silk dyers as well as academics, merchants, pharmacists, and physicians.
- Five merchants/traders came from eminent old Basel families noted for wealthy merchants, manufacturers, scientists, jurists, artists, philosophers, theologians, physicians, academics, and politicians.
- A seminary teacher, a German whose family origins are not noted, served the Mission for six years, then returned to his home in Württemberg.
- A German postmaster (Oberpostmeister Kellner) from Württemberg was a founding member of the Mission but served on the governing Committee for only one year before leaving to follow Frau von Krüdener when she was pressed to leave Basel.

22. Cf. Vogelsanger, *Pietismus und Afrikanische Kultur,* pp. 46ff.

By the year 1900, some eighty years later, the social composition of the Committee had not changed. In that year there were thirteen members. Two (again including the inspector at the time) were theologians from Württemberg who were associated with Tübingen University. Another Württemberger among the thirteen was from a family of tanners; exceptionally, he had begun as a missionary and worked his way into the administration of the Mission and onto the Committee, the only case of such dramatic internal mobility in the Mission's first century of existence. The other ten members were drawn from the economic, social, and political elite of Basel, essentially replicating the profile from the earlier period: merchants, bankers, manufacturers, academics, politicians, and jurists. A picture of the leadership taken at any interval during the Mission's first century would show the same pattern, and the family names of some Committee participants span the entire period.

Indeed, family is the key to understanding this leadership. There were, in all, forty Swiss men who served on the Committee between 1815 and 1900. Their participation in the established institutional leadership of local churches, in the economic life of the region, and in the government of the city/canton of Basel has been amply documented elsewhere and need not be repeated here.[23] My investigation of the family records for these forty men indicates that they were also part of a tightly knit and endogamous network of social interaction. Fully eighteen of the forty were married to a person from a family with one or more members who also served or would later come to serve as a member of the Committee. To this basic tabulation I added the connections that linked Committee members by marriage to persons who served the Mission in ways other than Committee membership (for example, as members of important commissions). Finally, I looked for close kinship connections besides marriage (for example, son, father, cousin, brother) that tied Committee members to other important members of the Mission community. Taking all of these connections together, the investigation reveals a remarkably dense interpersonal network: thirty-three of the forty men who served on the Committee had relatives in responsible positions in the Mission, compared with seven who did not.

Generations of shared family devotion to the Mission's work was the rule, not the exception. A founding Committee member named Daniel LaRoche, whose family name is still among the most prominent in Switzerland, offers

23. Schlatter, *Geschichte der Basler Mission*, 1:133ff.; Waldburger, *Missionare und Moslem*, pp. 39ff.; Troeltsch, *Social Teaching*, 2:687; Wyss, *Soziale Politik des Konservativen Bürgertums*; Sarasin, *Stadt der Bürger*.

an apt illustration. He, his brother, two brothers-in-law, and a nephew served at different times on the Committee, and three other relatives were teachers in the Mission seminary or members of commissions presiding over different areas of the Mission's activities. Other noted families were just as deeply attached to the Mission, in some cases, like the LaRoche family, serving throughout and well beyond the period covered by this analysis. Sarasin, for example, is a family name that was prominent among the most active Committee members and financial supporters of the Mission in the nineteenth century; that family name is still attached to the private bank that handles the organization's accounts, and a member of the bank's directorate sits on the Committee as this is written.[24]

In short, the founding of the Mission was accomplished and its leadership was provided by representatives of a visible and stable religious, social, political, and economic elite. It is interesting, however, that as time went on this same elite did not continue to be the principal source of the Mission's day-to-day financial support. To be sure, Committee members and their families sometimes contributed large sums to the cause, including grants to support specific activities and to buy the compound of land and erect the buildings that still serve as the headquarters of the Mission (see plate 18).[25] Other wealthy and well-placed individuals in Switzerland and Germany who remained outside the immediate leadership group were also dependable supporters. Soon after the founding of the Mission, however, the Committee decided to broaden the financial support base far beyond their own relatively narrow social circle. The strategy was to reach down the social hierarchies of the time to tap the zeal and steady generosity of ordinary Pietists. The *Hilfsvereine* (support groups) that church women created for this purpose in turn organized collections and put together efficient networks of subscribers, most of whom were "common folk" of modest station attached to congregations throughout Europe.[26]

In adopting this strategy the Mission consciously followed the earlier experience of the important English missions.[27] The Church Missionary Society in London, for example, with a controlling board at least equal in eminence to that in Basel, had learned quite quickly that the weekly accumula-

24. See Sarasin, *Stadt der Bürger.*
25. Schlatter, *Geschichte der Basler Mission,* 1:255ff.
26. Schlatter, *Geschichte der Basler Mission,* 1:26-27, 38ff., 333ff.; Eiselin, "Zur Erziehung," p. 103; Tschudi-Barbatti, "Die Halbbatzen-Kollekte."
27. In this as in other ways, imitation played an important part in the isomorphism that can be observed among nineteenth-century missions. See DiMaggio and Powell, "The Iron Cage Revisited."

tion of pennies from children and from mission enthusiasts among the lower-middle and working classes could easily exceed the contributions of the well placed and wealthy.[28] In the early years of its existence the Basel Mission's version of this arrangement, called the "halfpenny collection" *(Halbbatzenkollekte)*, was so successful that surpluses generated out of those accumulating small contributions could be invested at interest and held in reserve against future needs.[29] The concept of "class collaboration," which I have used primarily to describe the membership and internal affairs of the Mission, also captures the essence of this funding strategy.[30]

An interesting analogue to this strategy was used in Africa. After the Mission was fairly well established on the Gold Coast, Africans who were part of the Mission community were expected to contribute money to support the programs that had been introduced by the missionaries. Special appeals were made in periods when the economies of Europe were depressed and contributions through the *Halbbatzenkollekte* fell off. In March 1898, for example, Inspector Oehler had the following missive distributed "To the Pastors, Catechists, Elders and Congregations connected with the Basel Mission on the Gold Coast" (the original is in English):

> [In] 1896 as well as in 1897 the accounts of our society showed a deficit; and we are afraid that 1898 . . . will be the same. . . . And this, notwithstanding many of our friends here in Europe do their utmost to keep up their subscriptions and offerings according to their ability; but a great number of our friends are really poor and not in a position to do more again, and several circumstances have combined to draw upon the liberality of those who are willing to give. In some parts of Württemberg hailstorms and inundations have done great damage and partly spoiled the crop. . . . I am quite sure, that you yourselves will derive the greatest blessing if you cheerfully and willingly accede to our request.[31]

28. Murray, *Proclaim the Good News,* pp. 14ff.

29. Schlatter, *Geschichte der Basler Mission,* 1:26-27, 136ff.; see also Eiselin, "Zur Erziehung," pp. 53-54, and Tschudi-Barbatti, "Die Halbbatzen-Kollekte."

30. "Hegemony" is another concept that describes an asymmetric arrangement of power that reflects class divisions but is supported by a legitimating cultural rationale accepted by participants at all levels. Discussions of hegemony usually begin with reference to Gramsci, *Selections.* See also Bottomore et al., *Dictionary of Marxist Thought,* pp. 193-96, 201-3.

31. BMA D-9,1c,4.

In 1914 a similar request was made in order to make up for the losses to the *Halbbatzenkollekte* caused by the growing war in Europe.[32]

The religious rationale for extending this financing principle to the Gold Coast was that by taking *material* responsibility, Africans gave evidence of their *religious* maturity. The November 17, 1898, pamphlet, "To the elders and congregations of the Basel Mission in the Twi district," makes the point clear (again, the original is in English):

> This is . . . the will of God, that the congregations learn to supply their own wants. . . . God will be more pleased with you if you willingly and joyfully contribute for His work among you than if you spend your money for things which are less necessary or not necessary at all. . . . [If] you give cheerfully from gratitude towards God, from love for His word, and from willing obedience towards your superiors, then it will be a joy to those who collect and to those who give. This will also be an encouragement for the missionaries who do and suffer so much for you. For your sake they leave father and mother, seperate [*sic*] themselves from their children [and] spend their health and strength in your country, which has fitly been termed "the white man's grave," where all of them fall sick and many of them die. It will be a joy as well to the Home Committee who only seek the salvation of your souls and the best of your country.[33]

The practical consequence of this collaborative arrangement in Africa, as in Europe, was an economic union that effectively bound leaders (in this case missionaries and, more remotely, the Committee in Basel) and (African) converts together in a common enterprise across the great social distance that divided them.

Origins of the Rank and File

Most nineteenth-century missions actively sought missionaries to work in the field who came from more modest circumstances than the founders and directors. Clear documentation for such a pattern exists for a number of missions that were contemporaries and in some cases collaborators of the Basel Mission, including organizations from as widely dispersed locations as Nor-

32. BMA D-9,1c,10b.
33. BMA D-9,1c,10a.

way,[34] Germany,[35] Britain,[36] and North America.[37] To be sure, young people born into the social strata that provided the leadership for these missions had many options to choose from. Their upbringing led them to expect prosperity and positions of high social regard as their normal due, and such expectations did not incline them in large numbers toward a life of subordination and personal humility devoted to the "poor and unsaved" in remote parts of the tropical world. From 1815 to World War I, none of the children of the founders or governing circle was posted abroad as an ordained Basel missionary, although, as I have already indicated, many of them joined the cause at home in positions of support, leadership, training, and administration.[38]

Quite apart from the scarcity of upper-strata candidates for work in the field, organizational considerations also supported a positive preference for a uniform and relatively modest missionary recruitment base. It was received wisdom among missions of the time that uniformity in beliefs, education, and experience contributed to predictability and efficiency in training and was the key to rank-and-file conformity. Peter Williams confirmed this in his examination of the recruitment practices of four important nineteenth-century British missions, including the CMS, the Wesleyan Methodist Mis-

34. Simensen, ed., *Norwegian Missions,* pp. 34ff.

35. Ustorf, *Mission im Kontext;* Gründer, *Christliche Mission und Deutscher Imperialismus.*

36. Oliver, *Missionary Factor;* Moorhouse, *The Missionaries;* Piggin, "Social Background"; Piggin, *Making Evangelical Missionaries, 1789-1858;* Williams, "Recruitment and Training"; Beidelman, *Colonial Evangelism,* pp. 159ff.

37. Coleman, *Presbyterian Missionary Attitudes,* pp. 20ff.

38. Some offspring of prominent families went abroad in *nonmissionary* roles, but their numbers are very small in relation to the roughly two thousand Mission workers from more typically modest backgrounds. I found fewer than a dozen examples. Ernst Preiswerk-Heintze, the son of a Committee member, went to the Gold Coast as a Mission merchant *(Missionskaufmann),* not as a missionary, in 1876. Pauline Hoch-Ecklin was a missionary's wife in India; her brother was a Committee member. Marie Huber-Streckeisen was also a missionary wife in India; her father was a relative of a Committee member. Five other persons from prominent "Old Basel families" not directly tied to the Mission included Sophie Im Hof (on the Gold Coast as a teacher and governess from 1896 to 1900); Maria Stähelin (who worked with children in India from 1903 to 1928); Anna Wuhrmann (a teacher in Cameroon from 1911 to 1915 and again from 1920 to 1922); Anna Linder, a nurse in China from 1913 to 1921; and Adolf Burckhardt, *Missionskaufmann* to India, 1872-81. Benedikt LaRoche, whose father was on the Basel Mission Committee, went to India as a theologian for the Church Missionary Society. He died on his way back from India in 1821. Christoph Burckhardt, from a branch of that powerful family that was not directly involved in the governance of the Mission, was a teacher in the Basel Mission Seminary and later went to Egypt and Syria as a theologian for the British and Foreign Bible Society.

sionary Society, the London Missionary Society (LMS), and the China Inland Mission.[39] Those in charge of these organizations believed the relatively lowly origins of the recruits would make them amenable to hierarchical discipline (pp. 142, 147ff.). More specifically, they believed the missionaries they recruited would be "'improved' socially by the process of training," and that in return they ought to "show their gratitude by the acceptance of authority" (p. 155). True to this implicit bargain, Williams says, recruits expected their acceptance as missionaries to "obliterate" their modest class origins and inscribe a new identity on their social accounts (pp. 142-43, 147ff.). It was naturally expected that they would repay their debt with loyalty to the organization that had accepted and so elevated them.

The Anglican bishop's sharply phrased comment quoted earlier about the "inferiority" of the missionaries and the "superiority" of the governing committee in the CMS makes it plain how firmly that organization embraced the principle of internal class distinctions. In the early years of the nineteenth century, in fact, it proved difficult for the CMS to find recruits "tough enough" and from "appropriately modest" backgrounds to staff its expanding overseas programs.[40] It is very significant that, rather than turning to middle-class recruits in England, which it considered a less than desirable solution,[41] the CMS relied instead upon the Basel Mission to find, train, and remand to it candidates who typically came from agrarian, craft, and semi-industrial origins in Germany. Paul Jenkins has reported that roughly a hundred Basel-trained missionaries entered the service of the CMS in this way between 1820 and 1850.[42] And between 1815 and 1820, before the Basel Mission had established stations of its own abroad, all the graduates of its seminary were absorbed by other missionary organizations in this way.

When the Basel Mission began to send out missionaries in its own name in 1821, it did not depart from these precedents. Like most other missions, it filled its roster with men from social origins markedly different from those of the governing group. The *Brüderverzeichnis* in the archive registers each individual's place of birth, his occupation at the time of acceptance into the seminary, his father's occupation, and his career path in the Mission. There were

---

39. Williams, "Recruitment and Training." The parenthetical page references in the following text are to this work.

40. Moorhouse, *The Missionaries*, pp. 48-49; see also Beidelman, *Colonial Evangelism*, pp. 159ff.

41. Williams, "Recruitment and Training," p. 155. I would note also, though Williams does not, that the CMS apparently did not consider recruits from the urban proletariat to be candidates to fill this need.

42. See table 1 in Jenkins, "Church Missionary Society," p. 45.

applicants from neighboring France and from as far away as Sweden, a few came from middle- and upper-middle-class urban backgrounds, and a handful were converted Jews. In the late eighteenth and nineteenth centuries, however, the Pietist movement retained particular strength in the villages and towns of southern Germany, and the preferred entrants to the seminary came from agrarian and craft origins in that area. Representatives from the industrial proletariat of large urban areas were notably absent. Regarding uniformity, one Committee member even expressed doubt about encouraging young people from Switzerland to apply for admission. He was convinced that the Swiss, compared with the Württembergers, were more difficult to assimilate into the daily routine of the Mission House. This was especially likely if they were from the French-speaking parts of Switzerland.[43] The "sameness" in the Pietist beliefs, backgrounds, and circumstances of young Württembergers distinguished them from the Swiss, he believed, and this homogeneity made them especially attractive to an organization that placed discipline, humility, and conformity just after faith on its list of essential Christian virtues.

In addition to recruitment from a relatively homogeneous social base, the Mission actively suppressed any outward signs of difference in status that remained after its recruits joined the seminary. "At the moment of entry into authentic mission service," said Christian Gottlieb Blumhardt, the first inspector of the Mission, "[seminarians are] completely torn away from their previous ties."[44] Displays of personal wealth were not allowed, and moreover, any significant personal assets of the missionaries had to be used in a manner approved by the Committee.[45] In the early years it was intended that their private means would actually be held in trust for them by the Mission until their resignation or retirement.[46] To avoid even the appearance of favoritism, welldisposed contributors to the Mission were not permitted to sponsor specific individuals among the seminarians.[47]

43. In BMA *KP* 56 for 1885, see the entries for May 27, p. 126; June 3, pp. 135-36; August 26, p. 182; October 7, p. 209; and December 2, p. 261.

44. Blumhardt, *Hausordnung*, p. 4.

45. In the contract, the principle was stated as follows: "The missionaries are to manage their assets in such a way as to cause no offense; they may not trade in houses or goods, and may not deposit sums in any bank not authorized by the administration" ("Verordnungen, die personliche Stellung der Missionare betreffend," version of 1868, BMA Q-9,11,2).

46. Waldburger, *Missionare und Moslem*, p. 44.

47. This restriction appears in section 14,2 of the versions of the *Hausordnung* circulated after 1848.

Principles such as these are likely to prevail wherever a similar premium is placed on uniformity and conformity. They are strikingly similar to those found in military academies, for example, judging from the description given by Sanford Dornbusch.[48] This military parallel, by the way, is neither abstract nor accidental. The next chapter will review how the Pietists and the Prussian military bureaucracy were drawn to each other, each incorporating much of the imagery and language of the other into its own organizational principles. The point here is that, to the extent they were "standardized" through the selection process, seminarians, like cadets, could be regarded by the organization as *tabula rasa*. By gaining acceptance into the Mission and cutting themselves off from their previous stations, seminarians agreed to subordinate themselves to, and serve under conditions almost entirely determined by, the Committee and the inspector. Seminarians were screened for sameness, entered the seminary as equals to each other, were equally dependent on the institution for their livelihoods, and came, over time, to be distinguished from each other chiefly by the marks and honors they earned *inside* the organization. It was an arrangement carefully calculated to produce uncritical obedience.

It is clear what the leadership's reasons for these recruitment strategies were, but the motivations that brought the rank-and-file members to the organization are another matter. Weber maintained that those likely to be vulnerable to missionary endeavors were typically from the economically least stable strata of society.[49] These were the people, he said, "for whom rational conceptions are the least congenial." But this too-facile psychological generalization does not go very far in explaining the desire to become the person doing the missionary work, any more than it explains why well-placed, well-educated, and eminently practical groups such as the "Basel aristocracy" (for whom "rational conceptions," as we shall see, were quite congenial) provided the leadership for struggling evangelical organizations. It is necessary to look more deeply into their reasons for participation.

At the time of the founding of the important nineteenth-century missions, other studies have suggested that young people were intrigued by the prospect of contending with practical problems in the field, or they were simply drawn to the promise of freedom (of an acceptable sort) from parental and church control.[50] For many, a simple youthful sense of adventure in exotic settings was also an important factor.[51] According to Michael

48. Dornbusch, "The Military Academy."
49. Weber, *The Sociology of Religion*, p. 101.
50. Williams, "Recruitment and Training," pp. 156, 172, 183.
51. Moorhouse, *The Missionaries*, p. 62.

Coleman, describing nineteenth-century missionaries to Native American tribes, "[t]hose who read the soaring prose of the evangelical literature were motivated to one degree or another by the wonder, the sense of adventure, and the romance involved in doing the glorious work of the Lord."[52] Like explorers, missionaries sometimes enjoyed great public renown and admiration. William McLoughlin does not equivocate about the public image enjoyed by missionaries to the American frontier: "In [this period], missionaries were heroes. In fact, most churchgoing Americans considered them far more heroic than the frontier heroes we honor today — Daniel Boone, Davy Crockett, Kit Carson, Buffalo Bill, and the rest."[53] David Livingstone, who served for many years with the LMS and was also seen by the public at large as an intrepid explorer, is perhaps the best European example. Geoffrey Moorhouse describes Livingstone as a man whose "lustre for the British [was] second only to that of Queen Victoria."[54]

It would be difficult to estimate how many young people in Europe and elsewhere were initially drawn to the missionary life by their fascination with this one man's public persona. The appeal must have been strong, even though few could expect to have a missionary career like his, and despite the odd dissonance between the independence suggested by Livingstone's adventurist image and the subservience and restrained style of life that were waiting for most missionaries. In the case of the Basel Mission, such essentially personal attractions to excitement may well have been important to some who applied for acceptance, but no one who highlighted such motives in the formal application or revealed them openly when interviewed would have been accepted into the seminary. Inspector Blumhardt expressed irritation with the "glory" that sometimes seemed to surround even the most inexperienced missionaries, regarding it as essentially unearned and unbecoming.[55] Enthusiasm — the energetic zeal of the truly reborn — was expected, but in ways that I will discuss more fully in the next chapter, that eagerness had to be tempered by piety, modesty, and self-abnegation.[56]

In addition to whatever popular appeal they were responding to, more deeply rooted social and historical factors were also at work in shaping the choices of the common Basel missionaries. The familiar world of the tradi-

52. Coleman, *Presbyterian Missionary Attitudes*, p. 24.
53. McLoughlin, *Champions of the Cherokees*, p. 3.
54. Moorhouse, *The Missionaries*, p. 111.
55. This attitude was sharply expressed to a visitor to Basel from the CMS of London. The reference for this conversation is a travel diary in the CMS archive in London, reference G/AC, 18/1, 1820-1834, 476ff., dated on its receipt in London on January 8, 1830.
56. Schlatter, *Geschichte der Basler Mission*, 1:23.

tional Württemberg agrarian village or town, to which the average applicant was culturally tied, was being unsettled by pressures on the land caused by population growth and by the gradual industrial transformation that was taking place in many parts of Europe.[57] The changes in Baden and Württemberg were more gradual than elsewhere in Germany, and were slowed by a positive preference for keeping the region agricultural.[58] Nevertheless, in each generation fewer young people could be sure of making a living as farmers or in traditional village-based crafts. Many were therefore compelled by social and economic insecurity to choose among the other options then open to them.

Emigration, usually to America, was one such option, but this was an uncertain prospect at best. Taking employment in the emerging urban/industrial sector was a second possibility, but as Troeltsch pointed out, those who embraced the Lutheran social ethic at that time would have looked upon industrial work and urban life with profound misgiving.[59] For those who were especially devout, as the Pietists certainly were, the Mission could represent a more attractive option than either emigration or joining the urban proletariat. The work of the foreign missionary was new and unfamiliar to them, to be sure, but it could offer an answer to material uncertainty as well as an outlet for religious fervor. The new life would be spent honorably in the company of coreligionists and in a context governed by familiar moral values.

Material uncertainty in the lives of prospective recruits, like the observation of the social separation between them and their leaders, is a common theme in mission history. The British were in the forefront of the nineteenth-century evangelical missionary movement, and the origins of the ordinary British missionaries have been traced to the less secure strata of that society. Most came from positions in society that were either just emerging in the modern economy or were passing into a state of decline.[60] Before they applied to be missionaries many had been mechanics, shop assistants, or skilled artisans (printers, drapers, and shoemakers, for example, were especially common), all occupations that were threatened by the Industrial Revolution. Stuart Piggin describes their circumstances this way:

57. Jenkins, "Villagers as Missionaries"; Jenkins, "Sozialer Hintergrund und Mission"; Fulbrook, *Piety and Politics*, pp. 36-39; Eiselin, "Zur Erziehung."

58. Borscheid, "Unternehmer, Arbeiter, Industriekultur"; F. H. Fischer, *Der Missionsarzt Rudolf Fisch.*

59. Troeltsch, *Social Teaching*, 2:540ff., 677ff. The same Pietist attitude toward the industrial proletariat that kept the Mission from recruiting from that social base may have caused young Württembergers to prefer the Mission to life as an industrial worker.

60. Piggin, "Social Background"; Williams, "Recruitment and Training."

They were not the human fodder of the Industrial Revolution, the help-less, exploited factory workers. . . . But they were victims of the Indus-trial Revolution in another sense — the coming of machinery meant that most of the old and honoured trades of Britain were doomed to eventual extinction. Furthermore, the needs of *laissez faire* capitalism, which then dominated the British economy, for cheap labour, ended ar-tificial restrictions on entry into the trades. As [these trades] became more unattractive the emerging professions [which included the mis-sionary calling] provided a natural outlet.[61]

There were also those who entered the mission life from the lower rungs of the British clergy and from emerging professions such as accounting, chemistry, dentistry, law, and engineering. Hardly more security character-ized their lives. Their experience, Piggin says, was one of always having to "campaign for greater recognition in the industrialising society to which they owed, if not their origin, then their increased importance."[62]

In a similar way the unsettled backgrounds of many of the Basel Mission's recruits had "pushed" them toward the missionary movement, though not, to be sure, from the ranks of the emerging professions. Just as important, the reli-gious goals of the Mission exerted a strong positive "pull" upon them. More-over, for many of the recruits the agrarian social ethic of traditional Lutheranism retained its strong attraction.[63] Those chosen by the Mission for duty on the Gold Coast in particular could join the evangelical cause without abandoning their commitment to that set of Lutheran values. As I pointed out in chapter 1, the centerpiece of the Mission's Gold Coast strategy was to bring Africans into economically self-sufficient agrarian "Salems" whose visible suc-cess in improving the moral and material standard of living was to be the bea-con leading the remaining "heathens" out of their "darkness."[64] Central to that strategy was the teaching of material self-sufficiency to the native converts who populated those villages. Because of the demands of this practical village program, the Mission had to have agents who, in addition to being evangelists, had training in useful trades and crafts of precisely the sorts that were most common in the villages and towns of southern Germany. The serious inten-tion, then as today, was to transfer "appropriate" technologies to West Africa, that is, technologies carefully chosen to promote the economic independence

61. Piggin, "Social Background," p. 42.
62. Piggin, "Social Background," p. 35.
63. Jenkins, "Villagers as Missionaries"; Troeltsch, *Social Teaching,* vol. 2, chap. 2.
64. Vogelsanger, *Pietismus und Afrikanische Kultur;* cf. Heise, "Prefatory Findings."

of the emerging convert communities. The cover photograph, taken alongside the Mission House in 1890 or 1891, and the pictures reproduced in plates 8, 10, 12-14 and 25 are clear portrayals of that principle in action.

The Mission's need for personnel with a certain profile of beliefs and skills intersected neatly with the search by many young Württembergers for a productive and morally upright role in a materially changing world, a role that did not ask them to abandon what they knew and cherished. The first twenty-five successful seminary applicants who were eventually assigned to the Gold Coast clearly reflect this meshing of needs (see Table 1 on p. 54). Included in this early generation of missionaries were three shoemakers, five weavers, four skilled carpenters, a sail maker, a glazier, two pot makers, a baker, two farmers, a servant, a lathe operator, a student, two teachers, and a scribe (stenographer). In following these pursuits the recruits typically did not duplicate the occupations of their fathers, but the overall profiles of the two generations were quite similar. This picture changed gradually during the nineteenth century, reflecting developments taking place in the modes of production in Württemberg,[65] but up to the period preceding World War I these developments had done little to close the distance between missionaries and the Mission's governors (see Table 2 on p. 55). As with the first contingent, if the members of this later generation of missionaries had not found acceptance by the seminary, few were on a path that was likely to take them far from their status and class origins.

For the small number of women who served in Ghana in a capacity other than that of a missionary's spouse, the record is different. The *Schwesternverzeichnis* (a document in the archive that parallels the *Brüderverzeichnis*) displays the records of only twenty-nine European and two African women who fit into this category. Looking just at the Europeans, one was the daughter of a prominent family in Basel's commercial "aristocracy," two were daughters of a factory or mill owner, and two others were from professional families (one law, the other medicine). The fathers of the remaining twenty-two were civil servants (two), pastors (four), missionaries (four), businessmen (four), teachers (five), craftsmen (a master tailor and a wagon maker), and one farmer-vintner. Only the last three of these can be regarded as replicating the pattern found among the male missionaries. This practice of recruiting women from a class and status position different from and usually above that of the men will be apparent again when I present information on the missionaries' wives.

---

65. Eiselin, "Zur Erziehung."

TABLE 1

Social Origins of the First Twenty-five Basel Missionaries Assigned to the Gold Coast of West Africa, Beginning in 1828

Missionary's Occupation	*Father's Occupation*
Servant	Barber
Shoemaker	Trader
Ribbon weaver	Wine merchant
Shoemaker	Linen weaver
Sailmaker	Linen weaver
Private teacher	Teacher
Glazier	Glazier
Cabinetmaker	Butcher, innkeeper
Weaver	Linen weaver
Linen weaver	Linen weaver
Carpenter, cabinetmaker	Carpenter
Cabinetmaker	Teacher
Shoemaker	Farmer
Student	Glazier
Lathe operator	Lathe operator
Weaver	Linen weaver
Carpenter	*
Pot maker	*
Scribe	Trader
Baker	Farmer
Pot maker	Pastor
Farmer	Village mayor
Weaver	Farmer
Teacher	Innkeeper
Farmer	*

SOURCE: *Brüderverzeichnis,* Basel Mission Archive

*Information not available

Upward Mobility

In exchange for the technical skills and religious energy the recruits brought with them, the Mission offered a formal education that could be attractive to people of their backgrounds. Fulbrook has pointed out that Württemberg

TABLE 2

Social Origins of the Last Twenty-five Basel Missionaries Assigned to the Gold Coast of West Africa before the Break Caused by World War I

Missionary's Occupation	*Father's Occupation*
Saddlemaker	Cartwright
Gardener	Master carpenter
Gardener	Teacher/librarian
Gardener	Beer brewer
Cabinetmaker	Farmer
Gardener	Farmer
Cabinetmaker	Farmer
Cabinetmaker	Cabinetmaker
Farmer	Teacher, farmer
Miner	Miner
Builder	Gardener
Mechanic (operator)	Evangelist
Tailor	Master tailor
Book salesman	Preacher
Farmer	Farmer
Baker	Shopkeeper
Farmer	Farmer
Instrument maker	Evangelist
Gymnasium teacher	Basel missionary
Apprentice teacher	Blacksmith
Mechanic (operator)	*
Book salesman	Pastor
Mechanic (operator)	Basel missionary
Book salesman	*
*	*

SOURCE: *Brüderverzeichnis*, Basel Mission Archive

*Information not available

was unusual in its support for public education; as early as the seventeenth century the expectation that schooling could lead to personal advancement was well established.[66] This education was not equally available to all, how-

66. Fulbrook, *Piety and Politics*, pp. 69, 78-80.

ever, and more important for the issue at hand, the desirable positions to which it could in principle lead were not reliably tied to demonstrated merit. In the clergy, for example, there were simply not very many vacancies for young people from modest social origins, no matter how religiously inclined, intelligent, or well educated they may have been. More than that, a discriminatory law was passed in 1749 that severely restricted the ability of the children of craftsmen and farmers to aspire to social advancement through the church.[67] The rhetoric of advancement and the relative openness of the educational system encouraged aspiration, but the reality of class exclusiveness in the church hierarchy worked in many cases to frustrate those hopes.

It is against this background that the attractiveness of the Basel Mission must be judged: it offered an alternative path to the desirable profession of the pastorate.[68] Jarle Simensen and Vidar Gynnild made a virtually identical observation about the recruits to the Norwegian Missionary Society (NMS): "The Missionary School provided a chance — probably the only one — for further advancement into higher education, with the status of an ordained missionary minister as the final goal."[69] Piggin, writing about the situation in Britain, says it would have been difficult for the recruits to nineteenth-century Protestant missions (recall the bishop's reference to "an inferior sort of men") to get into the established church hierarchy, even though their training ranked them in the better-educated part of British society.[70] Coleman has pointed out that Presbyterian missionaries in North America, who typically came from modest backgrounds in country areas and small towns, "would have had up to seven years of higher education at a time when few Americans even entered a college or university."[71] According to Peter Clarke, essentially this same pattern held generally among missions wherever the evangelical movement was strong.[72]

From these and other studies it is clear that objective upward social mobility was a common experience for nineteenth-century missionaries.[73] What

67. Hahn and Mayer, *Das Evangelische Stift in Tübingen;* Eberl, "Die Klosterschüler in Blaubeuren, 1708-1751"; Eberl, "Die Klosterschüler in Blaubeuren, 1751-1810." Albert Ostertag (*Entstehungsgeschichte,* pp. 77-78) describes the demoralizing effect of a similar 1798 decree, quickly rescinded, that extended the prohibition to the children of the petite bourgeoisie, an act that threatened to block the religious ambitions of Christian Gottlieb Blumhardt, the man who later became the Basel Mission's first inspector.

68. Waldburger, *Missionare und Moslem,* p. 47.

69. Simensen with Gynnild, "Norwegian Missionaries," p. 31.

70. Piggin, "Social Background," pp. 57, 344.

71. Coleman, *Presbyterian Missionary Attitudes,* pp. 20-21.

72. Clarke, *West Africa and Christianity,* pp. 56-57.

73. For still other examples, see Ustorf, *Mission im Kontext;* Gründer, *Christliche*

is harder to establish with any certainty, because it is a question of motivation that must largely be inferred, is the extent to which missionaries were *subjectively* attracted by the prospect of that social "betterment." Many of the recruits to the NMS, according to Simensen and Gynnild, had left the countryside to join the teaching profession as a first step away from their origins, and then quite openly made the move from teaching to the NMS because it meant a further stride toward an even more highly regarded profession.[74] Piggin has confirmed the same pattern among missionaries in Britain.[75] Teachers and ministers who applied to the major evangelical organizations had ordinarily started from modest circumstances and were motivated by an honest determination to move out of the "labouring classes." For them, Piggin says, it was clear that "religious conversion and social ambition were not mutually incompatible."[76] As I indicated above, Williams has also offered evidence that the young people drawn to the LMS and CMS actively expected advancement, and that these two organizations, "particularly in the first decades, gained recruits, at least partially, because they *projected themselves* as steps in the ladder of advancement."[77] Finally, Moorhouse suggests that David Livingstone's religious determination and his desire for education were key factors in his escape from the cotton mills of Scotland. In the end his accomplishments carried him so far from his impoverished origins that, when he died, he was buried in Westminster Abbey.[78] Such a visible example would not have been lost on other aspiring missionaries of the period.

The consciousness of social advancement and the sensitivity to often invidious distinctions of rank within the missionary profession stayed with missionaries in the field. In his description of missions in East Africa, T. O. Beidelman said those who were not yet ordained sought ordination; those who did not have authority sought to move into leadership in their stations; and those who wanted to be known and recognized beyond their immediate workplace strove to create new stations because of the attention and approbation it brought them.[79] There was an interesting compensation in the field for the hierarchical subordination to which most missionaries were subjected: Because of their European origins and their technical and religious knowl-

---

Mission und Deutscher Imperialismus; Oliver, *Missionary Factor;* and R. Hoffmann, "Neupietistische Missionsbewegung."

74. Simensen with Gynnild, "Norwegian Missionaries."
75. Piggin, "Social Background," pp. 20ff.
76. Piggin, "Social Background," p. 23.
77. Williams, "Recruitment and Training," p. 229, emphasis added.
78. Moorhouse, *The Missionaries,* pp. 111ff.
79. Beidelman, *Colonial Evangelism,* pp. 162ff.

edge, they were expected to assume patriarchal and charismatic dominance over their converts, whom they perceived as below themselves in the hierarchy of the Christian enterprise.[80]

This was exactly the case in the Basel Mission on the Gold Coast. Africans were required to acknowledge their own inferior status in the Christian community and submit to the religious and temporal control of the missionaries in much the same way as the missionaries had been required to submit to the will of the Mission's governing committee. The social distance between Africans and missionaries was further reinforced by visible differences in their housing and standard of living and by the practice of assigning native personal servants to the Europeans and their families. This hierarchical separation compensated for the missionaries' subordination in one sphere (that is, with respect to the Committee) by raising them to superordinate positions in another (with respect to the native converts). At the same time, it reproduced the Pietist vision of authority in the field and further legitimated the general principle of social hierarchy that was so deeply rooted in Pietist thinking (a topic to which I will return at length in the next chapter). John Middleton argued that this hierarchical arrangement was also encouraged by native rulers on the Gold Coast, who objected to any social arrangement in the Basel Mission community that suggested egalitarianism. Inside that community, he says, "European missionaries were in the highest rank, as 'rulers'; then the princes [sons of native kings] . . . as indigenous pastors and evangelists; then ordinary 'commoners,' and then the artisans and [finally] servants of slave origin."[81] (See plate 19.)

For purposes of recruitment, other missionary institutions openly acknowledged and even publicized the social mobility that the missionary movement meant for many people, but this was not the case in the Basel Mission. Harboring the hope of personal betterment was seen by the leadership as a

---

80. Beidelman, *Colonial Evangelism*, p. 28.

81. Middleton, "One Hundred and Fifty Years." Still another kind of invidious distinction came into play in the Mission's internal affairs. Following the anthropological "wisdom" of the time, African natives were regarded as lower on the scale of "civilization" than native Christians in other mission fields (the comparison with India was especially sharply drawn). For this reason missionaries selected for posting to Africa were regarded as less "gifted" than those sent elsewhere. They were less rigorously trained in "intellectual" subjects such as ancient languages and abstract theology, and their esteem in the informal hierarchy in the organization was of a lower order (Waldburger, *Missionare und Moslem*, pp. 45-46). They responded to this diminution of themselves by holding up their willingness to confront the physical dangers of the African milieu as evidence of their superior Pietist devotion. According to Michael Coleman (*Presbyterian Missionary Attitudes*, chap. 4), American Presbyterians developed a similar hierarchy of "civilization" to map their strategies for seeking Christian converts in various Native American tribal societies.

sign of egoism that might outweigh the genuine calling for the evangelical life.[82] At one meeting in 1837 during which this problem was discussed, Committee members expressed dismay that so many applicants to the seminary seemed to be motivated by the desire to get ahead and to escape the poverty of their parents. As a result, one member said, "it gets harder to find the pearls among them."[83] Prospective missionaries were aware of this concern, and they seldom revealed such "ambition" in their applications or other writings they left behind; they were more likely to deny such aspirations explicitly. Each applicant was required to submit a brief autobiography, or *Lebenslauf*, as one of the requirements for admission to the Mission. In his account, Johannes Zimmermann (an important missionary whose career is discussed in detail in chapter 4) wrote at length about his futile search for suitable employment after leaving his village in Württemberg, but then reassured the Committee by saying, "I am able to swear before God that in my calling [to the Mission] I neither seek nor expect vain honor or comfort, and in your decision [about my acceptance] I am ready to acknowledge the will of the Lord."[84]

The criteria for admission to the Mission community included a decisive moment of conversion, self-effacing modesty, and zealous commitment to the Pietist evangelical calling, with all the personal asceticism those characteristics entailed.[85] To admit the desire or expectation for personal gain would exclude an applicant from acceptance by the Mission seminary or lead to his summary expulsion should it be revealed after he was admitted.[86] Indeed, it could be compromising for a seminarian to emphasize too strongly even the simple "eagerness for learning" (*Bildungseifer*).[87] All other

82. See Jenkins, "Villagers as Missionaries"; Waldburger, *Missionare und Moslem,* pp. 46ff.

83. This was the meeting of June 22, 1837 (BMA *KP* 14, p. 25). Concerns about the motivations of the applicants to the Mission were also discussed in detail on June 30, 1836 (BMA *KP* 13, p. 127). See also Waldburger, *Missionare und Moslem,* p. 217.

84. The *Lebenslauf* is part of Zimmermann's personal file (abbreviated PF), PF302, dated Gerlingen, April 22, 1844.

85. See "Bedingungen des Eintritts in die Evangelische Missionsanstalt zu Basel und Anweisung zur Meldung um Aufnahme" (Conditions of entry into the Basel Evangelical Mission establishment, and instructions for reporting for admission) (BMA Q-9,21,3a).

86. Waldburger, *Missionare und Moslem,* p. 46.

87. The stated reason was biblical. Following 1 Cor. 2:5 ("That your faith should not stand in the wisdom of men, but in the power of God"), the Committee argued that the natural wisdom that comes from a proper relationship to God was to be prized above formal learning, particularly learning of an advanced theological or technical sort. The result of this doctrinal position was to reinforce a preference for missionaries of middling, rather than outstanding, educational accomplishment.

motives, including that one, were subordinated to the emotional commitment to serve the cause. Personal ambition in any form that hinted at independence or aggrandizement was defined as a character weakness, not a Pietist virtue.

Official policy on the matter of missionary motivation was therefore clear. Nevertheless, whatever the Mission's preferences were and whatever its applicants may have said about the complexities of their own personal motivation, it is a fact that five years in the Mission's seminary profoundly changed their objective life circumstances. Acceptance by the Mission led to a more advanced education than most recruits could ever have achieved at home, and at the end of this training ordination as (most commonly) Lutheran ministers awaited them, an accomplishment that was largely beyond their grasp through other avenues. And these gains were only part of the story.

Marriage and Social Mobility

The marital alliances arranged for the missionaries were also socially advantageous for them. Different missions approached the matter of marriage in different ways, and it is important to indicate how the social standing of missionary families could be affected by this. In London, the CMS believed that marriage had a steadying influence on missionaries because it enabled them to live normal family lives and kept them from being tempted into sexual improprieties in the field. For an interesting reason, however, it was thought that they should not become engaged or married before they finished their training. Because their missionary education was expected to elevate them in the social hierarchy, any mates they may have selected before they were ordained would, assuming typically class-endogamous choices, be from a station lower than the one into which they were moving. Upon ordination, it was considered advisable to push them toward marriage to women from backgrounds "appropriate" to their new place in society.[88] In terms of what sociologists call "social capital," the missionaries profited first from their own direct social mobility and then again from the indirect "betterment" imparted to them by the class and status origins of their wives. Their children were born into solidly middle-class families.

In contrast to this comparatively open deliberation and straightforward policy on matters of marriage and class identity in the CMS, the Basel Mission Committee thought missionaries should, ideally, be single. Because so

88. Williams, "Recruitment and Training," p. 142.

many CMS missionaries were trained in Basel, the contrasting positions of the two institutions came into direct confrontation. The Basel Committee's preference for single missionaries came from the conviction that celibacy would allow all their loyalty and emotional energy to be focused on the evangelical task.[89] Thinking practically, the Committee also thought it would be less expensive to support single missionaries in the field and easier to move them from one station to another as needed.[90] Attitudes toward marriage were also colored by the general view of women that was held by the men on the Committee. Women were considered in most circumstances to be a dangerous distraction for men destined for the religious life, and contact with them was regulated from the time recruits entered the seminary. In the nineteenth century, movement in and out of the Mission House was closely monitored, but its isolation was nothing like that of a monastery or cloister. Domestic servants, the wives of Mission teachers, and the visiting mothers and sisters of fellow seminarians were sure to be encountered. Unplanned contacts were also likely to occur in church, in the community at large, and when students were summoned as guests, as they often were, to the homes of prominent Mission supporters. Unsupervised interaction in all these circumstances was strongly discouraged, but in spite of all caution, contacts inevitably did occur and were a persistent source of concern. Where serious attachments or grave transgressions were revealed, dismissal of the offending seminarian was the usual remedy.

Similar concern, with even more strictly drawn rules, governed contact with native women in Africa and elsewhere. To limit casual contact with women, unmarried male missionaries were to have only male servants. All traffic with single women, whether they were natives, Europeans, or even the intended brides of other missionaries, was strictly governed. If a missionary encountered a woman alone in a room, he was expected to leave if possible; otherwise he was to leave doors and windows open. In the outdoors, men walking near where native women might rest or bathe must always call out before approaching, in order to avoid unexpected contact with women who were by European standards less than fully clothed.[91]

As Waltraud Haas has pointed out in her work on women in the Basel Mission, it was only reluctantly that the governing Committee relaxed its position to the point of allowing missionaries to marry at all, and even then

---

89. Haas-Lill, "Missionsgeschichte aus der Sicht der Frau," p. 14.

90. Waldburger, *Missionare und Moslem*, pp. 72-74.

91. The details of these policies appear in *Regeln für das Verhalten gegen das weibliche Geschlecht in Indien und Afrika (nach den Angaben erfahrener Brüder)* (BMA Q-9,3,10, June 1893).

marriage was permitted only under carefully supervised conditions.[92] Being out of conformity with the practices of more influential missions like the CMS played a part in this reversal. On several occasions the severity of Pietist discipline brought unwelcome attention to the Basel Mission's policies. Because it often relied on the good will and active assistance of larger, politically connected societies like the CMS, the Committee had to be concerned with projecting an image of reasonableness. Ultimately, however, it was Pietist belief itself that exposed the contradictions of male exclusivity in the Mission and brought women's indispensability into sharp focus. This paradox requires some clarification.

In the Pietist worldview evangelical success meant more than just growing tallies of converted individuals. In the end success had to be measured by the development of permanent Christian enclaves, or communities, outside of which true and lasting conversion was thought to be impossible. Inside these Christian communities stability was fundamentally linked to the strength of the family unit. It soon became apparent that single male missionaries were ill suited to serve either as the model or as the repository of wisdom for such family-based settlements. They would have no families of their own to use as a point of reference, and they were not well prepared either by inclination or by training to minister to the women and girls who would be part of the native Christian settlement. Women as wives of the missionaries, as fellow workers (albeit unsalaried) alongside the ordained men, and as teachers for native girls and women in the emerging Christian community were simply indispensable for the creation and sustenance of such settlements. No degree of commitment to an all-male evangelical enterprise could be reconciled with that simple necessity, and once that was recognized, the marriage policy changed.

Examination of the written and unwritten criteria for spouse selection, formulated in 1837, makes it clear that marriage, once permitted, was always complicated by concerns about social class identity. It was possible for a man in good standing to apply for permission to marry after two years in the field. He could suggest who his marriage partner might be, and often that choice would fall on the widow of a colleague who had died (as very many did) in service in the field. In the absence of such an opportunity, however,

92. The first comprehensive formal statement of the marriage rules appears in the minutes of the Committee meeting of December 27, 1837 (BMA *KP* 14, 1837-39, p. 54). The fullest exposition of the policy appears in "Verordnungen über die persönliche Stellung der Missionare, Revidiert 1886" (BMA Q-9,21,7: section V). A comprehensive discussion of the evolution of these rules and their application appears in Haas-Lill, *Erlitten und Erstritten.* See also Konrad, *Missionsbräute;* Haas-Lill, "Missionsgeschichte aus der Sicht der Frau," pp. 13ff.; and Waldburger, *Missionare und Moslem,* pp. 72-74.

the general expectation was that the Committee would conduct a search at home for a bride of suitable background, character, piety, and commitment to the Mission's cause. As with most important matters defining the missionary's relationship to the organization, the Committee spelled out the reasoning in detail:

> Because the wife of a missionary is called not only to share the sacrifices and dangers of the mission life with him but also herself to perform her share of the Mission's work, it is also necessary to require of her that she possess the physical, spiritual, and motivational capabilities appropriate to the Mission Calling. The obligation of the Committee is to see that we do not accept wives in the Mission who do not possess this capability. Therefore, not only the marriage, but also marriage to the specific person intended by the missionary, depends on the permission of the Committee. This permission will be given only after the Committee has formed a judgment about the qualifications of the intended.[93]

The marital alliances that evolved out of this policy fell into a distinctive pattern. As we have said, the men in the organization had quite modest social origins. It is revealing to note, however, that they seldom married women from equally humble backgrounds. "Qualifications of the intended" in the quoted passage included possession of an "acceptable" class background, which usually meant that the woman would come from a higher economic and prestige stratum than her husband. The archival records in the *Brüderverzeichnis* and the *Familienregister* (register of families) indicate that the search for a bride often led to the daughter of a Pietist petit bourgeois or clergyman in the Württemberg region. In this way religious uniformity, cultural compatibility, and respectability were, from the Committee's point of view, reasonably assured. It was also in the nature of this selection process that most of the brides came from somewhat higher class and status backgrounds than their husbands and thus, just as in the CMS, contributed directly to the upward social mobility of the missionaries. The search of the records revealed that, in the aggregate, only four of the first twenty-five wives of Gold Coast missionaries came from the farm or craft backgrounds that characterized the vast majority of the husbands. The fathers of another three were clergymen, and the remaining eighteen brides came from the families of professionals, civil servants, and enterprise owners or managers.

93. "Verordnungen über die persönliche Stellung der Missionare, Revidiert 1886" (BMA Q-9,21,7: p. 13).

Comparing the origins of husbands and wives more directly, i.e., couple by couple, none of the women came from a background lower than her mate's, and fully fifteen of the twenty-five came from clearly higher social origins than the men they married. The situation at the end of the century was essentially the same: of the twenty-five brides in the years just before World War I, fourteen were from bourgeois or petit bourgeois families (their fathers were factory owners, merchants, teachers, or civil servants); five came from the families of clergymen (pastors or missionaries), and six were daughters of farmers or craftsmen. Again compared couple by couple, fifteen of the twenty-five women came from higher and none from lower social categories than their husbands, who continued to be recruited from modest farm and village circumstances.[94]

Among the men there were, of course, some exceptions to the overall pattern of recruitment from modest backgrounds. A small number of missionaries came from much higher social origins than the typical Württemberg villager. When the question of marriage was addressed in these cases, the search for a bride could become complicated. One case in particular reveals the circumstances that could lead the Committee to relax its normally unbending rules. It also shows how class considerations, indeed "class consciousness," colored their thinking. A missionary to the Gold Coast named Charles Strömberg engaged in a prolonged dispute with the Committee over his repeated requests for permission to marry. Strömberg was unlike the typical Basel missionary in two important ways: he was Swedish, not German or Swiss, and he came from a privileged social class background. When he entered the Mission House at the age of twenty-one, he gave as his father's occupation Swedish military treasurer or exchequer (Feldkämmerer). Letters in his personal file give further evidence of the privileged style of life and attitudes that went with membership in the class of professional military officers.

Strömberg's social origins set him apart and gave him a certain marginality in the circle of Württemberg Pietists who made up the majority of Basel missionaries, and his years in the Mission House did little to erase the difference in his mind. After he was posted to West Africa, his marriage requests

94. I compared these observations on twenty-five early and twenty-five late Ghana missionaries with one hundred early and one hundred late marriage records for missionaries from all the Mission's overseas postings. This comparison showed that the patterns of bride selection for the Cold Coast missionaries were not atypical. In this larger sampling, three out of four brides came from professional, clerical, bureaucratic, or bourgeois families. Between a fourth and a third were from the families of clergymen, and only a small minority came from the modest farm and craft backgrounds that supplied most of the men.

challenged Committee policy in three ways. He insisted on marrying a *Swede,* of his *own choosing* and of his *own social class.* At the outset the Committee wanted him to marry a German or Swiss woman selected by them from the same broad categories that provided the brides of most of his fellow missionaries. Strömberg reminded the Committee that his social class was the same as their own, and when he was accused of arrogance *(Hochmut),* he replied that it was not arrogance simply to want to associate with members of his own social stratum.[95] It is revealing that the Committee agreed with him in the end; concern for the class privilege of "one of their own" struck a responsive chord and was factored into their treatment of his marriage request from that point forward. In the months that followed the Committee and Strömberg considered six prospective brides — including, significantly, both Germans and Swedes, but all from higher-than-usual social class backgrounds — and passed over each one for one reason or another. Ironically, before this search could come to a successful conclusion, Strömberg confessed to a drunken and unsuccessful attempt to have sexual intercourse with a young African servant woman and was dismissed from the Mission.[96]

In Strömberg's view of things, the Committee's initial suggestion to marry a partner much like those found for other missionaries represented to him a clear prospect of downward social mobility. On the whole, however, his case was exceptional; upward social mobility through education, ordination, *and marriage* was a fact of life for most of the Basel missionaries. Put simply, they entered the seminary as members of the farmer, artisan, or laboring class, earned the educational credentials of a solidly middle-class professional, and formed marital alliances with families whose class locations further enhanced their social capital. Those gains are visible in the material features of their

95. BMA, letter from Strömberg to Committee, copy in personal file (PF488), dated September 21, 1865.

96. Strömberg's performance in Africa produced mixed evaluations (BMA D-1,7, General Conference to Committee, March 14, 1865). His intelligence and skill were recognized, but he was considered unpredictable and moody and was thought to have damaged his resistance to temptation by his sexual preoccupation and by "too much spiritual and intellectual study." When his career in the Mission ended, he continued to set his own course. He refused to follow the Committee's decision that he go to America (to a remarkable degree, the Committee continued to direct the personal lives and fates of those it dismissed), insisting instead on returning to Sweden. In time he became a scholar of some repute and remained active in missionary affairs. Something of the sharpness of the feelings between the Committee and Strömberg is captured in the language of his dismissal (BMA KP 36, June 14, 1865, p. 61): "Brother Strömberg, in consideration of the admitted scandal as well as his weakness for drinking, his great irritability and changeability and chiefly his entire past, is expelled from the service of the Basel Mission. Where he goes is up to him."

lives in Africa (plates 20, 21, and 22 document how they progressed from comparatively crude to comparatively commodious living quarters), and they are visible in quite another way in the improved "life chances" of their children and grandchildren in Europe.

Consolidation of Gains

It is clear from the record that the missionaries were able to pass their mobility gains on to their children, and in this way their experiences take on significance for the analysis of class in the larger society. It is likely that this pattern of consolidation was common among nineteenth-century missions, but to my knowledge it has not been carefully documented.[97] It is an important matter, sociologically, because by transmitting their own gains to their offspring, the missionaries in effect transmitted the aggregate changes they were experiencing into the larger social structure. From the point of view of social change, therefore, this intergenerational transmission may be even more consequential than the simple upward mobility of the missionaries themselves. It is certainly a hypothesis that merits further investigation. In the Basel organization the children born to missionaries abroad were usually sent to Europe after they reached the age of seven. If relatives did not take them in, they were brought up in the Mission's children's home *(Kinderhaus)*, which had been erected in the same compound as the Mission House and seminary in Basel. As a rule the costs of their education and care were assumed by the Mission.[98] Almost none of these children fell back into the craft or farmer class circum-

97. I have tried without success to replicate this part of my analysis among the missionaries of the LMS, the CMS, and the Wesleyan Methodist Missionary Society. None of the archives of these three prominent British missions contains systematic information about the parents or the progeny of their members. The closest approximation is an undated CMS report from the early 1860s in which the leadership concluded that its children's home was "providing well" for the education of its missionaries' children. Among those who had recently passed through the school and taken paid positions in the labor force, eighteen had become missionaries, nine had become businessmen, six had become professionals (medicine, law), thirteen were schoolteachers, three were army officers, four had become civil servants at home or in the empire abroad, and four were governesses. It is not possible to match the records in this report case by case to the demographics of the parents and grandparents, and for this reason it is no more than suggestive about the consolidation of mobility between generations.

98. The terms of the Mission's agreement to provide for the education of the missionaries' children are set out in detail in "Verordnungen, die persönliche Stellung der Missionare betreffend, 1868" (BMA Q-9,11,2: section B, 8ff.).

stances from which their fathers had come; to the contrary, most of them consolidated or exceeded in their own work and family lives the gains their fathers had made. This conclusion is based on three clusters of information from the Mission archive and Württemberg church records in Stuttgart.

First, the occupational attainments and marriages of the offspring of twenty-five early Gold Coast missionaries were traced. This search did not start with the very earliest contingent of missionaries (the four who went out to Ghana in 1828) because none of those men was married and all died within two years of their posting. Rather the analysis began with the first missionary who survived long enough and succeeded well enough to be given permission to marry and then had children who, in turn, survived into adulthood. Second, the experiences of the grandchildren of these same early missionaries were also explored, but with data that are necessarily more limited. Finally, the adult occupations and marriages of the children of the last fifteen missionaries sent out before the start of World War I were traced to determine whether the patterns observed among the early missionaries continued in later cohorts. The numbers are tedious, but the pattern underlying them is quite revealing.

Before the findings are discussed, a word of caution is in order. These observations cover a small sampling, not a complete enumeration, of the experiences of the nearly 250 missionaries and their families who were involved with the Gold Coast mission between 1828 and World War I. The relevant facts had to be reconstructed child by child, as it were, from the various records that exist for the individual missionaries. The records are quite good for the children of those who stayed with the Mission until death or retirement. For the children of missionaries who resigned before retirement or were expelled from the Mission, however, the records are thinner; they typically end with the recording of the births that occurred during the parents' period of service to the Mission. The data are even sparser, of course, for the grandchildren. Even with the gaps in the files, however, the patterns that emerge are compelling enough to suggest clear intergenerational consolidation of the upward social mobility experienced by the missionaries.

Children of the Early Missionaries

The twenty-five early missionaries whose records I examined had, in all, 167 children; 117 (70 percent) survived their early years. Names and sexes of 8 of these children were not recorded; the remaining 109 included fifty-eight males and fifty-one females. It was possible to trace the adult occupations of thirty-nine of the fifty-eight men and the occupations and/or marital alliances of forty-two of the fifty-one women. Among the thirty-nine males, none became a farmer or industrial worker. Four became craftsmen: specifically, an ivory carver, a carpenter, a bookbinder, and an upholsterer. These are the only sons among the thirty-nine who can be said to have (approximately) replicated the social origins of their missionary fathers. Of the remaining thirty-five, twelve became pastors, one was a church official, and seven followed their fathers into the Basel Mission. In other words, twenty of the thirty-nine (51 percent) found their way into religious callings. Another six were schoolteachers, two became university professors, four followed professions such as engineering or medicine, two were businessmen, and one was a clerk. In short, the male offspring of the early missionaries achieved social positions that ranked in prestige clearly above those from which their fathers had originally come. When the positions achieved by these sons are compared with their mothers' class and status origins, the movement is, of course, less striking because most of their mothers came from significantly higher social class and status origins than the missionaries they married.

Of the forty-two daughters for whom data are available, eleven took positions of paid employment outside the home as adults. Eight of these were schoolteachers, one was a missionary (but not for the Basel Mission), one a minor employee in the Basel Mission House, and one became a deacon in her church. Only one of these eleven employed women was married; she was a schoolteacher whose spouse was a Basel missionary. For the thirty-one women for whom no formal paid employment outside the home is recorded, only their marriages are available as an (imperfect) index of their adult social "destinations." None of them married into a farm, craft, or proletarian family. Nine married pastors or church officials, three married teachers or school officials, one married a university professor, one a businessman, and fully nineteen marriages with Basel missionaries are recorded.

Simple addition shows that twenty-nine of the forty-two female children (69 percent) were tied by marriage to the clergy, the church, or the Mission. The nine who married pastors and the nineteen who married missionaries can certainly be said to have worked for a religious organization, although they would not have been regarded or compensated as "employees" of those organizations. Compared to their missionary fathers' origins, the adult destinations of the female children were relatively favorable. Again, however, if the placement is traced *mother*-to-daughter instead of *father*-to-daughter, the impression of upward movement is not as great for the daughters, given the social origins of their mothers. Viewed in this light, the evidence suggests that women (that is, the daughters of missionary couples) stood to gain less than men (that is, the sons of missionary couples). Put another way, the daughters' participation in social mobility and in the social changes that attended it was essentially annexed to that of the men they married.

Before looking at the next generation, it is important to stress again the role these children played in reproducing the overseas workforce of the Mission itself: seven of thirty-nine sons (18 percent) followed their fathers into the Mission, and twenty of forty-two daughters (48 percent) married Basel missionaries.

Grandchildren of the Early Missionaries

Turning to the second part of the consolidation analysis, partial data are available for fifty-eight grandchildren of the early missionaries. I will not reproduce all the details here, because they essentially reinforce what I have already reported for their parents. The records show no craftsmen or industrial workers, or marriages with the same, among the grandchildren, and only one of them became a farmer. *All fifty-eight either married or themselves became pastors, teachers, government employees, church officials, academics, lawyers, or physicians.* Unless a systematic and unlikely bias in the archive is assumed (specifically, one causing the disproportionate loss of the records of those who experienced *downward* mobility), the grandchildren's movement away from the agrarian, craft, and working-class backgrounds of their missionary grandparents seems to have been decisive.

It is also interesting, but not conclusive, that only one female among the grandchildren married a Basel missionary and only one male became a Basel missionary. This is to be compared with the twenty women and seven men from their parents' cohort (that is, the first generation of missionaries' children) who directly followed the Basel Mission life. The powerful attraction of the Mission as a calling, in other words, seems to have been seriously attenuated, though it did not disappear, by the second generation. To that same extent the contribution of the grandchildren to the direct reproduction of the Mission by joining it as missionaries or wives of missionaries was far less than that of their own parents. In a way this decline brings symmetry to what I said earlier about the reasons prospective missionaries had for joining the Mission and the way those reasons intersected with the recruitment preferences of the organization's leaders. The following sequence of actions and consequences can be detected: choices made by the grandparents (the original missionaries with whom the analysis began) resulted in the accumulation of social capital that moved their children and grandchildren (the first and second cohorts of missionary offspring) out of the situation in which becoming a missionary made the most sense. By the grandchildren's generation, the resemblance to the profile of the modest Württemberg villager had simply ceased to exist, and with the disappearance of that resemblance the balance of affinities that had led their grandparents into the movement was fundamentally altered. (Note that in stressing these changes, I do not mean to suggest that the later descendants severed all their ties to the Mission or lost interest in it altogether. Every year the Mission archive receives inquiries and visits from individuals interested in the mission careers of family members of one, two, or three generations earlier.)

The Children of the Prewar Cohort

The third and final piece of the analysis of the consolidation of gains concerns the children of the last fifteen married missionaries who served on the Gold Coast just before the war in Europe began. Eighty children were born to their families, of whom seventy-one (89 percent) survived to adulthood. This number included thirty-four females and thirty-seven males. Over half the women (eighteen of thirty-four) took employment outside the home as adults, compared with only about one-fourth (eleven of forty-two) who did so in the earlier cohort. These eighteen employed women included a pastor (she was the first female pastor of a Basel congregation and was connected at one time to the Mission administration), a physician, two nurses, two church workers (one in the Mission House), four office workers (a welfare worker, an interpreter, a secretary, and a clerk), six teachers, and a housekeeper (for her father). The marriages that are recorded for these women reveal alliances with doctors, teachers, pastors, businessmen, and one farmer, but not a single marriage to a Basel missionary is reported.

The thirty-seven male children assumed a wide range of middle-class professional positions. Among them were ten pastors or church officials, three dentists, two physicians, a chemist, and an engineer. There was also one government official among them, as well as an army officer, a teacher, a music director, a forester, a gardener, and one farmer. There were no craftsmen, no industrial workers, and no Basel missionaries. On this last point, it is significant that the internment of the Gold Coast missionaries during World War I caused a drastic interruption for the organization. When the actual incarceration of the missionaries and the exclusion from West Africa that followed it are added together, the hiatus lasted for a decade. It is possible that this interval broke the connection to the Mission for some families and lowered the number of children, males and females alike, who might have followed their parents into the life of the organization. Incidentally, it is also of interest that eleven of the thirty-seven male offspring of the missionaries died in the German army in World War II.

*   *   *

To summarize, the descendants of both the earlier and later cohorts of missionaries replicated or exceeded the upward social movement that their fathers had accomplished by being accepted into the seminary. Membership in the Mission community directly enriched the "cultural capital"[99] of the male missionaries, or more precisely that of their children, in lasting ways. This result was reinforced by the missionaries' marriages to women whose status was higher than their own. Even in the unlikely event that all the children or grandchildren who are missing from the archival records became urban industrial workers or returned to the agrarian and semi-industrial occupations from which their fathers and grandfathers came, the aggregate intergenerational movement away from the missionaries' origins would still be substantial.

For women, given their essentially middle-class origins, the evidence of social *gain* is less apparent for the single women who joined the Mission community or the women who married missionaries and contributed to the Mission's work as wives, mothers, and evangelical partners. This is a reflection of the patriarchal society from which they came, which severely restricted their occupational opportunities and often arranged their marriages for them. The male-dominated features of that society were carefully reconstructed, even celebrated, inside the Mission community itself. This is a point developed in more detail by Waltraud Haas-Lill.[100] The appropriate image, I believe, is one of men in the Mission who were able to ascend a ladder of "social betterment," but only with the hand reached down to them by the women who were already a few rungs higher on that ladder.

---

99. Bourdieu, *Reproduction;* Collins, *The Credential Society;* Portes and Sensenbrenner, "Embeddedness and Immigration."

100. Haas-Lill, "Missionsgeschichte aus der Sicht der Frau." See also Konrad's comprehensive recounting (in *Missionsbräute*) of the experiences of the women who joined the Mission as brides of missionaries. Among Catholic women, the situation in the nineteenth century may have followed a different dynamic. Helen Ebaugh ("Growth and Decline") has argued that joining religious orders takes place at a higher rate where opportunities for women are most restricted, because participation in the religious life represents social mobility.

Elective Affinities and Social Change

It bears repeating that the powerful personal zeal characteristic of Pietism was the ultimate source of the Basel Mission's moral energy. To give prominent place to the motivating force of those religious beliefs, however, does not mean that other, less manifestly spiritual interests receded into insignificance. The participants in the nineteenth-century missionary movement were influenced by all the changes — religious, economic, political, and demographic — that were transforming the societies in which they were rooted.[101] The decline of many familiar livelihoods was particularly important because the range of alternative employments affected the availability of rank-and-file missionaries. If the village economies from which the largest share of the Basel missionaries came had been able to sustain those young people in the pursuits of their elders, or if movement into the established local clergy had not been arbitrarily blocked for people who had the requisite fervor but not the requisite social credentials for entry, it is clear that many more would have chosen to remain close to home. In that case the Pietist evangelical energies of both those who became the leaders and those who became the followers in the Mission would have had to find quite different modes of expression. As it turned out, a category of relatively unattached and disadvantaged Pietist young people was emerging at the same time that the Mission's need for recruits began to grow. Without the "elective affinity" of the leaders' and followers' beliefs, interests, and circumstances, the Mission would not have emerged as it did, assumed the organizational shape that it did, survived as it did, or had the effects on the lives of its participants that it did.

I will conclude this chapter by speculating about how the interests of the different categories of participants were served by their membership and how the larger course of secular change might have been affected by the existence of organizations such as the Basel Mission.

Elite Interests

The prominent Pietists who had the enthusiasm and time to create the Mission and then watch over it sat at the pinnacle of the class, status, and power hierarchies in their community. The Mission was a sacred cause for them no less than it was for the missionaries who went abroad, and being a member of

101. McGuire, *Religion*, pp. 129ff.; Simensen with Gynnild, "Norwegian Missionaries."

the organization's governing circle surely added to their intrinsic religious satisfaction. If their experiences were at all like those of more thoroughly studied elites in the present century, however, it is probable that their shared nonreligious interests were also affected by their Mission activities. As Weber pointed out, interaction among elites crosses institutional boundaries, from religion to business to politics to family.[102] Ties formed on the basis of one set of shared interests reinforce those formed around other interests. More recent observers as disparate in their thinking as C. Wright Mills, E. Digby Baltzell, G. William Domhoff, and Pierre Bourdieu have pointed to the importance of these overlapping connections for sustaining and reproducing the prominence and privilege of elites.[103] Access to such cross-institutional networks of affluence and influence itself becomes a resource, a kind of cultural capital.

The Mission may have professed to have little to do with the marketplace of economic and political opportunity in Switzerland and Württemberg, but the connection in reality cannot be denied. Fulbrook has noted how Pietists commonly used religious fellowship to further their business dealings.[104] In Basel the influence went both ways: engagement in the Mission's affairs provided contact with some of the key business and political leaders of the region; and seen from the opposite angle, members of the Mission's inner circle used their business ties to win new adherents to the religious cause.[105] From all of this it is a reasonable inference that interaction ocurring in the context of the Mission's affairs intensified shared class identities at the same time that it enhanced the participants' social prestige and honor in the community. In the same connection, I have presented evidence that the Mission was the focus for the more intimate family alliances that connected the members of the Basel elite. Their endogamy and their decidedly familial loyalty to the organization, which in most cases must be measured in generations or even centuries, is a good index of the variety of long-term rewards — symbolic, spiritual, and material — that they derived from participating in its affairs.

When it came to the imposition of hierarchical control in the Mission, the Committee members were well served by the social distance separating them from the rank and file. There was little sharing of power across those lines of separation. The leaders showed no inclination to broaden official participation in the policy-making process as they had done in the area of fund-raising; not even the socially prominent leaders of the various *Hilfsvereine* in Eu-

102. Weber, *Protestant Ethic.*
103. Mills, *The Power Elite;* Baltzell, *Philadelphia Gentlemen;* Baltzell, *The Protestant Establishment;* Domhoff, *Who Rules America Now?;* Bourdieu, *Reproduction.*
104. Fulbrook, *Piety and Politics,* p. 150.
105. Schlatter, *Geschichte der Basler Mission,* 1:6.

rope, who were counted on to implement the Mission's broad-based fund-raising efforts, were given any regular part in internal decision making. One person who expressed the wish to be involved in internal matters was told by the inspector that his "rights of participation" extended only to the "right to pray" for the Mission, to collect money for it, and to broadcast its message as widely as possible. When the man countered that those "rights" looked more like "duties," the inspector then admonished him to regard them as the most beautiful of "privileges." The record notes that the man was satisfied with the wisdom of this counsel.[106] Committee members had religious reasons for maintaining such tight, centralized control over the organization's activities and for carefully managing its reputation in the world outside, but these reasons, too, were reinforced by their concern for their community standing and their commitment to social and political conservatism. I will turn to this subject at greater length in chapter 3.

Rank-and-File Gains

The mix of "pushes" and "pulls" that brought the rank and file into the Mission and held them there was equally complex. The missionaries' religious devotion to Pietism and the religious gratification they derived from their participation in the Mission were at least as strong as that of the leaders. It is not just a technicality that they came to the Mission of their own volition, and it was they, after all, not the Committee, who directly carried out the real evangelical work of the organization, often in circumstances that were as trying socially and psychologically as they were threatening physically. The Mission life did not promise to eliminate the social gap between them and those who controlled the organization — quite the contrary — but the profession to which they gained access, the ministry, brought them greater social honor than the other callings they were likely to have followed. Both inside and outside the Mission they gained respect and recognition — that is, social status — for the work they did, particularly for their willingness to sacrifice and confront personal danger in the name of a religious movement that enjoyed wide popular legitimacy in Europe at the time.

Beyond personal religious validation and *status* recognition, however, a theme of this chapter has been that the *class* positions of the missionaries, that is, their life chances in the emerging economic and employment structures of the time, were also improved by their participation in the Mission.

106. W. Hoffmann, *Eilf Jahre in der Mission*, p. 24.

Their uncertain material circumstances at home gave way to the prospect of a lifelong profession, and they experienced visible upward mobility as they moved away from farm, craft, and semi-industrial occupations in a pattern that allowed them to avoid either emigration or (from their perspective) descent into the class of urban industrial workers. Their children and grandchildren were able to consolidate that movement. Of course, the missionaries did not, in fact dared not, openly celebrate their class gains or even express the hope of such gains, and they remained clearly subordinate to the elite inside the boundaries of the Mission. Yet their material situations and those of their offspring were profoundly and permanently altered. Simply put, their children and grandchildren did not face life on the same material terms that they and their fathers had done.

The missionaries cannot have been oblivious to such considerations, and it is worth speculating about the effects of their awareness. A strong suggestion comes from the rapid decline in the attraction of mission work after the first generation of missionary offspring. Even in the records from the early period that I examined, few male grandchildren were "called" to the Mission and few of the female grandchildren chose to marry missionaries, and by the end of the period covered by the study, *all* of the children whose records I found were making their lives outside the Mission. In other words, the tie to the organization, if we measure this just by direct participation in it, was *relatively* short-lived for the rank-and-file families, indicating (to put it in perhaps unfairly crass terms) that they converted their acquired "cultural capital" fairly quickly into other channels of advancement, including, to be sure, other religious channels, judging from the number of ministers, church officials, and theologians among them.

It is interesting to speculate about why the governing group's direct attachments to the Mission were actually so much more enduring across the generations than those of the missionaries. I could be wrong, but I doubt that the purely religious gratification that came from participation differed significantly between leaders and followers; beyond that spiritual reward, however, there may well have been a difference in the relative balance of material compared to symbolic benefits for the two groups. For the Committee members, I suggest, symbolic gains (validation and enhancement of their prestige, or status, in the larger community) outweighed material gains (incidental improvement in their already privileged political-economic, or class, positions). The symbolic gains were directly tied to the visibility of the participation itself; they did not have to be converted into another currency in order to be appreciated, embraced, and passed on to succeeding generations. The prestige and respect earned by the rank-and-file missionaries are not to be dismissed, but their material gains had the potential for drastically altering the objective life circumstances of their families. Those gains could only be realized — fully exploited, as it were — when their children made their lives in the emerging new economic order outside the Mission community.

Unintended Consequences

"From the point of view of the social sciences," Anthony Giddens has said, "it is hard to exaggerate the importance of the unintended consequences of intentional conduct."[107] Certainly that is the point that emerged with greatest force from Weber's *Protestant Ethic,* and I would argue that nineteenth-century missions could also provide a model for such a judgment. As I have already pointed out, these organizations were deliberate agents of social change in the colonial world, but it is true of most of them — and certainly true of the Basel Mission — that they did not intend to disrupt the social order of the societies in which they originated. Both the leadership and the rank and file among the Pietists were distrustful of change at home and were accustomed to hearing themselves described as socially and politically reactionary.[108] Together they embraced a regime in the Mission that mirrored the traditional divisions of the larger community, but at the same time a Mission career was a pathway leading many families decisively out of their positions in the established social hierarchy. That mobility contributed, ironically, to the evolution of a class structure that abandoned many of the traditional virtues of the preindustrial period. However inadvertently this happened and however little they may have understood it at the time, the participants in the Pietist evangelical movement were on the cusp of a social transformation, living through the "adaptive upgrading" that marked the emergence of modern social and economic institutions.[109] If research on other missions confirms these changes, it will illuminate one of the ways in which that process of change actually took place.

Over a period of about ninety years the Basel Mission's Gold Coast undertaking involved only some 250 families. If the reference point is the broader demographic patterns and class structures of Germany and Switzerland, the accumulated effects of these few families' social mobility might well be lost

107. Giddens, *The Constitution of Society,* pp. 11-12.
108. Scharfe, *Die Religion des Volkes,* pp. 155-57.
109. I use this term without embracing the Parsonian view of social evolution (Parsons, *Societies*) from which it comes.

among the transformative effects of secular processes such as political innovation, the fragmentation of traditional landholdings, emigration, and industrialization.[110] If the Basel missionaries assigned to other outposts in Africa and to stations in India, China, Persia, and Russia are included, however, closer to two thousand families were involved, and on the average these families had four or five surviving children. When the ripples caused by the movement of these numbers are projected through two or three generations, the geometrically progressing secular effect of the Pietist missionary movement is more to be reckoned with.

This is even more apparent if the point of reference narrows to the Württemberg region. For this area, an important question is whether "social betterment" was more likely for those young people who joined the evangelical movement than it was for those who found other ways to support themselves and their families. By the time the Mission began its work in 1815, changes in the class structure in the region were well under way. Regardless of what the male applicants to the Mission did or did not consciously seek for themselves, what they actually gained by acceptance is undeniable in terms of their own immediate movement and the future class placement of their children. Staying on the farm or in the village or town was becoming less attractive as it became less secure. Compared with their other options (emigration or industrial employment in the cities), the Basel Mission may well have been the most promising avenue of escape that offered itself.

In the *Lebenslauf* I referred to earlier, Johannes Zimmermann described how he left his home in Württemberg seeking work in the cities and after several months found himself caught in a painful and humiliating relationship with an employer in Basel.[111] "The Lord led me into a severe school of suffering," he wrote, "in which I took employment with one of the wickedest and most brutal bosses in Basel, whose severe mistreatment I had to suffer patiently if I wanted to remain in the city." Zimmermann could find no other work in the Basel region but took comfort from his contact with two friends from his village who had joined the Mission seminary. He returned to Württemberg when he reached the end of his tolerance and resources, but he continued to apply for admission to the Mission. Eventually he was accepted and was able to join his friends there. There is little doubt that this acceptance transformed Zimmermann's objective life chances in measurable and positive

110. See Lehmann, *Pietismus und Weltliche Ordnung;* R. Hoffmann, "Neupietistische Missionsbewegung"; Jenkins, "Villagers as Missionaries"; Fulbrook, *Piety and Politics;* W. Fischer, "Staat und Wirtschart im 19. Jahrhundert."
111. The *Lebenslauf* is in PF302, dated Gerlingen, April 22, 1844. The cited passage appears in paragraph 6.

ways, and his example can be multiplied a great many times in the Württemberg region. Passage through the seminary was an acceptable and effective mechanism for "class refitting" (to coin a term) that allowed individuals and especially their progeny to escape the more corrosive effects of the social changes going on around them.

It also bears repeating that the missionary movement enjoyed widespread popularity throughout Europe and North America. Estimates are scattered and exact numbers are hard to come by, but Rev. Harvey Newcomb's world survey in the middle of the nineteenth century recorded the activities of scores of missions employing thousands of missionaries.[112] After a global tour of missions undertaken in the late 1870s, William Bainbridge estimated the number of North American and European missionaries abroad at just under 5,000.[113] Moorhouse reports that in 1901 the British alone fielded 2,750 male missionaries and their spouses, together with 1,700 unmarried women; the Germans in that same year sent out another 880 mission agents.[114] Coleman estimates for the year 1910 that 21,000 agents were being supported by Protestant missions in Europe and North America.[115] If the patterns of family size and intergenerational mobility shown by the Baslers are at all like those for participants in other missions, then cumulatively these organizations will have been more important in the reshaping of specific regions and in the emergence of the modern urban middle class than is commonly acknowledged. The movement they represented clearly ranks among the important social determinants of economic action.[116]

Contributing to such changes in the social structure in which it was embedded is one kind of evidence of the secular effects of the Pietist movement.[117] An interesting parallel can be seen in Baltzell's history of social philanthropy among the New England Puritans.[118] Viewed in the abstract, the motives driving the philanthropic and evangelical movements were similar. Both represented the desire to mount an organized Christian response to un-

---

112. Newcomb, *Cyclopedia of Missions.*

113. Bainbridge, *Around the World Tour*, p. 553.

114. Moorhouse, *The Missionaries*, pp. 273ff.

115. Coleman, *Presbyterian Missionary Attitudes*, p. 9.

116. "Social determinants of economic action" is the phrase suggested by Portes and Sensenbrenner in "Embeddedness and Immigration."

117. George Becker has carried on a lively debate with Robert Merton about whether contributing to the emergence of modern science was another such unanticipated outcome. See Becker, "Pietism and Science," "Fallacy," and "Pietism's Confrontation"; and Merton, *Social Theory*, pp. 628-66, and "Fallacy."

118. Baltzell, *Puritan Boston.*

acceptable social conditions; both involved the collaboration of participants from different class backgrounds; and both significantly expanded the opportunities open to their ordinary members. "Philanthropy," Baltzell points out, "transformed society, *inadvertently* bringing power and authority to the participants in the emerging world of careers open to talent" (emphasis added).[119] With only a small change of wording he could have been describing the unintended consequences of participation in the Basel Mission.

Changes taking place abroad suggest another parallel. Evidence that I reviewed in chapter 1 indicates that in the tropical world where missionaries did their work, the material impact of many missions was considerably greater than their strictly religious influence. Moorhouse relates the story of a noted English missionary who labored for the CMS for thirty years and at the end of his life could point to only eight "true Christian converts" in his station — an average of roughly one conversion for every three years and nine months he had invested in the effort.[120] The story is not an isolated one. In central Africa, Moorhouse reports, the LMS produced its first "definite convert" only after fourteen years of labor. Later, when the LMS baptized its twentieth convert, it had to balance that number against twenty missionaries who had died in Africa up to that point, a grim one-for-one exchange.[121] As I pointed out in chapter 1, the "harvest" of the early Basel missionaries was no more bountiful than those recorded by the CMS and LMS.

In sharp contrast to these meager early religious gains is the description I gave of the eventual long-term secular impact of the Mission on the social structure of Ghana. Along with religious instruction, recall that formal education and the transfer of "appropriate" European technology were at the core of the Basel Mission's program in West Africa. Individual Africans had different reasons for coming to the Mission, but once they were in the Christian community they found refuge from the surrounding social disorganization, received a solid formal education, and learned a wide range of practical skills that were of direct benefit to them. It was this education and these skills that eventually opened up opportunities in the economy and positions in the governmental apparatus that were emerging under colonial control.

The lives of the educated Africans and their families, much like those of the missionaries' children in Europe, were forever changed.[122] The long-term effects of this are apparent in Middleton's recent assessment of 150 years of

119. Baltzell, *Puritan Boston*, pp. 77-78.
120. Moorhouse, *The Missionaries*, pp. 321ff.
121. Moorhouse, *The Missionaries*, pp. 321-22.
122. Clarke, *West Africa and Christianity*, p. 59.

Christianity in Akuropon (Akropong), near Accra, Ghana.[123] This is the community in which the first significant Basel Mission station was built. Membership in the Presbyterian Church of Ghana continues to be the most important mark of social status in that community and is a coveted symbol of prestige for those striving for upward social mobility in the developing economy. Next to church attendance, the right to burial in a Presbyterian cemetery is the surest sign of social standing. Little of this was foreseen in the early days of the Mission. The Baslers' strategy had been to build self-sustaining traditional villages (in the Württemberg sense of "traditional") that would stand free of the modern and increasingly urban economic and political structures emerging under colonialism.

T. O. Beidelman and J. F. A. Ajayi are two scholars who have described how Africans elsewhere used the early missions to their own social and economic advantage.[124] The incentive to see missions in this way was provided by the Europeans' obvious power, technical sophistication, and material advantages. Clarke has said that this instrumental response to mission on the part of indigenous peoples was already apparent in Portuguese Catholic missions at least as early as the 1600s.[125] That church membership would function so effectively as a means of access to those modern structures is a clear example of the secular consequences of religiously motivated activities. How general this pattern is for the nineteenth-century missionary movement as a whole is a question of obvious historical importance.

* * *

The different categories of participants in the Basel Mission were brought together by elective affinities in their beliefs, interests, and circumstances. Similar influences can be seen at work in the organizational apparatus they built and sustained together.

123. Middleton, "One Hundred and Fifty Years."
124. Beidelman, *Colonial Evangelism,* pp. 12, 27ff., 188ff.; Ajayi, *Christian Missions.*
125. Clarke, *West Africa and Christianity,* p. 10.

Plate 1. Ref. no. D-30.09.039 "Miss Kies with her teachers," Aburi, between 1888 and 1890. Photographer F. Ramseyer.

It is easier to illustrate practical aspects of education than its biblical nature, but the importance of the Basel Mission's persistent efforts over many generations to teach "women's handwork" should not be underestimated. The modern profession of seamstress in Ghana probably derives from this aspect of missionary education.

Plate 2. Ref. no. QD-30.014.0006
"Christiansborg, the Mission's Middle School." Photographer unknown, probably c. 1870.

The series QD-30.014 from which this picture comes is one of two albums with the oldest photographs from Ghana in the Basel Mission Archive. It is very likely that this photograph of the Mission's main Ga/English secondary school (Christiansborg is the Danish name of the suburb of Accra known traditionally as Osu) dates back to the third quarter of the 19th century.

Plate 3. Ref. no. QW-30.006.0013
"Aburi Girls' School 1900. Miriam [evidently the indigenous teacher] on the left. Miss
H. Brugger on the right." Photographer unknown.

Neither here, nor in Plate 2, are the names of the missionary teachers' indigenous colleagues known with any certainty.

Plate 4. Ref. no. D-30.03.043
"The brass band of the Middle School in Christiansborg." Photographer unknown.
c. 1901.

Neither the breadth of the Basel Mission's educational endeavor nor its impact in
modern Ghana should be underestimated. In the little-known dynamics of Ghana's
musical history in the colonial period it is likely that many "high-life" musicians made
first contact with western music and its instruments in the Basel Mission's school music classes.

Plate 5. Ref. no. QD-30.014.0017
"Akropong, houses for Christians, and the orange-tree alley." Photographer unknown, probably c. 1870.

One prototype of the Basel Mission's Christian villages, or Christian quarters, in Ghana, with stoutly built houses, probably originally put up by the West Indian returnees. Note the wooden shingles on the roofs — a type of roofing straight out of peasant life in central Europe that was introduced by the Basel Mission in Ghana, and proved very influential in indigenous architecture till it began to be ousted c. 1900 by corrugated iron.

Plate 6. Ref. no. QD-30.04.0020
"The Basel Mission Bookshop in Accra," photographer unknown, early 20th century.

Architectural evidence of the effort the Basel Mission put into the development of literature in English, Twi, and Ga for the then Gold Coast.

Plate 7. Ref. no. QD-30.044.0034
"The Basel Mission Trading Company trading post at Akuse on the Volta River," between 1888 and 1908, photographer F. Ramseyer.

This is a collecting point for palm oil, a major export commodity for indigenous farmers in this part of Africa since the beginning of the nineteenth century. Note the many large barrels made on the spot by Basel Mission trained craftsmen for storage and transport (numbered for proper commercial control!), but also the use of corrugated iron for roofs and walls — a melange of what was centuries-old European village technology and the newest products of the industrial world.

Plate 8. Ref. no. D-30.013.012
"Rev & Mrs Bauer and pupils from Begoro [with the Catechists Adade, Ewi and Aye]." Unknown photographer, end of the 19th century.

An illustration of the Basel Mission effort to root education in rural life, but also a key photograph in the discussion about the kind of technology transfer which happened in this mission in 19th century Ghana. Note that while a number of European tools are on display — an axe, a saw, a spade, etc. — many of the pupils are carrying the kind of hoe characteristic of African production.

Plate 9. Ref. no. QD-30.011.0090
"The African John Anum, carpenter in Aburi, with his daughter Catherine." Photographer Wilhelm Locher, from the 1860s.

Series QD-30.011 is the second album with the earliest Basel Mission photographs from Ghana. This portrait deserves prolonged reflection. John Anum's name and his place in this album suggest that he was a member of the Christian community in Aburi. But he is dressed traditionally. The sign of his trade — a ruler in his left hand — is very discreet. It looks as if Wilhelm Locher was taking a photograph not only of a mission-trained craftsman but of paternal and filial love in a strongly indigenous context — a most unusual image in Africa of the 1860s.

Plate 10. Ref. no. QD-30.011.0020
"Christiansborg. Shoe-maker Bohner's workshop." Photographer Wilhelm Locher, from the 1860s.

The social and pedagogic unit of the master and his apprentices, still a major feature of the society from which Bohner came, has clearly established itself here in the framework of the Basel Mission on the West African coast.

Plate 11. Ref. no. D-30.24.039 "The blacksmith Maniesen with his family." Photographer Wilhelm Erhardt, between 1899 and 1912.

Although blacksmithery is, of course, an ancient precolonial craft in most parts of Africa, the way this family presents itself suggests strongly that Maniesen was a product of Basel Mission training.

Plate 12. Ref. no. QD-32.032.0046
Original caption illegible. Photographer O. Schultze, early 20th century.

This is a photograph of pupils from a school participating in the building of a new church in Christiansborg/Accra early in the 20th century. It seems that pupils, perhaps of the Christiansborg Middle School, were forming the human chain to transport the roofing materials up the ladder to the roof. Note the handcarts in front of the church, products of the wheelwright's shop in Plate 13.

Plate 13. Ref. no. QE-30.007.0102
This is the Basel Mission's wheelwright's shop in Christiansborg, Accra, before 1914, photographer unknown.

The archive series QE-30.007 is an album with many photographs from Cameroon — but some from Ghana. We do know that the Basel Mission had a wheelwright's shop in Accra at the end of the 19th century. It seems very likely that this photograph was taken there — documenting the transportation to West Africa of village crafts from central Europe, but also again the importance of the central European institution of apprenticeship in this mission.

Plate 14. Ref. no. QW-30.007.0011
"Mr Evans with the agricultural course for mission teachers, Aburi, 1911." Photographer unknown.

Mr. Evans was not a Basel missionary, but presumably a government official playing the part of what later generations called an agricultural extension office.

Plate 15. Ref. no. D-30.22.052
"Women carrying headloads of cocoa to the coast." Photographer Rudolf Fisch, between 1900 and 1911.

For centuries head-loading was the only feasible form of transport in southern Ghana. Although the Basel Mission sought to develop other forms of transport — hand-carts, barrels rolled along paths, motor lorries — long-distance head-loading remained an activity which was part and parcel of economic activity even at the time of the cocoa revolution.

Plate 16. Ref. no. QD-32.024.0102
"Buying cocoa and rubber in the Kumase trading post of the Basel Mission Trading Company." Photographer: F. Ramseyer, between 1898 and 1908.

The European trader asserts his centrality in this image. But indigenous initiative was crucial in seizing the opportunities offered by the trade in wild rubber in the 4th quarter of the 19th century, and of cocoa from the 1890s.

Plate 17. Ref. no. D-30.11.054
"The new church in Larteh." Photographer: W. Erhardt, between 1899 and 1912.

Pre-1914 Basel Mission history in Ghana is punctuated in all regions by major building efforts executed and financed either by the mission or the local community. Many Basel Mission settlements like that in Larteh were on hill-top sites. Even in 1908 there were virtually no mechanical means of easing the work of building. The application of human muscle power to preparing the local building materials and shifting them and the imported items onto the building site deserves attention as a social history phenomenon of its own.

Plate 18. Ref. no. QS-30.036.0071
View of the Basel Mission House from the south, late 19th century, photographer unknown.

A late nineteenth century photograph of the Mission House in Basel, the location of the Basel Mission's headquarters and, not least, its seminary.

Plate 19. Ref. no. D-30.09.024
"Sons of the Akropong Akwapim, who [were] agents of the Basel Mission. Photograph [taken] during the [Basel Mission Twi District] Synod 1909." Photographer unknown, apparently a reproduction from a published half-tone plate.

This photograph documents a paradox that non-Ghanaians find it hard to grasp and expound. In their clothing and their description as Basel Mission agents these men stress their role in church and modernization. But their traditional identity as members of prominent families is the reason for them being grouped and photographed like this. Each one will have had a traditional anchorage in Akropong society which, at any moment, will have influenced his thoughts and actions — and his participation in Mission activities — to an extent which is rarely understood by the outside world.

Plate 20. Ref. no. D-30.16.006
"The Ramseyer's temporary quarters in Kumase." Photographer: F. Ramseyer, 1896.

On the final subjection by the British of the kingdom of Asante in 1896, the Basel missionaries Fritz and Rosa Ramseyer, who had been held hostage in Kumase from 1869-72, were invited by the colonial government to start a Basel Mission station there. Fritz Ramseyer's photographic record of the next few years (during which the Basel Mission station was destroyed by the Asante uprising in 1900 and then rebuilt) is the best we have of the founding of a 19th century mission station.

Plate 21. Ref. no. D-30.16.048
"The dining-room in the mission house in Kumase." Photographer: Fritz Ramseyer, probably 1897 or 1898.

The contrast between the life-styles and -techniques of a pioneer and an established mission station is well exemplified in Plates 20 and 21. It would not be too much to say that they reflect not only the range of situations the missionaries faced in Ghana, but also the range of their experience in Europe — starting in rural families very near the bread-line but gaining middle-class status by their education and experience in Basel.

Plate 22. Ref. no. D-30.14.008
"Mission House in Abetifi [with Mrs. Ramseyer standing in the garden]." Photographer:
Fritz Ramseyer, between 1888 and 1895.

This classical Gold Coast Basel Mission house, built in the late 1870s, has been beautifully
restored in 1998-89 by funds contributed by the Swiss ambassador in Accra, Dr. Peter
Schweizer. With its original shingle roof, and its combination of broken stone walls and
half-timber construction it well illustrates the application to the tropics of ideas in the
vernacular rural architecture of substantial farmhouses in South Germany and Switzerland. The houses were oriented east-west, so that the low sun in the morning and evening
strikes the narrow and not the long walls, thus minimizing the heat taken up by the walls
and transmitted to the rooms inside. It is only one room wide (which is apparent also in
Plate 21), thus allowing for maximum through draft. The roof is set off a little above the
ceiling of the upper floor to allow for maximum air movement to insulate the living
quarters from the fierce temperatures on the roof at midday.

Plate 23. Ref. no. QS-30.014.0029
"For me it would be easier to die than to leave the mission." Photo Studio Brunner, Winterthur, undated, but before 1879.

A portrait of the powerful *Inspektor* (executive head) of the Basel Mission, Joseph Josenhans, with an epigram reflecting his complicated situation as someone living in relative safety in Europe and sending his troops out to very likely death in "the white man's grave."

Plate 24. Ref. no. QS-30.002.0237.02
The Zimmermann-Mulgrave family, probably taken during a furlough in Europe in 1872-73, studio unknown

Shown are the Basel missionary Johannes Zimmermann and his wife Catherine Zimmermann-Mulgrave with the children from this marriage and from her earlier marriage to the Liberian George Thompson. The young European woman on the left is probably a cousin of Johannes Zimmerman.

Plate 25. Ref. No. D-30.02.015
"Basel Mission Factory Lorry Review," unknown photographer, c. 1914.

A photograph redolent of the power of the Basel Mission immediately before 1914. With the worst of its health problems solved by advances in tropical medicine c. 1900 and the population of its part of Ghana benefiting from the cocoa revolution, it seems to have been the Basel Mission Trading Company which took the lead in introducing motor-transport to Accra and its hinterland.

CHAPTER 3

Authority and Discipline

In nature as well as in the realm of the Bible and human history, God is a god of order. If any individual person or association of persons devoted to a businesslike purpose want to please Him and take part in His blessed grace, this can only take place on the path of order, which He in His wisdom has drawn in legible strokes in the nature of things and in the heart of man.[1]

Let every soul be subject unto the higher powers. For there is no power but of God: the powers that be are ordained of God. Whosoever therefore resisteth the power, resisteth the ordinance of God: and they that resist shall receive to themselves damnation.[2]

Frogs must have storks.[3]

The prominent Pietists who established the organizational apparatus of the Basel Mission in the early 1800s were resourceful individuals with extensive leadership experience in religious and secular organizations in their communities. For all their efforts to create something new, however, and despite their prominence in public and private affairs, they could not build a missionary

1. Blumhardt, *Hausordnung*, p. 2.
2. Rom. 13:1-2.
3. Luther, "On Secular Authority," in Höpfl, ed., *Luther and Calvin*, p. 30.

institution entirely as they wished, nor, having established it, were they free of constraints in the way they governed it. They were alert to the examples provided by the evangelical missions that preceded them, and like the builders of any organization, they had to work within the hierarchical precedents and cultural rationales for leadership that were characteristic of their own time and place. Special care had to be taken not to threaten the interests of established political leaders or challenge too directly the convictions of those religious authorities who remained non-Pietists and who scrutinized the Mission's activities, especially in the formative years, with a critical eye and not a few misgivings. A framework had to be found that was compatible with the talents and expectations of those recruited to be missionaries in the field. In all of this, care had to be taken to stay within the range of what was acceptable in Pietist belief.

Basel in the late eighteenth and early nineteenth centuries was an island of relative religious tolerance, and this influenced the decision to establish a missionary society there. But it was a nervous time that was convulsed by the example of the French Revolution and its aftermath, reverberations from which were felt in several forms. There was increasing tension between Basel and the relatively disenfranchised countryside surrounding it; the Swiss cantons experienced a temporary loss of their independence; and the Napoleonic Wars threatened more than once to engulf the city.[4] In this climate important secular and church leaders needed reassuring that the evangelical movement did not spell more disorder and that the energies of the Mission's members could be held in check. I have already pointed out how uneasy some local notables had been about the role of Juliane von Krüdener, the one woman who was visibly influential in the creation of the Mission, and how their concern led to her separation from the Mission and her virtual expulsion from the city. It was because of her charisma and visibility and the potentially troublesome beliefs of her followers that her movement was seen as a potential threat to community order.[5] Managing such external points of concern in the community while protecting their own freedom of action demanded considerable sophistication and impressive diplomatic skill from the Mission's leadership. In fact, when the city government finally gave official permission to create the Mission seminary in 1815, the founders received the news with relief but also with surprise. They had expected more determined opposition, especially from certain members of the government who were attracted to Enlighten-

4. Meier, *Basler Heimatgeschichte,* pp. 558-59.
5. Ostertag, *Entstehungsgeschichte,* pp. 337ff.; Schlatter, *Geschichte der Basler Mission,* 1:16ff.

ment philosophies and sympathetic to the political example of the French Revolution.[6]

Inside the Mission the overseers had to be equally mindful of the rank-and-file members, whose frame of mind and whose objective interests and capabilities were crucial to the development of the organizational structure. There was a published list of criteria and procedures for admission to the seminary,[7] but beyond this the exchanges between aspiring applicants and the organization were structured by an unwritten script that set out the attitudes and competencies that the applicants must display and at the same time defined the categories of sober assessment that recruits could expect from the Mission's gatekeepers.[8] Aspiring seminarians often had friends who had preceded them into the Mission, and from them they learned to approach the organization with an appropriately supplicant demeanor, which the officers of the organization matched by a display of their own dominant positions. Quite apart from this imbalance in the dialogue, however, it is clear that the zeal and skills of the would-be missionaries were indispensable to the organization and that the rank and file were active agents in the construction of their own religious lives. As Giddens has put it, "all forms of dependence offer some resources whereby those who are subordinate can influence the activities of their superiors."[9] The petition to join the organization represented a vital personal choice for the applicants, a choice that for them was shaped by their own beliefs and their own personal circumstances. The Mission leadership, on the other hand, like the leaders of any organization that is not governed by overt coercion, had to make a claim to authenticity that would be credible to these "lower participants."[10]

To discover the limits of the seminarians' "readiness to obey," the framers had to be alert to those young people's talents, to the opportunities they had forgone by electing to join the Mission, and indeed, to their keen awareness of their identity as Pietists. On their side, the prospective missionaries expected to be provided with the resources and institutional structures they needed for

6. Schlatter, *Geschichte der Basler Mission*, 1:15ff., 21. More extensive discussions of the political and religious context immediately surrounding the Mission's creation appear in Ostertag, *Entstehungsgeschichte*, pp. 317ff., and Eppler, *Basler Mission, 1815-1899*, pp. 9ff. See also Meier, *Basler Heimatgeshichte*, pp. 250-54, 559, 615.

7. "Verordnungen über die persönliche Stellung der Missionare, Revidiert 1886" (Regulations concerning the personal position of the missionaries) (Basel Mission Archive [BMA] Q-9,21,7).

8. See Jenkins, "Villagers as Missionaries."

9. Giddens, *The Constitution of Society*, p. 16.

10. Mechanic, "Power of Lower Participants."

translating their religious energy into long-term collective action. For this purpose, as we shall see, not just any structure would do. Pietism had a special preoccupation with collective discipline and had developed an extensive stock of moral prescriptions about authority and obedience. Authoritative rules, reverence for the hierarchical structures thought to be necessary for the implementation of those rules, and norms about the effective use of time, material resources, and human energy — all were intrinsically important. For this reason it is useful to regard Pietism as an *organizational* movement or *organizational* ideology at the same time it is regarded as a *religious* phenomenon.

To be sure, rigorous temporal control in ascetic Christian movements can be traced back at least as far as the Benedictine Rule of the sixth century.[11] For Pietism, however, there was more to it than this general heritage. All the participants, including the immediate incumbents of leadership positions in the Mission, the wider circle of prosperous and influential Pietist supporters, and the ordinary seminarians and small subscribers to the missionary cause, had to be convinced that governance in the organization faithfully expressed the moral priorities of the movement in which they were all devout participants. Moreover, the mandate for discipline did not stop at the physical boundaries of the Mission per se. As I pointed out in chapter 1 when I described the impact of the Mission on the culture of Ghana, the same authoritative precepts that were in force inside the institution were taken as a moral template for the Christian communities established abroad. This collection of shared understandings among the members about what must be done, and how, made up the Mission's "rationalizing myths."[12] For the members the organizational *medium* was part of the religious *message* (to borrow an overworked phrase from the present), and this intimate connection between discipline and belief magnified the importance of the Mission structure. This helps to explain why the controlling group held on to the key features of that structure with such tenacity, even when there was a high price to be paid by doing so, and why the ordinary members went along with them, long after the same structure's inherent weaknesses were apparent to any careful observer. I will come back to how this doctrinal commitment conditioned the survival of the Mission in chapter 5.

Max Weber argued that all these factors — time, place, political and religious context, organizational precedents, and the moral premises that commanded the attention of the participants — will leave their traces in the so-

11. Walker et al., *History*, pp. 157-58; Hollister, *Medieval Europe*, pp. 60ff.; Forell, *Christian Social Teachings*, pp. 84ff.
12. Meyer and Rowan, "Institutionalized Organizations."

cial architecture of an institution. The Basel Mission had deliberate points of commonality with other organizations, but it also developed distinctive permutations on those shared themes and displayed enduring contradictions and difficulties that were all its own. What is most interesting about its structure theoretically is that it integrated in a lasting and virtually seamless way all three of the forms of legitimate authority that Weber made familiar in his historical discussion of imperative control. Those who constructed the Mission and occupied its administrative center through the years believed they had been divinely called to guide the organization. The plausibility of this religious claim, which is a form of *charismatic* justification for exercising control, was essential to their continuing acceptance by their subordinates. Because of their prominence in society, those same leaders thought of themselves as members of an exalted hereditary status group, and this led them to replicate in the Mission the patriarchal responsibilities and privileges that defined their *traditional* roles in the larger community. Finally the families they represented had for generations been, and would continue to be, key players in the political economy of their region. They had extensive experience in national and international business firms and government agencies, which at the time were becoming increasingly rationalistic and contractual, that is, *bureaucratic*, in form. This experience was reflected in the Mission's written charter of duties, regulations, and contractual agreements, in its detailed division of labor, its preoccupation with punctuality and dependability, and its commitment to systematic record keeping and precise accounting practices.

Leaving aside "sheer force," which he regarded as inherently unstable, Weber believed that appeals to these three forms of legitimate authority essentially define the alternative strategies available to decision makers who must coordinate large-scale collective enterprises. In their "pure" forms, charisma, tradition, and rational-legalism (bureaucracy) contain points of mutual incompatibility,[13] and much of Weber's effort went into explaining the historical tendency in modern societies for the rational-legal form to become the predominant one, gradually displacing the other two.[14] This is the side of Weber's argument that is most familiar in organizational sociology; it parallels in many ways the argument about instrumental rationality and "disenchantment" in his sociology of religion.[15] When this interpretation is taken too literally, however, it reifies the categories of authority, exaggerates their

13. Weber, *Economy and Society*, 2:1111ff.
14. *From Max Weber*, p. 51.
15. Weber, *Protestant Ethic*; McGuire, *Religion*, pp. 232-35.

differences, and encourages a vision of social change that is both too deterministic and too simplistic. A "tendency" toward separation into discrete forms of authority followed by the supersession of one decision strategy over the others does not mean that such outcomes are inevitable. Explaining instances in which the differentiation into discrete types does not occur can contribute as much to the understanding of imperative control as the study of examples in which it does. I will discuss the circumstances that led to the Mission's particular organizational "gestalt" in some detail, but first I need to set the theoretical context for my analysis with a critical reconstruction of Weber's argument about the points of convergence and tension among the three types of authority.

Building a Structure

In Weber's discussion of imperative control, he made a forceful statement about how difficult it is to reconcile charisma with either traditional or bureaucratic authority: "Since it is 'extraordinary,'" he said, "charismatic authority is sharply opposed to rational, and particularly bureaucratic, authority, and to traditional authority. . . . Charismatic authority is specifically irrational in the sense of being foreign to all rules. . . . [It] repudiates the past . . . [and is] a specifically revolutionary force."[16] Wolfgang Schluchter's summary of Weber's argument neatly captures the logical contrasts: with charisma, "valid" means *newly revealed;* with tradition, "valid" is *what has always been;* and with bureaucracy, "valid" refers to *what has been legally enacted or contractually imposed.*[17] When they are stated in such stark terms, it is difficult to imagine a situation in which decisions proceeding from one of these principles could avoid undermining decisions based on either of the other two. The claim that past solutions offer the best answers to present problems is unlikely to satisfy either the impatient charismatic or the reckoning bureaucrat; similarly, what is newly revealed is, by definition, as unlikely to confirm what comes through generations of traditional practice as it is to validate what emerges from a process of rational-legal calculation; and finally, principles of rational-legal reasoning cannot be counted on to generate solutions that echo received wisdom of either a revealed or a traditional sort.

What is "logical," of course, is itself a culturally and historically bound notion, and that is precisely the point that has to be made in order to understand

16. Weber, *Economy and Society,* 1:244.
17. Schluchter, *Western Rationalism,* p. 84.

authority in the Basel Mission. Weber recognized that living actors with complex real programs of action in mind will assemble organizational strategies from the elements available, acceptable, meaningful, and useful to them, not from an abstract understanding of what is logical in any supposedly universal sense. In reality, Weber said, the three types of authority rarely exist in pure form, and they may "appear together in the most diverse combinations."[18] The "revolutionary force" of charisma, for example, only applies to the exercise of that type of control in its original form *(in statu nascendi)* by a prophet, warrior, entrepreneur, or demagogue. In historical terms such episodes may only be flash points, useful for establishing the definition of a concept but not typical of any variant that persists beyond its founding moment. In its institutionalized forms, charisma may be found mated to structures that, in Weber's terms, are in principle "alien to its essence."[19] More to the point, charisma has to develop a firm institutional base in order to survive. At the same time, a traditional or bureaucratic regime is immeasurably strengthened if it can call upon the immediate energy or the cultural memory of revealed truth and provide leaders who, in the eyes of the led, can lay claim to an inherited relic of the mystery and credibility of the founder.[20] Far from being a revolutionary force, charisma in these "routinized" settings can become the very bulwark of traditional or bureaucratic authority; in many religious organizations in particular, it is simply indispensable for any kind of sustained collective action in which the rank and file are expected to be involved.[21]

In short, complex combinations of the different forms of authority can survive, and the Basel Mission is clearly such a case, that blur the edges of their differences and soften their potential incompatibilities. The key point, according to Weber, is that charisma, standing alone, "cannot remain stable, but becomes either traditionalized or rationalized, *or a combination of both*."[22] The specific direction or directions charisma takes is determined by the larger institutional context,[23] and particularly by the nature of the surrounding economic order.[24]

18. Weber, *Economy and Society,* 2:1133; see also Schluchter, *Western Rationalism,* pp. 128ff.

19. Weber, *Economy and Society,* 2:1122-23.

20. Bendix, *Max Weber,* pp. 301, 312ff.; Weber, *Economy and Society,* 2:1148-49.

21. Weber, *Economy and Society,* 2:1139ff.

22. Weber, *Economy and Society,* 1:246, emphasis added.

23. *From Max Weber,* p. 54.

24. Weber, *Economy and Society,* 1:246, 254. Combinations of charisma and bureaucracy, or charisma and tradition, would be fairly common, Weber argued, compared with combinations of bureaucracy and tradition or of all three forms.

It is also important to note that stable combinations of the various modes of authority will emerge only if the accommodation of the forms to each other alienates no essential constituency, as might happen, for example, if one important group believed that its conception of what is religiously necessary is absolutely negated by competing principles of, say, practical efficiency or traditional privilege. "In general," Weber wrote, "it should be kept clearly in mind that the basis of every authority, and correspondingly of every kind of willingness to obey, is a *belief,* a belief by virtue of which persons exercising authority are lent prestige."[25] It follows that stability for the more complicated configurations of authority (those that try to incorporate more than one decision strategy) will be possible only where there is a unifying collection of beliefs that bridges the differences of underlying principles and lends prestige and plausibility to those exercising leadership, whatever the form their leadership may take at a given moment. This belief system, which, needless to say, is "seldom altogether simple," determines the "willingness to obey," that is, the critical band *inside of which* an overall structure of decision making and the specific directives that flow from it will be accepted as legitimate by participants, but *outside of which* they will be rejected or resisted.[26] It is the breadth of this zone of acceptance,[27] in turn, that conditions the probability of survival of an organizational form. Where it is broad, leaders have wide latitude in the directives they can expect to see obeyed; where it is narrow, they can hardly afford a misstep if they wish to preserve their credibility. However rare and tortuous it may be, a cultural rationale that is able to reconcile charismatic, traditional, and bureaucratic modes of decision making will produce an associated zone of acceptance that is very broad indeed.

For the Basel Mission the religious movement that we now call Württemberg Pietism provided just such a system of bridging beliefs. It preserved the belief in divine ordination — the gift of grace — in the leadership of religious affairs; it taught that such ordination was most likely to fall on leaders from established traditional strata; and it embraced the appropriateness of rigid schedules, written rules, and contractual agreements for implementing decisions made by those leaders. Several historical developments that coincided with the late eighteenth- and early nineteenth-century popularity of this movement help to account for its ability to absorb these diverse beliefs.[28]

25. Weber, *Economy and Society,* 1:263, emphasis Weber's.

26. Weber, *Economy and Society,* 1:263.

27. Chester Barnard ("Cooperation," pp. 93ff.) used the phrase the "zone of indifference" to refer to essentially the same idea.

28. On the relationship between nineteenth-century Pietism and earlier expressions of the Pietist movement, see Beyreuther, *Geschichte des Pietismus,* pp. 331ff.

Familiar farm and village social and economic arrangements still enjoyed strong cultural support, but the influence of urban and industrial political economies was growing. Many among the traditional elites who were attracted to the evangelical movement, for example, voiced support for Luther's view that agrarian communities and traditional values represented the biblical ideal, but they were also becoming increasingly committed to the modern economy in their own lives. These same transformations can be seen at work reshaping the lives and the life choices of the men and women of much lower estate who were to become the recruitment base of the missionary movement.

These currents converged in special ways in Basel. The city was strategically placed, early to industrialize, and wealthy. Until the time of Napoleon its membership in the neutral and comparatively stable republican federation of Switzerland kept it relatively free (but never unmindful) of the political intrigues and shifting alliances that contributed to instability elsewhere in Europe.[29] Albert Ostertag, an early member of the Mission's governing committee, offers an apt description of the city in the days just before the founding of the Mission.[30] Most notable, he says, were its lively trade and business energy, which were enhanced by its position on a great commercial thoroughfare, the Rhine, and at the point where the border of Switzerland intersects with those of two other populous lands, France and Germany. Those advantages contributed to Basel's material prosperity and independence, but along with its increasing integration into the modern economy the city was also deeply invested in tradition. In its civic life it was dominated by its ancient guilds, whose "aristocratic" rule took the form of venerable customs and laws that layered the population into discrete and relatively fixed social categories. Governance, though republican in form, was by no means democratic or egalitarian. At the same time, however, the city was relatively tolerant of both modern scientific thinking and religious variation, as long as the established Protestant churches, established economic arrangements, and established political structures were not challenged by them.

This distinctive blend of openness and conservatism made the creation of the Basel Mission by the German Society for Christianity possible, and it strongly influenced the shape the Mission would need to assume in order to preserve its credibility and legitimacy.[31] As I pointed out in chapter 2, the

29. Troeltsch, *Social Teaching*, p. 687; Wyss, *Soziale Politik des Konservativen Bürgertums;* Meier, *Basler Heimatgeschichte*, pp. 250-54, 558-59.

30. Ostertag, *Entstehungsgeschichte*, pp. 9-14.

31. Gründer, *Christliche Mission und Deutscher Imperialismus*, pp. 22ff.

Swiss and south German families of the founders had long been prominent socially, economically, politically, and religiously in their communities. Ultimately it was the money and, more important, the prestige and credibility of this elite group that were exposed to risk by the Mission's activities. The structure they put together was carefully crafted to protect their interests from any potential harm. They recognized from the beginning how crucial it was to reconcile "the enthusiasm, without which the work would have had a hard time emerging," with "the sobriety, without which it would not have achieved steady development or won wide trust."[32] Day-to-day governance was placed in the hands of the Committee, whose membership I have shown was drawn almost entirely from the founders' own social circle. The Committee in turn engaged as inspector a man of acceptably eminent academic, religious, and social standing who would oversee daily Mission administration, set the theological tone, preside over weekly decision-making meetings, and represent the organization's public face. Wilhelm Hoffmann, one of the early incumbents of this elevated position, called the closed circle comprised of himself and the ruling Committee "the beating heart" (das schlagende Herz) of the organization.[33]

As important as the organization's founders and directors were, the experiences and expectations of the rank-and-file missionaries were also of fundamental importance in shaping the Mission. The leadership expected complete compliance and great personal sacrifice, not excluding death, from its subordinates, but it would be a mistake to assume that the missionaries were merely passive human material in the hands of an omnipotent leadership. Erich Beyreuther writes of the Pietists' willingness to sacrifice "life and blood" for their cause, and Wilhelm Schlatter has documented the specific form that this call for personal sacrifice took in the Mission.[34] Nevertheless, the young men and women who took part were under no obligation to join the evangelical cause, and the devotion, piety, and courage required by the missionary life were not qualities that could be simply "hired" or created by command.

Despite their imperious bearing, therefore, the leaders had to extend trust

32. Schlatter, *Geschichte der Basler Mission,* 1:23. The passage in full reads: "Eine Verständigung dieser beiden Temperamente des Glaubens erschien unmöglich; der Enthusiasmus, ohne welchen das Werk schwerlich in damaliger Zeit zustande gekommen wäre, und die Nüchternheit, ohne die es sich niemals hätte stetig entwickeln und ein grosses Vertrauen gewinnen können, standen gegeneinander."

33. W. Hoffmann, *Eilf Jahre in der Mission,* p. 20.

34. Beyreuther, *Geschichte des Pietismus,* pp. 343-44; Schlatter, *Geschichte der Basler Mission,* 1:217-18.

to their subordinates and be trusted by them in return. All their resources, prestige, and determination would have been unavailing without subordinates who for reasons written in the record of their own experiences were ready to submit to the rigorous discipline of the missionary life. In point of fact, the recruits were moved by their own religious beliefs to accept the Committee's claim to revealed wisdom and charismatic religious legitimacy. They were also moved to compliance with "duly constituted authority" by the traditional expectations associated with their modest social origins. And finally, they were familiar with contractual subordination because of their direct or indirect knowledge of the increasingly rational and contractual economy that was emerging around them. Had these influences — these elective affinities — not been present, the history of the Mission would be very different.

Inherited Charisma and Pious Emotional Attachment

In terms of specific doctrinal beliefs, Pietists were noted for an intense emotional fervor that began with the conversion experience, or spiritual "rebirth," and expressed itself, among other ways, in uncritical readiness to obey established authority, whether that authority was religious or secular and whatever the specific form it might take.[35] Other missions characterized by equal evangelical fervor moved toward more decentralized and egalitarian organizational forms.[36] The strong centralization embraced by the Baslers mirrored in many ways the teachings of Luther and Calvin, both of whom argued that subordination to established order was the proper expression of Christian humility.[37] In the Mission the members of the governing committee justified

35. Weber, *Protestant Ethic,* pp. 137ff.; Forell, *Christian Social Teachings,* p. 257.

36. The Wesleyans, the Moravians, and the nondenominational LMS are good examples. Roland Oliver, in *Missionary Factor,* pp. 41-44, says the LMS was so decentralized it had at times virtually no leadership in the field and therefore was unable to get anything done that required coordination. In the eyes of the organization, the missionaries were independent and absolutely equal to each other. There is no better example than David Livingstone (in his adventurous mode) of the independent missionary working outside the confines of church structures.

37. For Luther's views see his essay of 1523, "On Secular Authority" (pp. 1-43 in Höpfl, ed., *Luther and Calvin*); see also the discussion by Troeltsch (*Social Teaching,* pp. 529, 574-75, 617ff.). For the views of Calvin see the selection from the *Institutes of the Christian Religion* titled "On Civil Government" (pp. 47-86 in Höpfl); also see Troeltsch's summary (pp. 619-23, 901, 904) and the discussions by Kai Erikson (*Wayward Puritans,* pp. 50-54) and Fred Graham *(The Constructive Revolutionary).* See Ernst Cassirer (*Philosophy of the Enlightenment,* pp. 134-97, 239-40) for a discussion of the confrontation as well as the

their "right" to occupy the center and to prevail over the organization's affairs on the grounds that *specifically* they, as individuals and as representatives of a special social group, had been directly called by God to create and control the organization.[38]

The Mission's founding mythology is revealing in this regard. Several stories identify the decisive moment of the organization's creation with Basel's "miraculous" escape from a siege during the Napoleonic Wars. In 1815 the city's governors allowed the armies allied against Napoleon to gain a tactical advantage over their foes by marching over its Rhine river bridge. In retaliation for this breach of neutrality, a nearby garrison loyal to the French bombarded the city. According to one account, the Pietists of Basel took the city's survival as a divine signal to create the Mission: "[A] torrent of bombs was opened upon the town. But the Lord sent a violent east wind, which had such an effect upon the fire of the enemy, that the bombs were exhausted in the air before they could reach the houses. In consequence of this remarkable deliverance, the people of God resolved to establish a mission seminary, to train up pious teachers for the heathen."[39]

Ernst Stähelin has reproduced a series of letters written by the principal founders of the Mission in which variations on this theme of divine intervention are expressed. One version was that the bombs were God's way of telling Peter Ochs, a key figure in the local government and a leader of the Francophile party, that he should reconsider any objections he had to the establishment of a Pietist seminary.[40] Essentially similar accounts are rendered by other Mission chroniclers.[41] Such stories allowed the founders to assume an aura of personal specialness beyond the halo of "office" or "inherited" charisma that attaches to some extent to all religious functionaries.[42] It enabled them to appeal to the zeal of the members and it provided legitimacy for the way power was divided in the Mission. Johannes Hesse described from his own experience a meeting in which Inspector Josenhans, who presided from 1850 to 1871 and with whom the Mission's spirit of discipline is most identified (see plate 23), was asked how "the will of God" could be recognized. The answer given without hesitation was that God's will manifested itself "in the

---

points of reconciliation between Reformationist (Lutheran and Calvinist) and Enlightenment thinking.

38. Hesse, *Joseph Josenhans*, p. 163; see also Eiselin, "Zur Erziehung," p. 49.

39. Newcomb, *Cyclopedia of Missions*, p. 171.

40. Stähelin, *Christentumsgesellschaft*, pp. 295-311.

41. Ostertag, *Entstehungsgeschichte*, pp. 317-35; Eppler, *Basler Mission, 1815-1899;* and Schlatter, *Geschichte der Basler Mission*, 1:19ff.

42. Bendix, *Max Weber*, pp. 312-13; Weber, *Economy and Society*, 1:248, 251ff.

will of the Committee." Hesse's account continued as follows: "[In saying this] the Inspector was not thinking of [his own] infallibility but only wanted to emphasize that a missionary . . . was best assured of fulfilling the will of God by doing everything his superiors told him to do."[43]

The frequent references to divine insight and guidance were meant to produce a sense of awe, and many of the seminarians took the message quite literally.[44] Their accounts of life in the Mission House and the letters they wrote from the field seldom failed to display the reverence — and sometimes the fear — with which most of them regarded the Committee or the humility and supplication with which they approached that body, particularly the inspector. Cornelia Vogelsanger's description of the seminarians' attitudes toward Inspector Josenhans makes this point succinctly: "Josenhans was not just feared," she said, "but fanatically loved by many of his students. It appeared that his domineering personality did not make it possible for [them] to maintain any inner distance from him. He embodied in the patriarchal world of the Basel Mission an outsized father figure who dispensed fear and love, punishment and grace just like the Old Testament God to whom he knew himself to be responsible."[45]

This complex of feelings sharpened the students' eagerness to obey directives from above, whatever the form those directives might take. One seminarian, Friedli Heinecken, described his sense of the inspector's position in this way: "He was for us a consecrated personality; one submitted cheerfully to his decisions; his word was authentic."[46] Hesse, himself a member of the inner circle of the Mission, offered a similar (and at the same time much more analytical) characterization. In his view any close observer could see that the insistence on the unerring judgment of the inspector and Committee could cause injustice and injury. The inspector and Committee could err, after all, and dissenting subordinates could occasionally be right. Nevertheless, "admitting an error on the part of the Inspector or the Committee was simply never done." Hesse quoted Inspector Josenhans as saying, "The Committee takes nothing back. . . . [It] always knows best what must be done," and as further insisting that, however great the likelihood of injustice might have been, it was always "a lesser evil than the weakening of authority."[47]

The personal qualifications that governed admission into the seminary reveal the premium that was placed on the acceptance of authority as some-

43. Hesse, *Joseph Josenhans*, p. 177.
44. Hesse, *Joseph Josenhans*, p. 177.
45. Vogelsanger, *Pietismus und Afrikanische Kultur*, p. 60.
46. Heinecken, "When Grandfather," p. 390.
47. Hesse, *Joseph Josenhans*, p. 177.

thing religiously and organizationally necessary.[48] The decisive criterion for acceptance was a personal rebirth *(Wiedergeburt)* that signaled complete emotional surrender to the larger Pietist cause. An applicant had to describe the exact moment of his own conversion experience, and the authenticity of the conversion had to be confirmed by a witness, usually the candidate's own local minister, who was known to the Mission. Entry was impossible for anyone who did not pass this spiritual test. Upon acceptance the individual surrendered his or her self-reliance, independent thinking, and individual initiative, or else these inclinations would be extinguished by the organization. The leadership were untiring in their efforts to identify, then counsel, and if necessary dismiss anyone who continued to display such qualities of individuality, which in the context of the Mission were regarded as "character defects." In the view of Inspector Josenhans, a seminarian must be severely tested before it could be determined whether he was fully receptive to the Mission's training and therefore could be trusted to carry on the Pietist cause without question. Evidence of an "unbroken spirit," if it persisted, could disqualify a seminarian from further study in the Mission House.[49] The source of this language is Psalm 51, the "penitent psalm," which says the sacrifice most pleasing to God is "a broken spirit and a broken and contrite heart."[50] As Josenhans himself put it in the passage that introduced chapter 1: "It is necessary to smash [a seminarian] down mercilessly in order to determine conclusively whether he is capable of bearing the discipline."[51] By their immersion in this philosophy of revealed wisdom and by their commitment to the program of subordination that was justified by it, the missionaries were socialized for obedience throughout their lives in the organization.

Every leadership of a movement that makes extraordinary demands upon the personal devotion and sacrifice of ordinary members has to be able to make some such claim to special wisdom and special mandate, even when it is difficult to reconcile with other elements of the movement's philosophy. In his essay on authority, for example, Luther argued against hierarchical differences in power when he said that "there neither can nor ought to be any supe-

48. These requirements appear in the document "Verordnungen über die persönliche Stellung der Missionare, Revidiert 1886" (BMA Q-9,21,7, p. 5).

49. The German phrase is *ungebrochener Sinn,* sometimes replaced by *ungebrochenes Herz,* or "unbroken heart."

50. Ps. 51:19 reads in German, "Das Opfer, das Gott gefällt, ist ein zerbrochener Geist, ein zerschlagenes Herz wirst du, o Gott, nicht verachten." In the King James Version the corresponding verse is number 17: "The sacrifices of God are a broken spirit: a broken and a contrite heart, O God, thou wilt not despise."

51. Quoted by Hesse, *Joseph Josenhans,* pp. 212-13.

riors amongst Christians . . . except Christ alone," but having said that, he also found room for the principle of divinely ordained leadership in Christian communities. Such governance, he insisted, is not about the superiority or power of one earthly group over another, but rather is about service, or calling. It exists only as a channel for the "furtherance of the Word of God."[52] In his treatise on civil government, Calvin drew upon the teachings of Paul to reach a much simpler conclusion, namely, that "all power exists by divine ordinance . . . there is none that is not established by God."[53]

The idea seems to be timeless. The famous Rule established by the founder of the Benedictines at Monte Cassino phrased the claim to divine knowledge by clerical leaders in this way: "The obedience we pay to superiors is paid to God: for he tells us: 'He that heareth you, heareth me.'"[54] In Helen Ebaugh's experience in a Catholic religious order 1,400 years later, the idea was stated in this way: "The voice of the superior had a divine ring, for we were taught that God made his desires known through every command and suggestion of superiors."[55] The Catholic charismatics whose story is told by Mary Jo Neitz demanded recognition from the bishops for their leaders on the grounds that those "renewed ministers," as they were called, had been chosen by God and therefore were authentic.[56] Stephen Warner found essentially the same claim shaping the debate over leadership of the Mendocino (Calif.) evangelical movement of the 1970s.[57] Susan Rose has factored gender into the equation in her description of authority in a charismatic fellowship in which not leadership alone but "divinely mandated patriarchy" was accepted as a general organizing precept.[58] In chapter 5 I will argue that the ubiquity of this principle of obedience is due in part to its ability to relieve "inspired" leaders of mundane accountability for the less welcome consequences of their decisions.

52. In Höpfl, ed., *Luther and Calvin*, p. 33.
53. In Höpfl, ed., *Luther and Calvin*, p. 52, emphasis added. Calvin's reference was to the thirteenth chapter of Romans.
54. Reprinted in Forell, *Christian Social Teachings*, p. 88.
55. Ebaugh, *Out of the Cloister*, p. xii.
56. Neitz, *Charisma and Community*, p. 165.
57. Warner, *New Wine*, pp. 239-48. Stephen Warner's account of this pivotal debate includes a description (pp. 243-45) of a lightning display that is remarkably reminiscent of the storm and bombardment that the founders and leaders of the Basel Mission took as a signal of divine intentions.
58. Rose, "Women Warriors."

Status Privilege and the Weight of Tradition

In addition to its charismatic religious underpinning, the Mission's structure was also grounded in the notion that people born to traditional privilege are naturally entitled to make decisions for those of lower estate. This justification came from several sources. The belief in legitimate status distinctions and the commitment to patriarchy were important parts of the cultural history of Pietism, and both the governing group and the ordinary missionaries, despite the vast differences in their origins and experiences, came to the Basel Mission prepared to act out that heritage. To be sure, those who constructed the Mission were acutely aware of the progressive and egalitarian thinking put into play by the Enlightenment and by the French and American revolutions,[59] and key Mission documents, including the *Hausordnung* that served as the official charter for the Mission House,[60] made cautious use of the language of democracy and individual freedom. Later on I will describe how the Pietists struggled in their thinking as well as in their rhetoric to come to terms with these themes, but for now the point is that they identified themselves in the main with the conservative reaction against those currents of liberal change.

The "libertarians" in Basel in the early nineteenth century, that is, those who were publicly identified with the ideals of "liberty, equality, and fraternity," were seen by Mission supporters as their strongest opponents.[61] The French Revolution and the "rationalist" or "deist" philosophies associated with Kant, Rousseau, and Voltaire were frequently held up by Pietists as sources of much that was wrong with the European societies of the time.[62] A striking indication of how this distrust of the new thinking could be expressed at the level of practical action is seen in the words of the missionary Johannes Zimmermann, who became one of the Mission's more effective and articulate agents on the Gold Coast (his recruitment to the Mission was described in the previous chapter; his accomplishments as well as his troubles are highlighted in the next). In his search for the proper social outlines for the Christian community he was trying to create in Africa, Zimmermann had this to say about the liberal thinking abroad in Europe at the time: "Ever since the French Revolution, an unbiblical conception [*unbiblische Anschauung*] of personal freedom and equality, all mixed up with humanistic and Christian

59. Gründer, *Christliche Mission und Deutscher Imperialismus*, pp. 22ff., 30ff.
60. Blumhardt, *Hausordnung.*
61. Schlatter, *Geschichte der Basler Mission*, 1:19ff.; Ostertag, *Entstehungsgeschichte*, pp. 292ff.
62. Ostertag, *Entstehungsgeschichte*, pp. 79ff., 292ff.

ideas, has made itself known and has . . . dissolved the divinely ordained units of family, community, and state; confused property rights; displaced the worth of human beings and human life, the family and its honor; and, in the place of the natural units of family, community, populace and state . . . has set the sterile tree of freedom."[63]

When revolution again threatened to sweep through Europe in the late 1840s, the Mission once more put itself firmly on the side of the endangered traditional structures.[64] According to Inspector Josenhans's biographer, much of the iron rule that he established in the Mission between 1850 and 1871 was inspired by the trauma he lived through in Germany in 1848 as he watched the principle of monarchy being assailed by the populist and republican movements.[65] About one particularly terrible night in June of that year, Josenhans wrote to his wife, "For a long time the danger was very great. In addition to all the terror, fear, and misery there was also a fearsome savagery and satanic rage. Some [of the demonstrators] laughed out brightly and cried *Vivat!* [To life!] while others were cursing the authorities."[66] Josenhans emerged from that period of trial convinced that traditional social and religious structures had been shaken to the core, and that they must be made safe against any such future threats.[67] He labored hard to build just such protection into the Mission's recruitment procedures, its hierarchy, and its principles of daily governance. Disobeying traditional authority figures was simply not to be tolerated.

The Swiss members among those who provided leadership and financial support for the Mission were essentially in agreement with such a program. Most were personally identified with the Swiss Reformed churches, which, being Calvinist, were increasingly attuned to urban, commercial, and industrial concerns.[68] Despite their essentially bourgeois origins, however, when it came to defining their place in the social order, they thought of themselves as a natural hereditary social elite; this much was clear from the discussion of their origins and motivations in chapter 2. They held and promulgated the belief that they sat at the apex of the venerable traditional order, and that their social station conferred unquestionable "aristocratic," even "quasi-monarchical" deci-

63. Quoted by Vogelsanger, *Pietismus und Afrikanische Kultur,* p. 126.
64. According to Martin Scharfe (*Die Religion des Volkes,* pp. 141-70), the conservative and counterrevolutionary sentiments of the Mission were characteristic of nineteenth-century Pietism.
65. Hesse, *Joseph Josenhans,* pp. 75ff.
66. Hesse, *Joseph Josenhans,* pp. 77-78.
67. Vogelsanger, *Pietismus und Afrikanische Kultur,* pp. 44ff.
68. Troeltsch, *Social Teaching,* pp. 540ff., 625ff., 642.

sion-making rights upon them inside the Mission.[69] For their part, I have noted that the German theologians in the Mission's central leadership typically came from Württemberg, which at the time was the seat of nineteenth-century Pietism and the source of the largest group of rank-and-file Basel missionaries. When the Mission was established, Württemberg was still a kingdom, and there was a close alliance there between the Lutheran church, with which most German Pietists were identified, and the traditional class of large landowners.[70] One inspector of the Mission, Hermann Praetorius, himself a German, came from a position as minister to the court *(Hofvikar)* in Württemberg,[71] while another, Wilhelm Hoffmann, also a German, became a spiritual adviser and ecclesiastical administrator to the Prussian court in Berlin after he retired from the Mission.[72]

In short, although the Swiss and German leaders of the Mission were not themselves titled members of a true landed aristocracy, they pulled the mantle of inherited superiority about themselves and knew well what forms of authority such claims could be made to serve. This complemented rather than conflicted with their belief in their own divine call to the mission cause, which I discussed earlier as the source of their claim to institutional charisma. It stood to reason that God would settle his preference for leadership of the Mission on those already accustomed traditionally to performing that function. According to Troeltsch, this was a conception of leadership that could easily be traced to the social thinking of Martin Luther.[73] It also echoed two Calvinist concepts, namely, the idea of predestination, which could issue in the belief that "the minority, consisting of the best and the holiest, is called to bear rule over the majority,"[74] and the belief that temporal structures of authority, so long as they do not violate the laws of God, are in effect divine ordinances.[75] The convergence of the two principles of leadership was virtually seamless: traditional authority was reinforced by divine nomination, and

69. W. Hoffmann, *Eilf Jahre in der Mission,* p. 27; see also Wyss, *Soziale Politik des Konservativen Bürgertums.*

70. Fulbrook, *Piety and Politics,* chap. 6; Troeltsch, *Social Teaching,* pp. 523ff., 617ff.

71. Praetorius became co-inspector in 1881 and died in Africa in 1883. See Schlatter, *Geschichte der Basler Mission,* 1:306ff.

72. Hoffmann was inspector from 1839 to 1850. He later became *Hof- und Domprediger* (minister to court and cathedral) under Friedrich Wilhelm IV, and in that station served for two decades as the king's confidant. He was, according to the Mission historian Wilhelm Schlatter (*Geschichte der Basler Mission,* 1:216), the most influential churchperson in Prussia.

73. Troeltsch, *Social Teaching,* pp. 561ff.

74. Troeltsch, *Social Teaching,* p. 618.

75. Troeltsch, *Social Teaching,* pp. 618-20.

conversely, charisma was made more effective by being anchored in a traditional structure of authority.

The origins of the ordained missionaries, as we have seen, were modest compared with those of the leadership, but they, too, were receptive to the principles of traditional governance. Even though the pressures of urbanization and proletarianization were increasing in the Württemberg region,[76] the Lutheran agrarian social ideal with its patriarchal patterns of village and town authority survived in the communities from which the largest group of Mission recruits came.[77] In his *Open Letter to the Christian Nobility,* Luther had argued forcefully for the Christian necessity of this traditional way of life: "This I know well, that it would be much more pleasing to God if we increased agriculture and diminished commerce, and that they do much better who, according to the Scriptures, till the soil and seek their living from it, as was said to us and to all men in Adam, 'Accursed be the earth when thou laborest therein, it shall bear thee thistles and thorns, and in the sweat of thy face shalt thou eat thy bread.' There is still much land lying untilled."[78] Troeltsch's summary of the Lutheran hierarchy of social values gives a broader view that is also useful in understanding the Mission's perspective on social structure:

> [T]he forms of social organization which ought to be maintained and which, above all, have a right to be protected and morally recognized, are the classes which live most near to the natural order: the main class of feudal and peasant agriculturists who, in direct contact with nature, produce goods without any intermediaries between the producer and the consumer; the class of officials and soldiers who are needed for the natural task of caring for the common weal, to which belong the vassals who were liable to military service, the class of workmen in the towns who produce goods which cannot be made by the peasantry; day-labourers, servants, and other functionaries, who are to be exhorted to frugality and obedience; finally also the merchant, whose services are indispensable for exchange, who in addition to the net cost may raise the price to one which will secure his existence.[79]

76. Lehmann, *Pietismus und Weltliche Ordnung;* R. Hoffmann, "Neupietistische Missionsbewegung."

77. Jenkins, "Sozialer Hintergrund und Mission"; Troeltsch, *Social Teaching,* pp. 540ff., 555-57.

78. In Forell, *Christian Social Teachings,* p. 159.

79. Troeltsch, *Social Teaching,* pp. 555-56.

Given their agrarian and Lutheran origins, it is not difficult to see why most of the rank-and-file members of the Mission community took the southern German village or town, with its notions of family, authority, and obedience, as their natural point of reference. By contrast, there is irony in the way the "commercial aristocrats" from the Basel elite embraced this agrarian ideal. Many of them were factory owners, merchants, and bankers tied into the emerging international economy, and almost all of them were far removed — generations removed — from primary production for the local economy. Nevertheless, they took the agrarian ideal for the Mission because of the intrinsic Christian virtues they associated with it, especially as far as the "simple folk," both at home and in the "heathen world," were concerned. They were determined to have as many of its features as possible reproduced in the self-contained communities of converts that the missionaries were expected to create on the Gold Coast.[80] When it came to administrative authority inside the Mission, the Committee members translated their acknowledged social superiority into a role in loco parentis that closely paralleled the paternalistic authority held in village society by fathers, elders, church authorities, and local aristocrats or social notables. The official written guide that defined the relationship between the Committee and the missionaries began with the call for "unconditional submission" *(unbedingte Hingebung)* on the part of the missionaries and "fatherly care" *(väterliche Fürsorge)* on the part of the Committee.[81] Discussions preserved in the Committee's records show that discontent with this arrangement was expressed on very rare occasions by seminarians and missionaries who found the distance and demeanor of their "superiors" to be condescending. One such complaint was entered by a young man (later dismissed) who questioned a rule that required seminarians to accept dinner invitations from prominent Mission benefactors. He was offended by the condescension and attitude of noblesse oblige that he thought were shown by the hosts, but the Committee did not consider this to be sufficient grounds to excuse him from the obligation.[82]

Marriage rules occasioned similar complaints. The small number of upper-status recruits who found their way into the seminary were sometimes offended when their freedom to marry "within their station" was set aside by the

80. Schlatter, *Geschichte der Basler Mission,* 3:72-73, 84-91; Oliver, *Missionary Factor,* p. 24; Brokensha, *Social Change at Larteh,* chap. 2.
81. Schlatter, *Geschichte der Basler Mission,* 1:233.
82. The case involved the seminarian Johann George Epple, who was dismissed in 1878 after an accumulation of such delicts. See Basel Mission Archive (BMA) *Komiteeprotokolle* (Committee Minutes; hereafter *KP)* 49, June 26, 1878, pp. 156-57, and November 27, 1878, p. 268.

Committee (see the discussion of missionary Strömberg in chapter 2). The missionary Zimmermann, whose appeal for special marriage treatment will be discussed at length in chapter 4, was not in this select upper-status group. When he asked the Committee's indulgence for his violation of the rules of betrothal, he did so using language closer to the typical rank-and-file perception of the matter of paternal authority: "Were my relationship to you merely that of a subordinate to his superior, it would be hard for me [to approach you], but in fact I have known since I took up the path of the Mission that the relationship that binds me to you is also, perhaps even more so, one of a son to his father, and that gives me the courage to lay my case before you openly."[83]

In general, expressions of dissatisfaction with authority and requests from the rank and file for special dispensation from the rules were infrequent and exceptional. Most of the time the familiar principle of "People like us have always provided the lead for people like you" prevailed and rendered a wide range of decision making familiar and acceptable to the Mission membership. The social distance separating leadership from rank and file that supported this patriarchal principle continued well into the present century. Like the model of the agrarian village, the patriarchal principle was replicated in the field, where missionaries exercised "fatherly" dominance over converts because of their "superior" European origins, and Christian Africans were expected to submit to the missionaries in recognition of this supposed natural superiority.[84]

To recapitulate, in the same way that the charismatic claims of the Mission leadership were validated by the Pietist beliefs of the young people recruited to the seminary, so were the traditional status distinctions that prevailed in the organization a continuation of the familiar reality of those recruits' daily lives. Neither the idea of religious revelation nor the notion of traditional status obligations conflicted with their experiences in the towns and villages to which they were culturally and emotionally tied. In addition to these themes of revealed authority and traditional obligations, Pietism also expressed a highly developed need for the strict measuring out of time, effort, and responsibility. In some quarters this emphasis on uniformity and accountability caused the movement to be called, aptly, "Precisionism."[85] In the Mission it took a form that provided a strong overlay of modern bureaucratic calculation.

83. D-1,3, Ussu, 1851, no. 19, June 2, 1851, p. 1.

84. Vogelsanger, *Pietismus und Afrikanische Kultur*, pp. 60-61. The Baslers were not the only missionaries who felt justified in providing both religious and secular leadership for their convert communities. T. O. Beidelman (*Colonial Evangelism*, p. 28) and Michael Coleman (*Presbyterian Missionary Attitudes*, pp. 15ff., 38ff., chap. 5) have discussed permutations of this same principle in other missions, both in Africa and elsewhere.

85. Troeltsch, *Social Teaching*, p. 682.

Bureaucratic Obligations and Legal-Contractual Ties

In some ways the relationship between the Basel Mission and the young people attracted to it was as "instrumental" (that is, attuned to calculated "means-ends" rationality) in outward form as any they might have encountered in paid employment in the emerging industrial and commercial sectors of European society. It was a central theme of chapter 2 that recruits, by virtue of their acceptance into the Mission, experienced significant improvement in their "life chances" in the changing material marketplace. Once they agreed to join the seminary, they were parties to an exchange in which they conceded, in writing, the administration's right to make decisions about discipline, training, posting, duties, pay, marriage, benefits for families, and conditions for termination of the relationship. If they violated the employment contract or for any reason resigned or were dismissed before they reached the point of ordination, they could be called upon to repay the Mission for the accumulated costs of their education and support.

Despite the contract's careful legalistic language, its form permitted significant asymmetries (perhaps more accurately called "exclusions") that clearly favored administrative prerogative. The missionaries, for example, were diffusely bound by the terms to which they agreed: in essence, virtually all their time, hour by hour, was committed to the organization's needs, and little remained under their private control. For the Committee the situation was just the opposite: these men reserved for themselves a wide area of discretion, recognizing only a "moral obligation" to do their "fatherly best" for the missionaries, depending on the priorities they set for the organization and on the circumstances and the resources available. The document called "Regulations concerning the Personal Position of the Missionaries" sets out this asymmetry, but does so in unmistakable bureaucratese: "These regulations rest on the proviso, established from the beginning, . . . that whoever surrenders himself to the service of the [German Society for Christianity] acknowledges the basic premise of unconditional submission on the Missionaries' side and fatherly care on the Committee's, in contrast to any possible juridical determination of the reciprocal relationship between the Society and its missionaries."[86]

86. "Verordnungen über die persönliche Stellung der Missionare, Revidiert 1886" (BMA Q-9,21,7, p. 5). The passage in German reads: "Diese Bestimmungen ruhen auf der von der Gesellschaft von Anfang an festgehaltenen Voraussetzung, wer sich in den Dienst der Basler Gesellschaft begebe, sich zu dem Grundsatz unbedingter Hingebung auf seiten der Missionare und väterlicher Fürsorge auf seiten der Kommittee bekenne, in Unterschied von aller juridischen Feststellung des gegenseitigen Verhältnisses zwischen der Gesellschaft und ihren Missionaren."

The Committee reserved to itself unconditionally the right to dismiss a subordinate at any time, which could mean, in effect, the right to set the contract aside unilaterally.[87] It was explicitly understood that the Mission, by accepting a recruit, in no way obliged itself to pay him a particular salary or pension or even to post him to a foreign station at all. In the relevant passage in the "Regulations" the imbalance is clear to see: "The recruits . . . place themselves in a position of unconditional service to the Society, but without the latter in any way being legally bound to post them [to a station abroad], to keep them in service, to pay them a salary, or to support them. The obligations of the Society reach only as far as its resources, and it is in that relationship in which all its recruits and employees stand, [namely,] a relationship of pure personal trust, in the final analysis grounded purely on faith."[88]

The imbalance in the language of these agreements exemplifies how contractually binding bureaucratic provisions were wedded to the more diffuse obligations associated with traditional hierarchies and religious commitments. Hesse's firsthand description of the spirit in which the Committee's business was conducted is a good summary: "The most remarkable feature of the Committee is its absolutely patriarchal character. . . . [It] does not stand in any legally circumscribed relationship [*Rechtsverhältnis*] either to the missionaries or to the local support groups, let alone to the so-called mission communities. It can do what it wants; no one can prescribe anything for it."[89]

"Patriarchal above, legalistic below" fairly describes the form of the relationship that bound the leaders and the followers. Whatever else can be said about their association, however, it is important to remember that the members of the Mission community were always coreligionists and coparticipants in a social movement. To use Weber's terms, the relationship was *communal* before it was *associative,* where "communal" means based on shared values and "associative" means instrumental or rationalistic in nature.[90] For the sake of accuracy, therefore, it is critical to stress that the vague "moral obligations" that defined the Committee's side of the exchange was not a screen for exploitation or purely capricious administrative action. The leadership did structure the relationship between the strata in the Mission in a way that preserved their own administrative freedom of action, yet beneath the complexities of the collaboration (for such it always was), the tie between them and their subordinates began with shared objectives and reciprocal confidence, or, as the

87. Schlatter, *Geschichte der Basler Mission,* 1:232ff.
88. "Verordnungen über die persönliche Stellung der Missionare, Revidiert 1886" (BMA Q-9,21,7, p. 2).
89. Hesse, *Joseph Josenhans,* p. 173.
90. Weber, *Economy and Society,* 1:40-43.

passage cited earlier phrased it, "a relationship of pure personal trust . . . grounded purely on faith." As we have already seen in the discussion of social mobility, it was only if they succeeded as missionaries that the seminarians could look forward to higher status, a secure if modest standard of living for themselves and their families, and an education and therefore further improvement in socioeconomic outlook for their children. So far as I have been able to determine, however, the Committee never violated the moral pledges it made to the seminarians on these matters. Social honor and a dignified retirement, often in the place of their origin in Württemberg, waited at the end of the missionaries' careers. The Mission also took pains to provide for the material needs of the survivors of those who died in service.

In addition to the formal ties established at the point of entry to the seminary, a great deal of attention was paid to daily procedural detail in the Mission. In his reminiscences about the time he spent as a member of the Mission Committee, Albert Ostertag observed that the religious seriousness of the Basel notables who created the Mission was matched only by their practically tireless energy in trade and business.[91] The commercial and industrial firms and other secular organizations to which many of the founding elite were attached tied them into regional, national, and international markets,[92] and there is evidence to suggest a close connection between the evolution of those broad exchanges and the increasing reliance on contractual social relations throughout European society.[93] These are the infrastructural "relational networks" that figure so prominently in institutional theories of organizational development. As Richard Scott has put it, "modern social systems are likely to give rise to elaborate relational networks that stretch from the center to the periphery of the society. Linked to both nation-building and state-formation processes, these networks provide 'nooks and crannies' as well as lattices and supports for a rich collection of organizations."[94]

Given the participation in such networks by prominent Pietists, including many of the Mission's founders, it is not surprising that so many "rationalistic" features ("rationalistic" in the organizational, not the philosophical or theological, sense) are visible in the Mission structure. The influence ran both ways. Robert Wuthnow has argued that the borrowing of business and government organizational models by religious groups has long been part of a global pattern that parallels the development of the modern world econ-

91. Ostertag, *Entstehungsgeschichte*, pp. 9-10.
92. Fulbrook, *Piety and Politics*, p. 150; Schlatter, *Geschichte der Basler Mission*, 1:6.
93. Kieser, "Organizational"; Scherer, "New Typology for Organizations."
94. Scott, "Introduction," p. 14.

omy.[95] In the case of the Basel Mission, the clear evidence of the "practical" and "businesslike" strains in the framers' thinking was counted among their most important qualifications for leadership.[96] At the same time, however, at least two prominent Committee members led the fight in Switzerland for more progressive policies regarding child labor, workplace hazards, health insurance, sanitation, savings, and social security. For them such measures reconciled Pietist regularity and reciprocity (again, *väterliche Fürsorge*) with the exigencies of modern industrial production. Because of governmental resistance at home, some of those business practices, considered at the time too radical, were introduced in the Mission's industrial experiments in Africa and India long before they were deemed acceptable in the industrial communities of Switzerland and Württemberg.[97]

In 1816 Christian Gottlieb Blumhardt, the first Mission inspector, prepared the first version of the *Hausordnung*, which in effect was the Mission's organizational charter. It was periodically revised and extended over the years, but its fundamental principles remained constant. It provided a refined codification of rules and an elaborate division of labor for the Mission House; as a result, virtually every activity between waking and sleeping was covered by written prescriptions. The opening words of this document (which I highlighted at the beginning of this chapter) bear repeating here because they show the exquisite intertwining of the business and the Pietistic versions of disciplined regularity: "In nature as well as in the realm of the Bible and human history, God is a god of order. If any individual person or association of persons devoted to a businesslike purpose want to please Him and take part in His blessed grace, this can only take place on the path of order, which He in His wisdom has drawn in legible strokes in the nature of things and in the heart of man."[98] Consistent with the Mission's "businesslike" view of "the nature of things and the heart of man," the Committee then laid down unbending bureaucratic rules concerning punctuality and channels of communication, and established precise specifications of the qualifications and duties attached to every position in the organizational hierarchy. There were thirty-nine such positions, from the inspector down to the gatekeeper. The measuring and use of time, which is a critical feature of bureaucracy as well as a principal value of Pietism, was prominently featured in the regimen they created. They took the inspiration for this preoccupation from

95. Wuthnow, "International Realities," pp. 24-25.
96. R. Fischer, *Basler Missionsindustrie in Indien, 1850-1913.*
97. Vogelsanger, *Pietismus und Afrikanische Kultur,* pp. 48, 82ff.
98. Blumhardt, *Hausordnung,* p. 2.

the biblical maxim "Use the time well, for anyone unwilling to work should not expect to eat."[99] At 5:00 A.M. the seminarians arose, and by 6:00 they were expected to have washed themselves and made their beds. The hour between 6:00 and 7:00 was devoted to work and prayer, and at 7:00 morning service began, lasting a half hour. After these preliminaries, the day was arranged as follows (with slight alterations during the winter months):

7:30	Breakfast
7:45	The monitor (a student officer) makes his report to the teachers
8:15	Lectures and work, uninterrupted until 12:15
12:15	Midday meal
12:15–2:15	Free time, to be used in workshops, gathering wood, or gardening
2:15–4:00	Study or lectures
4:00 (winter)	Vespers
4:15–7:00	Study or lectures
7:00–9:00	Evening meal, followed by free time and more manual work
9:00	Evening service, followed by study and prayer
10:00–10:15	Bedtime

The language and sense of the rules formalized by the *Hausordnung* grew naturally out of principles that were deeply ingrained in Pietist belief.[100] Although his construction of the Mission's organizational outlines was in many ways a pioneer effort, Inspector Blumhardt's first version of this foundational document drew heavily on his experiences with the system of discipline at Tübingen University.[101] Moreover, both the *Hausordnung* and other organizational documents in the Mission contain unmistakable echoes of seventeenth-century Pietist writings. These included such tracts as *Rules for the*

99. The quoted verse, from 2 Thess. 3:10, appears on page 3 of the *Hausordnung*. In German this verse is written, "Kaufet die Ziet aus, den wer nicht arbeiten will, der soll nicht essen." In the King James Version the verse appears without the reference to time: "For even when we were with you, this we commanded you, that if any would not work, neither should he eat."

100. A close analogue to the "bureaucratism" of the Mission can be seen in the spiritual underpinnings of "contractarianism" in New England Puritan thinking. See Zaret, *The Heavenly Contract.*

101. Waldburger, *Missionare und Moslem*, pp. 43-46; Ostertag, *Entstehungsgeschichte*, p. 77.

Preservation of Conscience and Good Order in Social Intercourse or Society, written by the theologian August Hermann Francke, who has been called the "organizational genius" of German Pietism.[102]

Still other organizational considerations that influenced the Mission's framers are of interest. It is no accident that the precise listing of jobs and obligations in the *Hausordnung* resembled the outline of the Prussian military bureaucracy, which in the eighteenth century was directly, and heavily, influenced by Pietist thinking.[103] Pietists initially were resistant to militarism, but the aversion was not mutual. Military interests, most notably the eighteenth-century Prussian kings, were strongly attracted to the discipline they saw in Pietism. Mary Fulbrook describes the developing affinity between the two in this way:

> [Friedrich Wilhelm I] was much impressed by the conscientiousness implanted by a Pietist education; and when Francke [the Pietist leader] refused to accept two soldiers' sons in his orphanage at Halle, the King employed Pietists to establish and run a military orphanage at Potsdam. Halle-trained Pietists were also employed to staff the new Berlin *Kadettenhaus.* Many Pietists were chosen as *Feldprediger,* or army preachers, who were an elite of pastors directly appointed by the King and destined for considerable advancement in their later careers. Pietist Feldprediger took very seriously their religious and educational duties among soldiers, whose levels of morality, literacy, and religious knowledge were in Pietist eyes abysmally low. As the officers of the army were being converted into a service nobility owing primary allegiance to the centralised state, so the common soldiers were transformed from illiterate, ill-educated and unwilling forced recruits into Bible-reading, God-fearing, conscientious and obedient troops, easily disciplined and organised for motivated combat. Pietists may have helped to make some soldiers into better Christians; they certainly contributed to making them better servants of the King.[104]

102. Forell, *Christian Social Teachings,* p. 264. The tract and the commentary appear on pp. 265-70. Mary Fulbrook's discussion (*Piety and Politics,* pp. 154ff., 165-67) of Francke's influence indicates how widespread the organizational consequences of his beliefs were, spreading in his own time throughout the military and state structures of Prussia.

103. See Waldburger, *Missionare und Moslem,* pp. 74-75; Fulbrook, *Piety and Politics,* pp. 49-55, 166-167; Beyreuther, *Geschichte des Pietismus,* pp. 154ff., 338ff.

104. Fulbrook, *Piety and Politics,* pp. 166-67.

By the time of the Mission's creation the reluctance of prominent Pietists to identify themselves with military thinking had lessened considerably, and members of the Mission Committee had become positively fond of military metaphors. One person compared the inspector to a general, the Mission House to a parade ground *(Exerzierplatz)*, and the overseas mission arena to a battlefield *(Schlachtfeld)*.[105] Elsewhere, the goal of the Mission's strict internal order was described as "the training of a well disciplined fighting squad [*Streiterschar*] for the Mission war."[106] As I pointed out earlier, Inspector Josenhans assumed leadership of the Mission not long after his unsettling experiences in the revolutionary year of 1848 caused him to strengthen his commitment to monarchy for the German nation. He insisted on the need for the Committee to "hold all the strings in its own hands." His reasoning is encapsulated in this remark: "To be sure, this [principle of centralization] is not democratic, not at all republican, to say nothing of liberated, but it should not be [any of those things]. Mission service is war service. What is needed [in such service] is uncompromising commands and unconditional obedience."[107]

The *Hausordnung* to which I have referred at length was aimed primarily at the governance of daily life in the Mission House in Basel. When individual missionaries were posted to their field assignments abroad, they took with them similarly detailed written instructions that not only spelled out their professional responsibilities as preachers of the gospel, but also resolved such mundane questions as the makeup of a proper missionary wardrobe (how many shirts, frocks, and handkerchiefs were acceptable, and of what styles and materials they should be), the daily allowance of wine, the quantity and style of home furnishings (how many chairs, plates, and pots, of what design and quality), and the proper use of mosquito netting. Even decisions concerning individuals' acute medical needs in Africa were sometimes remanded up the hierarchy to the Committee in Basel for resolution,[108] which is perhaps the most striking illustration of how far the principle of centralized decision making could be taken.

A startling example of this is to be found in the Committee minutes for February 6, 1871. In a letter posted from the Gold Coast on November 28, 1870, it had been reported that the missionary Emil Borel could not perform his du-

---

105. Quoted by Vogelsanger, *Pietismus und Afrikanische Kultur*, p. 59.
106. Schlatter, *Geschichte der Basler Mission*, 1:243.
107. Hesse, *Joseph Josenhans*, p. 164.
108. According to a general set of instructions that applied to all missionaries, questions of illness fell under the Committee's oversight. No missionary who was ill could return to Europe without the Committee's permission. See *Instructionen und Contracte von 1848-1876* (BMA series Q-3,3,26).

ties effectively because he was spitting blood and appeared to be tubercular. Permission was requested to relieve him of some of his duties so that he could recover. Given the normal movement of the mail over land and by ship, it was nearly three months later that the Committee received the letter and discussed the matter in its weekly meeting. The conclusion they reached after their discussion was that *vomiting* blood (common with fever and other ailments) could have been mistaken for *spitting* of blood (common to tuberculosis), and so, they decided, the request to relieve Borel of his duties for reasons of health was probably premature. It was denied. Fortunately for Borel, the Committee's judgment may have been correct in his case, if we can judge from the absence of further references to his illness in the Committee records.[109]

Together with the material and contractual elements of the missionaries' attachment to the organization, these rationalistic components of daily governance formed the third pillar of support for the Mission's structure of discipline. In keeping with sound bureaucratic practice, records were kept of all departures, trivial and substantial alike, from the Mission's extensive rules and procedures, and punishment for violations could be uncompromising, including summary expulsion from the Mission community.

Social Control: Supervision and Surveillance

In the daily reality of the Mission, the Committee's claims to divine inspiration, traditional prerogative, and bureaucratic empowerment gave its members a far wider range of legitimate decision making than they would have had if only one of those principles had prevailed.[110] Anchored as it was on those three points of validation, the official regime was further buttressed by four effective social control mechanisms. Two of these, public self-criticism and simple hierarchical supervision, were fairly straightforward in their operation and require little discussion. The other two mechanisms, which involved formalized *peer* control and informal *peer* surveillance, proved to be more complex and more problematic for the Mission. I need to discuss them at some length.

109. In reading this exchange, I was reminded of Robert Antonio's description ("The Contradiction") of how the obsession of the army of the late Roman Empire with "formal rationality" (rules, precedents, ceremony) undermined "substantive rationality" by distracting it from the barbarians attacking the periphery of the empire. The Mission Committee's formalistic way of dealing with the problem of Borel's quite substantive illness has a similar ring.

110. Bendix, *Max Weber*, pp. 318ff.; Scott, *Organizations*, pp. 287-89.

Confession and Hierarchical Oversight

As a cornerstone of discipline, public confession of wrongdoing is as old as Christianity.[111] In the Basel organization, teachers and administrators expected seminarians and missionaries alike to admit their misdeeds freely to superiors, often in the presence of their peers. The rules also required seminarians and missionaries to keep diaries that chronicled their moral lapses along with their accomplishments, and these were available for examination by superiors so that the progress of their religious conversion could be charted.[112] In addition to these measures of self-control, the Mission's moral paradigm was guarded by teachers and other officials who supervised the students' lives in the seminary and reported all violations of discipline, through proper channels, to the Committee. Similarly direct hierarchical controls followed the missionaries to the field, where senior colleagues, station chiefs, and district supervisors enforced the rules and kept detailed records of their efforts in that regard. Together these two mechanisms, personal confession and direct supervision, provided the Committee with a steady flow of information, often in writing, about the obedience or lack of obedience of every subordinate. But these provisions were never considered sufficient by themselves to ensure Christian conformity. For reasons rooted deeply in Pietist philosophy, the members of the Mission were also enlisted to exercise surveillance over each other, a policy that was referred to as "mutual watching."

Mutual Watching

Scrutinizing each other's behavior was an obligation the Basel missionaries had in common with the members of many other ascetic religious groups. Precedents for this principle could be found close to home in the philosophical legacy of their Protestant forebears in sixteenth-century Geneva.[113] Fred Graham's useful discussion highlights the subordination of individual needs to collective requirements in many areas of Calvinist life and stresses the role of informers in exposing wrongdoing among members of the religious com-

111. Boer, *Short History,* pp. 38ff.

112. These diaries were to be continued after posting to the field and were to be submitted, first to superiors in the field for their countersignature and then to the Committee, four times a year. See *Instructionen und Contracte von 1848-1876* (BMA series Q-3,3,26). Relatively few of these diaries survive in the archive in Basel, an unaccountable gap in an otherwise dense primary record.

113. Weber, *Protestant Ethic,* pp. 122ff.

munity.[114] Both policies show striking philosophical similarities to Basel Mission practices, and the similarity extends to the interpersonal strain that resulted from those measures. Kai Erikson documents similar conventions, and similar effects, among the New England Puritans.[115] While the similarity to the surveillance practices of the New Englanders was probably unwitting, the Baslers would have been directly aware of the experiences of the Genevans.[116] In any case, by legitimating and participating in such policies, the missionaries made themselves parties to their own subordination; every action they took in conformity with these surveillance practices served to reproduce the structure that controlled their own lives. It was a complex arrangement with complicated results.

There were both formal and informal ways in which mutual surveillance was organized. Three student offices, whose occupants were called the "Senior," the "Famulus," and the "Monitor," were filled in rotation by seminarians who were expected to report on every student whose behavior departed from the norms. According to the 1860 version of the *Hausordnung*, the Senior for each class "must freely and without coercion report anything that contradicts the honor of the Lord or the dignity of a future missionary."[117] With the timetable presented above in mind, he was expected to keep the peace among his fellows and to take the lead in class conferences and prayer meetings. He was to see that every individual awoke on time, made his bed, dressed cleanly, arrived at meals punctually, occupied the seat assigned to him in each of his activities, avoided disturbing the work of others, preserved the quiet of the Mission House, took exercise and fresh air, ate and drank moderately, kept his study desk clean, and refrained from leaving his clothing lying about. The Famulus was the Senior's assistant; he was charged primarily with routine housekeeping duties, but he was also expected "to report to the Senior any Brother guilty of breakage, uncleanliness, or any sort of misbehavior."[118]

Finally, of the three student-held offices, that of the Monitor was perhaps

114. Graham, *The Constructive Revolutionary*, pp. 163ff.

115. Erikson, *Wayward Puritans*, pp. 50-54, 185ff. I will discuss this parallel in detail in chapter 5.

116. Basel embraced the Reformation in 1529, and Calvin had found a Protestant haven there when he fled from France in the winter of 1534-35. On the first point see Meier, *Basler Heimatgeschichte*, pp. 208-11; on the second point see Höpfl, ed., *Luther and Calvin*, p. xxix, and Walker et al., *History*, p. 473.

117. The archive reference for this version of the *Hausordnung* is Q-9,31,11. The excerpt is from p. 38.

118. *Hausordnung*, Q-9,31,11, p. 37.

the most extraordinary.[119] Each student took on this position for one week when his turn came around. During that time he carried messages and rang the bells that regulated the hour-to-hour activities of the Mission House ("with the greatest precision . . . [and] . . . peacefully and respectably, not in a stormy or powerful way," according to page 41 of the *Hausordnung*). But in addition to this metronomic function, his most important task was to keep a set of books for the inspector in which all permissions to deviate from the official rules were recorded. In each case a note was made about who entered the request for an exception to a rule, what the reason for it was, and who approved it. Any exceptional behavior that he or anyone else observed that was not supported by the requisite requests and approvals could be considered illegitimate and was recorded and likely to be dealt with as such. The purpose was clear: these records kept the inspector and, through him, the Committee informed about the extent to which the rules were being followed in daily practice; they identified who was allowed to step outside them and why; and they revealed who the staff members were who were granting these dispensations.[120]

The positions of Senior, Famulus, and Monitor and the ways they were rotated gave every seminarian extensive experience in watching over and reporting on the behavior of fellow students, but the principle of peer surveillance by no means stopped with these formal provisions, nor did the Committee ever expect it to be confined to the Mission House environment. The leadership also appropriated the informal personal ties that developed among the seminarians and turned those relationships to organizational use, both in Basel and in the field. In the closeness of the Mission community, that the missionaries shared a common social background, the common experience of spiritual rebirth, and a common organizational rank created the potential for strong social bonds. It also gave them intimate knowledge of each other's feelings and behavior. All the shortcomings of colleagues that came to their attention in this way, whether trivial (for example, laughing too loud or too often) or serious (reading a forbidden book or concealing a relationship, however chaste, with a woman), had to be reported without delay and without discussion to superiors. In this way the miscreant was exposed and the

119. I have called this position the "Monitor" because of the surveillance duties it entailed. In German it was sometimes called the *Wöchner* (roughly, the "Weekly," I presume in reference to the periodicity of its rotation from one student to the next). At other times it was referred to by the Greek term *Hebdomadarius* (roughly, "weekly functionary").

120. This last provision required the Monitor to exercise at least nominal surveillance over his teachers and other formal superiors. This raises questions that cannot be answered here about the relationship between the Committee and the nonmissionary staff in the Mission House.

one who reported the misdeed gained in moral stature (if not in friendship) because of his piety and vigilance. The practice continued relentlessly in the field, with the troublesome results that I will relate in the next chapter.

Paradoxically, this principle of mutual watching was predicated on the Pietist version of Protestant individualism. It was, of course, a central Protestant belief that individuals were "responsible," in the sense of *accountable,* for their own individual transgressions and atonement. In a crucial way seminarians and missionaries also had to see themselves as "individual" in the sense of *morally separate* from all the other members of the religious brotherhood. The Committee admonished seminarians not to be drawn into "special" friendships, nor to see themselves as members of a "corporate" group with solidary interests vis-à-vis the leadership or the religious community as a whole.[121] When the situation demanded it, missionaries had to have the moral courage to stand apart from others and serve as overseer and censor of their behavior. It was recognized that it would take a strong friendship indeed to survive such personal exposure, even when the act of exposure (betrayal?) was committed in the interest of shared religious values.

Weber recognized the importance of this principle in his observation that ascetic collectivities, despite the rhetoric of brotherhood or sisterhood, often discourage close emotional relationships among their members.[122] Such ties are thought to "exceed moderation" and border on the "service of the flesh." More important, they dissipate collective strength by deflecting commitment into interpersonal emotional ties. The "brotherly love" professed by these groups is thus of an "impersonal" kind; what is expected from this love is not devotion to other individuals but rather devotion to the larger organic entity, that is, to the organization, which crystallizes the contributions of diverse individuals.[123] In this way the emotional energy and informal ties of the members are harnessed to larger organizational purposes, and "the active energies of the elect [can flow directly] into the struggle to rationalize the world."[124] The Mission's reliance upon "mutual watchfulness" to channel individual Pietist zeal into organized evangelical action seems to be exactly the kind of phenomenon that Weber had in mind. In effect, the religious principle that persons are morally individual and not part of a solidary interpersonal network became an underpinning for the organizational principle that separate individual interests must be subordinated to the good of the collective enterprise.

121. See Ebaugh, *Out of the Cloister,* for a contemporary parallel.
122. Weber, *Protestant Ethic,* pp. 108ff.
123. Bendix, *Max Weber,* p. 63.
124. Weber, *Protestant Ethic,* p. 224 n. 30.

Francke's list of *Rules for the Preservation of Conscience and Good Order* offers further insight into the Pietist values that lay behind the missionaries' willingness to bring down punishment upon their peers. The twenty-first admonition on his list of thirty reads:

> If it is up to you to punish others because of their sins, do not make excuses that the time is inconvenient if it is really fear and timidity that keep you back. Fear and timidity must be overcome like other evil emotions. But always punish yourself before punishing others so that your punishment will flow from compassion. Punish with love and great care and modesty in order that the other person may somehow be convinced in his conscience that he has done ill. Christ punished with one look when he looked at Peter who had denied him. Yet Peter wept bitterly. Christ would also punish with explicit and plain words. Love must here be your teacher. But do not participate in the sins of others.[125]

Watching, reproving, and informing on peers — all deeply ingrained in the Mission — are consistent with the meaning of "punish with love" in this passage.

An interesting episode in the Mission illustrates how these principles were viewed practically by those in charge. In 1872 several seminarians quite unexpectedly discovered a fellow student's secret betrothal to a young woman.[126] Before calling this breach of the rules (a grievous offense that could bring quick dismissal) to the attention of their superiors, as they knew they were morally bound to do, the group discussed the propriety of the forbidden relationship among themselves, concluding that it was an essentially innocent one. It was only after this discussion that they dutifully passed on what they knew to their superiors. The inspector brought it home to them quite forcefully that they had followed an entirely inappropriate course. He reminded them that they were not to discuss and certainly not to dispute or debate among themselves the Mission's rules or any of the decisions made by the leadership. They were not to be swayed by their feelings of personal loyalty in deciding whether, or how, to report an offense. And they were never to speculate or make judgments about the weaknesses, motives, or external circumstances that might cause the behavior of any one of their fellows to depart from the norm. Finally, they were certainly not to assess *collectively* the justice

---

125. In Forell, *Christian Social Teachings,* p. 268.

126. This disciplinary case (involving the dismissed seminarian Johann Dewald) and the object lesson that came to be attached to it is related in *KP* 43, April 17, 1872, pp. 89-90.

of the sanctions that might be applied in any given case. All such moral evaluations of rules, motives, and sanctions were to be left to the more mature, revealed wisdom of the Committee. In the future, the inspector told them, if they observed a behavior that might violate any rule or suggest any lapse of Christian virtue, they were *as individuals* to report it immediately, without reflection or discussion, to superiors. Since any activity not specifically prescribed was likely to be proscribed, the list of potential offenses was quite long and subject to definition only by those at the top of the religious and organizational hierarchy. In the pithy phrase used by one inspector in stating this principle, the Mission was "not a republic."[127] Most of the missionaries appear to have learned these precepts well. Sometimes they urged that even harsher treatment than the Committee had ordered be meted out to offenders, and not uncommonly they refused to associate with those who were stigmatized by having been officially punished.[128] As we shall see, it was the latter impulse that most clearly undermined the mutual solidarity the missionaries needed to succeed in their work.

The Hermeneutics of Freedom and Control

In describing the internal government of the Mission, I have concentrated on matters of control and orthodoxy. This emphasis is not misplaced because conformity was indeed the operating rule in the daily life of the organization. Yet I have alluded more than once to a paradox woven into much of the Mission's written history. The organization's leaders often enclosed their prescriptions for uniformity in the language of individual freedom and egalitarianism, even though Pietists made a point of standing apart from such liberal themes in the larger cultural discourse that surrounded them. If not ambivalence, there is certainly ambiguity in their logic, and it is an ambiguity that recurs with remarkable frequency in religious movements. For the purpose of understanding other organizations it will be useful to explain, first, why the Baslers were pulled into this hermeneutic struggle and, second, how their be-

127. Quoted by Hesse, *Joseph Josenhans,* p. 177. See also Vogelsanger, *Pietismus und Afrikanische Kultur,* p. 40. The inspector at the time was Josenhans, whose aristocratic, monarchical, and militaristic preferences for organizational discipline in the Mission have already been noted.

128. A clear example of this attitude can be seen in the discussion of the dismissal of Israel Doluchanyanz, an Armenian seminarian who, disappointed over being denied a posting to his preferred station abroad, caused disruption among his fellows in the Mission House. See *KP* 38, March 6, 1867, pp. 42ff., and March 13, 1867, pp. 45-46.

liefs on the matter were woven into the organizational structure they devised. Students of other missions will be able to judge how far this explanation can be generalized beyond Basel.

The paradox I refer to has its roots in Protestant beliefs about individual accountability and the "priesthood of believers."[129] Even Luther found it difficult to reconcile these themes, both of which imply independence and equality, with language that stresses unconditional submission to divinely constituted authority, which suggests that individuals rightly have no control over the direction they must take in their own lives.[130] Mutually exclusive meanings of "choice" come into play, and "freedom" is the word used to describe the exercise of both of them. In one meaning the freedom is of a "sterile" kind that is linked to the "burden" of choosing among the empty temptations of the material world. This is the "unbiblical conception of personal freedom" alluded to by Johannes Zimmermann, the Basel missionary whose opinion I quoted earlier. A person who carries the affliction of this kind of freedom is always constrained or oppressed by the need to make choices and, therefore, can never be "truly" free. Neitz captures this logic perfectly in her description of the thinking of Catholic charismatics in the 1970s: "They say that modern society's presentation of 'choice' offers, in reality, only 'bondage.'"[131]

"True" Christian freedom, in contrast, is achieved by giving up the tyrannical distraction of worldly choice and following instead, without lapse, the one correct course that provides a passage through the world's temptations. This is possible only in an authoritative structure so carefully contrived that by its nature it expresses the will of God. A charismatic priest quoted by Neitz clearly had something like this in mind when he referred to "God's healing gift of authority" (p. 158). Authority heals the affliction of worldly choice. These charismatics also speak of the freedom that comes from self-control, which they see as the discipline "developed by submission to God's representatives on earth who are in positions of authority." Again, surrender is the way to liberation (p. 159).

It was these same doctrinal currents that were at work as the Basel Mission's structure was taking shape. The definitions of freedom were complicated still further by the fact that the missionaries were part of a "free labor force," not fettered by traditional bonds, and thus they were "free agents" in the sense of being able to invest their labor and devotion elsewhere. In reality

129. See Luther's treatise "On Secular Authority," in Höpfl, ed., *Luther and Calvin*, pp. 33-34. The converse conception, "brotherhood of faith," is sometimes used.

130. Höpfl, ed., *Luther and Calvin*, pp. ix-xvi.

131. Neitz, *Charisma and Community*, p. 157. The parenthetical page references in the next paragraph are to this work.

their options in this regard were narrow because of the economy in which they had to make their way, and I have already discussed how this conditioned their availability to the Mission. Nevertheless, it is not a mere technicality that they came to the Mission of their own volition. Fulbrook points out that while Pietists were moderate, precise, and dutiful in matters involving religion, they were not timid or excessively self-denying (in today's colloquial sense of "puritanical") in the way they addressed themselves to the practical affairs of their daily lives.[132]

It would have been impossible — not to mention imprudent — for the Mission leadership to ignore these competing themes of freedom and choice. Yet to be true to the conservatism in Pietism and to the conservative interests implicit in their own social and organizational positions, they could not give in to the more radical egalitarian interpretations in vogue in the circles of non-Pietists around them. They had to find a way to harness the "freedoms" of the rank and file to the yoke of missionary service. The symbolic work that was needed to accomplish this is visible in the language of the *Hausordnung*. In composing that set of rules for the daily routine of the Mission House, Inspector Blumhardt invoked the symbolism of Christian freedom and spontaneity, but with the constant subtext of strict oversight by the inspector (himself at the time) and the Committee, who together presided over dire sanctions for willful nonconformity.[133] The rationale that Blumhardt offered for this juxtaposition of liberty and constraint was, in essence, that a person who is truly converted will have God's law of order and obedience to authority in his or her heart (a concept expressed in Rom. 2:15) and thus can be "free" of the burden of external laws and sanctions. A person free in this way will experience no sense of constriction or personal duress in following the will of God, and in fact will be in "natural" (read *unreflective*) accord with the Christian rule that prevails in the Mission House. A person (read *independent-minded person*) who needs reminding of the written Christian law of order, that is, who calls down official sanctions by any sort of nonconforming thought or behavior, or even suspicion of the same, is revealed as possibly unsuited to the missionary life and unprepared for true Christian freedom.

Codified rules and sanctions exist, in other words, not to bind the faithful as much as to expose and deal with the unfit or religiously unprepared. "Frogs must have storks!" as Luther put it.[134] The purpose served by rules is not to inhibit the mature Christian, whose behavior spontaneously finds its

132. Fulbrook, *Piety and Politics,* p. 34.
133. Blumhardt, *Hausordnung,* p. 4.
134. In Höpfl, ed., *Luther and Calvin,* p. 30.

way into the narrow channels of propriety. Such Christians will conform "freely" and virtually without thinking to the "order in the heart" and will never feel the weight of the written rules, let alone experience the full force of the official mechanisms of punishment. The person caught in the unchristian doubt that leads him or her to offer resistance to revealed authority is the one who is "unfree." In the *Hausordnung* this sinuous principle was stated in these words: "At the moment of entry into authentic mission service [the newly accepted seminarians] enter at the same time into the realm of unlimited evangelical freedom, at which point, on their own and completely torn away from their previous ties, they have to give account only to their invisible Lord and Master for their daily behavior. Whoever does not carry in his heart the complete law of freedom as an ever-present sentinel over his behavior is in danger of destroying the walls of Zion instead of building them up."[135] It was not directly stated in that passage, but the Committee and the inspector wanted it understood that it was they, through their superior wisdom, who were the ones qualified to judge when the "walls of Zion" were threatened[136] and what steps must be taken to guarantee their protection.

The result of this reasoning is a complicated but compelling tautology with important organizational consequences. As a guiding paradigm it served the Basel Mission well: only true Christians will have the law of God within themselves as a fully internalized model of true spiritual freedom. Such a person would never choose to question duly constituted authority, or be suspected of doing so, either in the Mission or in the secular world outside it. In effect the leadership was saying to the seminarians, "We will know that you have achieved complete Christian freedom when you show us absolute conformity." Only an "unfree" (and therefore "unfit") person would resist authority, disobey a rule, or deviate from the law of God to follow an idiosyncratic path and in so doing bring down both confusion and punishment upon herself or himself. Indeed, the displeasure of God can be inferred from the application of a sanction, which is in itself proof of wrongdoing sufficient to warrant dismissal. As Inspector Blumhardt phrased it: "[W]hoever shows himself not to be a law unto himself . . . but rather [is] in need of the wooden crutch of orders and prohibitions, entreaties and threats of punishment, in that same moment excludes himself from our circle."[137]

More about the complicated logic that tied freedom to conformity in the Mission can be gleaned from a letter that Inspector Blumhardt enclosed when

135. Blumhardt, *Hausordnung,* p. 4.
136. Again the reference is to Ps. 51:18.
137. Blumhardt, *Hausordnung,* p. 4.

he sent a copy of the *Hausordnung* to a colleague in the Church Missionary Society (CMS) in London. As a more prominent and more powerful mission, the CMS set a compelling organizational example for the Basel Mission. Moreover, the CMS continued until the 1850s to absorb into its own operations many of the young men trained in the Basel Mission Seminary.[138] It was important, therefore, for the Baslers to make the home board of the CMS understand the philosophy behind their own distinctive organizational discipline. As we have seen, the list of rules and responsibilities in the *Hausordnung* left almost none of the seminarians' daily activities ungoverned, and the formal and informal surveillance that prevailed left almost none of their behavior unscrutinized. The inspector insisted nevertheless that the "spirit of perfect freedom" prevailed in Basel, and that the community of shared belief and contented devotion to order rendered every kind of dictatorial organizational discipline superfluous:

> The Gospel of Christ is composed of laws of the most perfect order and [because these] laws are the foundation of all true Christianity, they constitute the domestic and economical order of our Institution. No kind of despotic discipline, as is generally the case in [other] seminaries, finds existence in our circle. Every brother is duly sensible to his important engagements and truly anxious to spend the time of his abode here to the best advantage; all desire to imitate the example of Him who for our sakes became poor and to walk as he walked, and act as he acted. When this spirit of simplicity, regularity and contentment reigns in an establishment of this kind, no despotic laws can possibly find existence.[139]

Images of personal freedom thus coexisted with rigid organizational control in the Pietist way of thinking.[140] Individuals were responsible for the con-

138. See Jenkins, "Church Missionary Society."

139. This letter (in English), labeled "Blumhardt to the Lay Secretary of the CMS, January 23, 1823," was in the CMS archive in London (now in Birmingham), reference G/AC, 18/1, 1820-1834.

140. Students of theory may find intriguing the similarity between the way Pietists reconciled institutional constraint with personal freedom and the proposition in functionalist theory which holds that effectively socialized individuals will naturally choose to accede to legitimate authority and to the values and guidance of "culture-bearing" elites. This notion underlies the "voluntarism" in Parsonian theory (Parsons and Shils, eds., *General Theory;* see also Selznick, "Institutional Vulnerability"). There is irony in the fact that Robert Merton's search (Merton, "Puritanism") for the connection between Pietism and science did not extend to a recognition of the parallels between Pietist thinking and much of social science theorizing.

sequences of their own actions, but the structure was designed to ensure that they were never fully the author of those actions. In principle, so it was thought, the true Christian instinctively reproduces the rules of the collectivity, freely conforms to its moral precepts, and experiences no alienation in being subordinated to the regime of authority. Christian correctness, personal freedom, and organizational conformity fuse together; in the resulting alloy they become, in effect, indistinguishable. "Willfulness," "self-determination," "self-confidence," and "creativity" often became negative judgments, words used to describe those whose actions took them outside the established guidelines of the organization. "Freedom," in contrast, came to be the word used to describe the actions of those who stayed within those guidelines. From the point of view of those in control of an organization, the advantages of having subordinates accept such a definition of discipline are obvious.

Conclusion

The convergence of the personal beliefs, collective interests, and historical circumstances of the nineteenth-century Pietists created a broad zone of obedience among the Basel missionaries, and it placed a variety of control measures at the disposal of the leadership. Both the leaders and the followers were prepared to deal with decisions and sanctions based on what are recognizable as charismatic, traditional, and bureaucratic rationales, and they could combine these three modes of authority or switch from one to another with no sense of inappropriateness. From these elements they wove a tapestry of authority that had a tight concentration of power at its center. By accepting the philosophical premises underlying this regime, the rank-and-file members elevated the organizational leadership above mere "authorization" (based on the narrow procedural license to make decisions within a defined range of decision types) to "endorsement" (anchored broadly in the beliefs and values of subordinates). Authority that enjoys both authorization and endorsement in this way, Richard Scott argues, "may be expected to be more effective and more stable than that which receives support from only one source."[141]

By helping to socialize and sanction new members as they were recruited, the missionaries assisted in reproducing the structure that controlled their own lives. Because of this, it could be said that they were truly complicit (collaborators, again) in the social construction and daily functioning of the Mission's hierarchy, but their complicity did not entail being formally recognized

141. Scott, *Organizations*, p. 289.

as "participants in decision making" in the sense of "shared initiative" in which that concept is used today. The point in calling attention to their complicity is not to minimize their subordination but simply to emphasize that the regime that subjugated them was partly of their own making. Paul Willis and Michael Burawoy have described essentially similar mechanisms at work in the construction and reproduction of social control in the secular world.[142]

All the members of the Mission community could take satisfaction from the strengths that were built into the organization's structure, but as a group they had to come to terms with the troubles that also had their origins in it. The next chapter addresses two fundamental contradictions that eroded the work of the Mission but were never fully resolved. The first is the need to rely on rule-breakers to accomplish what conformists could not undertake — a supreme irony in an organization that placed obedience among the very most important Christian virtues. The second is the destruction of brotherly solidarity caused by the requirement for relentless mutual watching.

142. Willis, *Learning to Labor;* Burawoy, *Manufacturing Consent.*

CHAPTER 4

Contradictions and Their Consequences

As sociologists use the term, a contradiction exists in an organization when a practice that is indispensable for one desired outcome inescapably undermines another. I will describe two such situations that complicated the work of the Basel Mission, both connected to the measures the Mission had devised to preserve internal order. As the discussion of authority in the preceding chapter has shown, centralization of control in the Mission conformed closely to Pietist values and was supported by three different legitimating rationales. Yet that arrangement left the missionaries with few opportunities and little official encouragement to use their own individual judgment in addressing the tasks assigned to them. Recall that for recruits to the Mission it was not enough to be attracted to the Pietist religious persuasion; they had to have been "truly reborn" and by that transformation made ready for a completely new life in the missionary cause. But the terms of their membership also mandated that they be prepared to submit unconditionally to the authority of their organizational superiors. Paradoxically, then, at the same time that the religious zeal of the members was a major resource for the organization, the leadership was committed to practices that could choke off the energy that flowed from that zeal. In the field, personal initiative was suppressed so effectively by the stress on control and conformity that many faithful rule-followers could not cope with extraordinary events that demanded creative solutions. When this happened, the organization could find itself dependent upon unpredictable rule-breakers — who were perhaps less thoroughly "socialized" than more conforming members, and certainly less bound by hierarchy — when challenges in the work called for fast and innovative responses. This was the first contradiction.

The second contradiction was tied to the practice of "mutual watching." I have described that practice as a critical element of social control in the Mission, but it was also a policy that could transform interpersonal solidarity into bitter interpersonal estrangement among the missionaries. An organization committed to "brotherly [and sisterly] love," in other words, insisted on methods of surveillance that could extinguish the simple collegial cooperation that was needed for a sustained collective effort. The origins and the consequences of these two dilemmas are the subjects of this chapter; how the organization survived them is the subject of the next.

The Relationship between Creativity and Deviance

According to the leadership of the Basel Mission, a primary task of the missionaries who went to the Gold Coast was to address the social wreckage and spiritual damage caused by three centuries of slavery and economic exploitation of Africans by Europeans.[1] Most Europeans of the time who encountered indigenous African societies characterized them as "uncivilized" and fundamentally "un-Christian" in their structure and customs.[2] Some Basel

1. For the Basel Mission's position, see Schlatter, *Geschichte der Basler Mission,* 3:1, and Vogelsanger's extensive treatment in *Pietismus und Afrikanische Kultur.* On the general opposition to slavery among evangelical missions, see Neill, *History of Christian Missions,* 2nd ed., p. 9; Moorhouse, *The Missionaries,* p. 36; Clarke, *West Africa and Christianity,* chap. 2. For a balanced discussion of the mixture of humanitarian and economic elements in the movement for abolition, see Hopkins, *Economic History,* pp. 112-16.

2. Moorhouse, *The Missionaries,* pp. 282ff.; Vogelsanger, *Pietismus und Afrikanische Kultur,* pp. 62ff. The exposure of seminarians to African culture came from talks by returning missionaries and from lectures on anthropology, or ethnology, as it was called. From the beginning of the missionary movement, most participants were convinced of the superiority of European culture, and the willingness to intervene in other cultures on such an ambitious level could be said to be predicated on some such conviction. Toward the end of the century many missions were attracted to social Darwinist theories of racial difference that assigned African natives in particular a lower place on the scale of psychological and cultural evolution (see the discussions in Ajayi, *Christian Missions,* pp. 263ff., and Gründer, *Christliche Mission und Deutscher Imperialismus,* pp. 337ff.). This conferred "scientific" legitimacy on attitudes of racial superiority and justified European domination of colonized regions. Attitudes and rhetoric became increasingly racist in some mission circles, but such negative opinions did not rule unchallenged. A very good example of the other side of the debate can be seen in the work of Sigismund Koelle *(Grammar* and *African Native Literature).* Koelle was a missionary for the Church Missionary Society (CMS), but he was educated in the Basel Mission Seminary. In *Grammar* (p. i) he responded forcefully to the racial attitudes he heard around him: "It has often been observed that the Negro race is not a genuine branch of the human family, and that they occupy a kind of intermediate position between irrational animals and rational man. This view is not only

124

missionaries came to disagree with this viewpoint after they had spent some time in Africa, but the aim of the Mission was not to credit, preserve, or restore native cultures. Nor was the goal simply to provide spiritual counsel or material aid to those Africans who sought them or were receptive to them. Rather, the intention was no less than the creation of an entirely new social structure around which stable communities built on a European model could be organized. In the 1840s this meant going as far as "repatriating" black families to the Gold Coast from the West Indies, on the assumption that their exposure to European (specifically, British colonial) culture and Christianity would have made them more amenable to Pietist social norms and religious ideals than indigenous native Africans were proving to be.

True to their usual practice, the members of the governing committee in Basel set this broad and ambitious goal of community building for the organization and then made the decisions and established the daily rules and regulations thought to be necessary for its implementation. No one who sat on the governing committee during the time that the program was first formulated was ever a missionary, and except for occasional evaluation trips by inspectors after the 1850s, visits to the Mission's overseas stations by members of that inner circle were not the rule. Direct personal experience with the uncertainties of life in the field, therefore, informed few of their orders and shaped little of the intelligence they imparted to the missionaries about what they were going to encounter in their assignments.[3]

To be sure, in the closeness of the seminary in Basel little initiative was required of anyone below the level of the governing committee. In the field,

---

opposed to the Bible, which speaks of the Negroes as men, but also to the results of an impartial examination of, and a closer acquaintance with, the Negro race itself. The genuine humanity of the Negroes can be proved in a variety of ways; and one of them is the *philological*. We confidently invite every man who can see in language the expression and counterpart of the mind to an examination of the Bornu grammar, and ask whether the richness of its inflection, the precision in the use of its forms, and its whole vital organism, is not an incontestable demonstration that the mind of a people, which daily weaves for its appearance so fitting and so artful a garb, must be allowed to claim fraternity with ours."

3. The Basel Mission was not atypical in this regard. See Moorhouse, *The Missionaries.* As an exception to the general pattern, the CMS moved sooner than most to incorporate into its leadership persons with extensive field experience. William Jowett, for example, had an illustrious career abroad before assuming a key coordinating role in London. By the 1830s his experiences were informing CMS policies overseas, and Jowett himself wrote supportive and informative personal letters to missionaries after they had been at their posts for a few months, because he knew from personal memory that this was likely to be a period of depression for them. A letter he wrote in 1836 outlining his opinions on these matters is in the CMS Archive, CI/L3, p. 109.

however, the very survival of the missionaries and, through them, the larger organization depended on how they dealt with the daily challenges they encountered. Moreover, in the days before the telegraph and steamship, communication between Europe and remote stations in Africa could take months to effect.[4] The missionaries were therefore far removed from timely direction from the center, yet they had to work in surroundings that were always dangerous, unpredictable, and imperfectly understood. In that environment they had to try to preserve their health and personal safety at the same time they were learning how to deal with traditional African societies, diverse economic interests (European planters, indigenous and European traders), and colonial authorities (administrators, police, military officers) who were sometimes helpful but just as often indifferent or actively hostile to their efforts. They had to confront all these struggles at the same time they were pursuing their basic religious objective, which was to find ways to bring into the Mission's orbit Africans who were themselves disorganized and demoralized by centuries of exploitation, divided by intertribal politics, and increasingly preoccupied with their own survival. These conditions were, in effect, "permanently extraordinary," never settled, and there was a chronic absence of *effective* behavioral guidelines for dealing with them. The collection of organizational precepts and principles formulated in Basel was reasonably well aligned with conditions in and around the seminary, but those rules and regulations were much less closely synchronized with conditions in the field.

Paradoxically, then, a condition of "anomie" (by which sociologists mean an absence of clear normative guidelines) existed for the missionaries despite the thick mantle of moral principles and internalized organizational controls they carried about with them when they left the seminary.[5] They were extensively trained in the minutiae of Pietist organizational discipline, reporting,

4. According to accounts by Geoffrey Moorhouse (*The Missionaries*), Lamar Cecil (*The German Diplomatic Service*), and Richard H. Werking (*The Master Architects*), the foreign services of the time faced similar problems of communication. Raymond Jones (*The British Diplomatic Service*) makes the interesting point that the telegraph actually reduced the effectiveness of foreign service officers because it encouraged them to evade responsibility by cabling too frequently for decisions on matters they should have resolved for themselves. Recognizing this, many reverted to the familiar and more deliberate methods of the post and personal messengers. In another permutation, missionaries abroad representing the Latter-Day Saints are discouraged from using email to stay in touch with home because the practice is thought to undermine their self-reliance.

5. Emile Durkheim draws a clear separation between *anomie* and *excessive regulation* (*Suicide*, chap. 5). The present analysis suggests that anomie can be the result of a misalignment between "excessive regulations" and the practical circumstances to which they are meant to bring order.

and record keeping. Moreover, when they were posted to the field they were given remarkably detailed guidelines for such matters as wardrobe, personal habits, hygiene, diet, housing and furnishings, and the distribution of supplies. But when it came to the details of their evangelical work per se, their mandates were necessarily phrased in very general terms. They were instructed to learn languages and minister to the unsaved, to build houses and workshops, to erect educational institutions, to impart technical skills, and to establish sound agricultural practices — in short, to create Christian communities. But beyond those written expectations, it was not possible for the leadership at home to anticipate all the specific problems the missionaries would face or all the specific decisions they would have to make outside the comparative tranquillity of the immediate mission compound. They could not be prepared adequately in advance to deal with the behavior of unpredictable colonial officials, the competition of rival missions, the reluctance of natives who found themselves the targets of the missionaries' attention, or interpersonal strife with fellow missionaries, devastating illnesses, or the loss of family members and friends. The slowness of communication to and from Basel aggravated their difficulties because many of the decisions that were sent to them from Basel, including those that came in response to their own requests for guidance, were moot before they could be implemented. The correspondence related to the illness of the missionary Borel related in chapter 3 is a good example.

"Trained incapacity," Robert Merton tells us, "refers to that state of affairs in which one's abilities function as inadequacies or blind spots. Actions based upon training and skills that have been successfully applied in the past may result in inappropriate responses *under changed conditions*. An inadequate flexibility in the application of skills will, in a changing milieu, result in more or less serious maladjustments."[6] The turbulent situation encountered in the field by the Baslers frequently called for quick intelligence and flexibility, but initiative and creativity were not capabilities for which they had been selected or that were often encouraged or rewarded in the seminary. Seminarians who showed even small signs of individuality were likely to be called *eigensinnig* ("self-willed" or "obstinate"); this pejorative label could be attached to their personnel records to call attention to potential trouble in the future. In the field many simply "hunkered down,"[7] waiting for orders to reach them from

---

6. Merton, *Social Theory*, pp. 195-206, emphasis Merton's. Merton attributes this apt term, "trained incapacity," to Thorstein Veblen, but does not give a citation. Stuart Piggin, in "Social Background," p. 344, uses the term "erudite inflexibility" to describe the same self-defeating syndrome in the training of British missionaries of the time.

7. This is the term used by Paul Jenkins (personal communication) to describe the missionaries' response to uncertainty.

the center before starting anything new. A small number fell into personal disorder, which expressed itself in such offenses as alcohol abuse or sexual misconduct, and were dismissed for their transgressions.[8] Others who remained officially in good standing were often disillusioned and demoralized by their lack of effectiveness.

To break this malaise required individual decisiveness by persons who could seize opportunities and make confident decisions in uncertain surroundings. But this kind of decisive behavior (which, not incidentally, had many of the elements classically attributed to personal charisma) was likely to be seen as arrogance *(Hochmut)*, and arrogance threatened the organization's ruling moral paradigm. The dilemma was clear: *The creative problem-solvers who were strategically essential for the Mission's survival and progress were frequently, almost by definition, norm-breakers.* And, as is often the case with nonconformists, they were as likely to depart from structured expectations in undesirable as in desirable ways. Therein lay the danger they posed for the organization, but the line must have been a hard one to draw. Punishment of a rule-breaker who was also a visionary could rob the Mission of flexibility and block its evangelical progress; but looking at it the other way around, openly encouraging a visionary who was also a rule-breaker threatened the revealed Pietist underpinning of the Mission's legitimacy, and it made the organization vulnerable to the unscripted consequences of that person's actions.

A number of prominent incidents in the Mission's history reflect this contradiction. During the first twenty-five to thirty years, when the survival of the organization was still in the balance, it was especially visible in the careers of three pivotal individuals, and I will use them as illustrations. From the Committee's perspective Andreas Riis, Simon Süss, and Johannes Zimmermann were guilty of one of the most serious offenses possible: each openly challenged the structure of control in the organization in a quite fundamental way. At the same time, each was identified with important accomplishments, each was taken seriously by the Committee and to an important degree protected by that body, and each was held up to the larger evangelical community in Europe as an example of the best in the Mission's work. In each case, therefore, retention versus dismissal represented a fateful choice for the organization. I refer to these individuals as "strategic deviants." They were *deviant,* it is clear, because their actions violated the basic norms of organizational discipline, but they were *strategic* as well, because for a time they contributed

8. I found fewer than twenty cases of administrative dismissal of Gold Coast agents for disciplinary reasons during the years covered by my study, out of a total of about 250 agents posted to the region.

in crucial ways to the Mission's progress.[9] Riis kept the Gold Coast effort alive when it was stretched virtually to the breaking point; Süss's efforts promised to expand the boundaries of the Mission's field of influence in ways that far exceeded the expectations of the leadership in Basel and outstripped the willingness of his fellow missionaries to take risks; and Zimmermann, as we saw in chapter 3, was influential among his colleagues and a key person in the strategy of village building and language study.

It was in the nature of the way the Committee did its business that the important accomplishments of the missionaries were announced to a wide and receptive audience in Europe, but outside the Committee's own tight circle, little was ever revealed about the controversies occasioned by the actions of men like Riis, Süss, and Zimmermann on the Gold Coast. The discussions in camera of each man's exploits, however, were extensive and often quite anguished, and the minutes of these discussions provide the clearest justification for the use of the term "dilemma" to describe what they meant to the organization. Summary dismissal without a second look could be the fate of lesser figures around them who violated the rules without laying claim to the same level of accomplishment.[10] The Mission's tolerance of Riis, Süss, and Zimmermann cannot, therefore, be attributed to any lack of attentiveness or resolve on the part of the governing group. The organizational reasons go much deeper.

Andreas Riis

During the early years the Danish colonial authorities placed serious restrictions on the Basel Mission's activities on the Gold Coast.[11] Its missionaries were confined to ministering to those few among the Europeans who showed

---

9. What sociologists call labeling theory (see Gove, "The Labelling Perspective") makes a distinction between "rule-breakers" (those who, technically, have violated a norm) and "deviants" (those who have been publicly labeled as offenders). The "strategic deviants" whose actions I describe fall somewhere between those two categories. They were recognized by colleagues and by the leadership as serious violators, but they escaped public labeling as long as they were credited with useful accomplishments alongside their violations.

10. A missionary named Mörschel, to take just one example, drank too much on board the ship that carried him from Hamburg to Accra, and upon arrival in Africa was almost immediately sent back to Europe (Basel Mission Archive [BMA], *Komiteeprotokolle* [Committee Minutes; hereafter *KP*] 72, section 346, April 3, 1901, and section 436, May 1, 1901. NB: This volume of the *Komiteeprotokol* has numbered sections, each dealing with a different subject, but does not have page numbers).

11. See Clarke, *West Africa and Christianity,* pp. 41ff.

an interest in religion and providing education for the blacks and people of mixed race who were attached to the Danish coastal settlement at Christiansborg. The hope of creating freestanding Christian villages of African converts seemed remote. In 1835 Andreas Riis broke out of this confinement by creating a Mission station several miles inland at Akropong (see plate 5). The bare outlines of Riis's career on the Gold Coast were widely reported in his time. Schlatter's comprehensive official history of the Mission recounts most of the highlights of his activities,[12] but with the exception of two innocuous paragraphs,[13] the controversies and conflicts surrounding him are, for the most part, not to be found in sources promulgated by the Mission itself. For unfiltered information about his activities it is necessary to consult the confidential minutes of the Committee's weekly meetings (Komiteeprotokolle) and the letters written to the Committee by the missionaries and Africans who worked with him. As a rule, neither of the latter two sources was shared with any audience outside the Mission leadership.[14]

The climate in Akropong was less threatening to the health of Europeans than the coastal region, but the new station created by Riis was outside the Danish zone of control. For this reason he ran into political difficulties owing to the colonial rivalry of the British and the Danes. In establishing the station he also moved well ahead of official Mission policy, which in this tentative time preferred to move carefully and avoid any political entanglements with contending colonial powers. Riis was tenacious in pursuing his projects, however, and after his efforts showed signs of lasting, most of them were accepted by Basel despite the Committee's private uneasiness about how they had come about. After all, Riis represented movement after several years of frustration and stagnation, and this was enough to push into the background the requirement for absolute conformity to the will of the Committee. In the early 1840s he proposed to recruit a number of black families and individuals (between thirty and forty people in all) from British-controlled Jamaica in the West Indies. He hoped these "repatriates," chosen for their religious devotion as well as their technical skills as farmers and craft workers, would form the nucleus of a black Christian community on the Gold Coast.[15] Although

12. Schlatter, Geschichte der Basler Mission, 3:27-39.
13. Schlatter, Geschichte der Basler Mission, 3:38-39.
14. This double system of reporting is not peculiar to missionary organizations. In the Mission's own time, Raymond Jones (The British Diplomatic Service, chap. 7) points out that the British diplomatic service erected a private system of communication and record keeping alongside the official ones because the latter, being potentially public, limited the flexibility of decision makers.
15. The reliance on blacks from the Americas to form the nuclei of mission commu-

there was trouble to come in Riis's relations with these settlers, it was thanks to this bold venture that the Mission's hope of creating "Christian Salems" amid the "heathen darkness" seemed realistic for the first time.[16]

For twelve years the Mission's outreach to the Gold Coast depended heavily on Riis's stamina and imagination and his willingness to follow his own inspiration, often seeking approval after the fact for whatever he was able to accomplish. The records show that the Committee considered abandoning the Gold Coast altogether during this precarious formative time, but as long as Riis persevered the conclusion was that the hardships could be borne and, in fact, must be accepted as part of the test God had set for the Mission. The willful insubordination that characterized many of Riis's actions was overlooked, and his accounts of his accomplishments were featured prominently and approvingly in *Der Evangelische Heidenbote (The Evangelical Message to the Heathens)*, a major publication that was circulated by the Mission among its sympathizers in Europe.[17] The ultimate recognition of Riis's indispensability appeared in his obituary, which acknowledged that without him the Gold Coast effort could not have continued.[18] One scholar, writing in 1958, described him as the "Moses of Ghana."[19] That comparison is hyperbolic, to say the least, but judging from the way Riis was held up to public view in his own time as an example of Pietist strength, it is less questionable to compare him to William Carey, the pioneering Baptist missionary to India, or especially to one of his far better known British successors in Africa, David Livingstone. Riis's public impact, however substantial, does not approach that of Livingstone, who was perhaps the leading media superstar of his day. Nevertheless, the comparison between the two men is apt in more than one way. In his discussion of prominent figures in the British missionary movement, Geoffrey Moorhouse described Livingstone as a man whose "lustre for

---

nities was not without precedent. It was a common practice in British spheres of influence in both East and West Africa, and the Basel Mission, in following their lead, had to have the permission and cooperation of British authorities to encourage former slaves and descendants of slaves to leave the West Indies for the Gold Coast. "Recaptives," or those liberated from domestic slavery in Africa, were also resettled in mission communities. See Clarke, *West Africa and Christianity*, pp. 32ff.; Groves, *Planting of Christianity*, 1:205ff.; Ajayi, *Christian Missions*, pp. 43ff.; and Oliver, *Missionary Factor*, pp. 14ff.

16. Schlatter, *Geschichte der Basler Mission*, 3:32-37.

17. See the following issues of *Der Evangelische Heidenbote*: nos. 15, 16, August 15, 1835; no. 12, June 15, 1836; no. 6, March 15, 1837; nos. 13, 14, July 1, 15, 1839; no. 3, March 1843; no. 4, April 1843; and no. 10, October 1843.

18. *Der Evangelische Heidenbote*, no. 10, October 1854, pp. 80-81.

19. Hans Debrunner, "The Moses of the Ghana Presbyterian Church," *Ghana Bulletin of Theology* 1, no. 4 (June 1958): 12-18. (Cited in Mobley, *Ghanaian's Image*, p. 21 n.)

the British [was] second only to that of Queen Victoria." More to the point here, Moorhouse also described him as a charismatic but contrary and contradictory personality whose adventurism put him at odds with the basic requirements of organizational discipline. "He would never yield anything of his judgment to anyone," Moorhouse wrote, "even to men with much greater experience than himself, and time did nothing to soften his craggy nature."[20] In a similar way, the Basel Mission's Riis, having shown his willingness to throw over the traces of Mission discipline, did not behave at all like a humble and obedient Württemberg villager. Moreover, many of his departures from Mission policy could hardly be counted as gains by the Committee.

His troublesome relations with Africans are the leading case in point here. It was the accumulated effects of these relationships that eventually brought his career as a missionary to an end. According to official policy, Basel missionaries were expected to live humbly and in close physical proximity to the natives; nevertheless, a person who failed to keep an imperative personal distance from Africans could be a candidate for dismissal. In part this was because it was believed that too much familiarity would lead a vulnerable missionary into all sorts of "temptation." One who was considered guilty of such a lapse of judgment might be called *verwildet,* an idea that is rendered approximately in English by the term "going native." But more basically, the policy of personal detachment existed because the breakdown of social distance violated the principle of hierarchy (dominated by Europeans, of course) that was considered essential to order in the Mission community. Riis's departure from the norm was that he actually thought this policy was *too lenient.* In his extremism he went far beyond both its letter and its spirit, so far that, in time, he alienated the very people the Mission was trying to attract. He became abusive and contemptuous of blacks and complained vocally when they were even present at meals.[21] At all costs, he insisted, one must avoid treating Africans like Europeans.[22] The West Indian families who had volunteered to join the Mission complained bitterly to other missionaries and to the Committee in Basel about Riis's cruelty and dishonesty and his disrespectful treatment of them.[23] Their voluntary move to West Africa came within ten years of the ab-

20. Moorhouse, *The Missionaries,* pp. 111, 114.

21. See the letter from Georg Thompson to the Committee, BMA D-1,2, Ussu, no. 19, July 28, 1845.

22. See in BMA D-1,2, Akropong and Ussu (1842-1848), the letter from the missionary Halleur to his brother, no. 4, March 31, 1844, and his letter to the Committee of June 7, 1844, no. 10.

23. Their concerns were voiced directly to the Committee (after a great many complaints to other Basel missionaries in Africa) in a letter in BMA D-1,2 (1842-1848),

olition of slavery in the West Indies, and Riis must have reminded them of the overseers who were such a prominent feature of the plantation economy.

In the end Riis gained a reputation for brutality, and his disregard for other missionaries, repatriates, and natives alike led some of his colleagues to threaten resigning if he were not recalled.[24] The chorus of disapproval from both blacks and fellow missionaries finally caused the Committee to summon him to Basel to reassess his role in the organization. The investigation into his activities, faithfully documented in the Committee's minutes, revealed a broad array of deviant directions that, according to his colleagues, his entre-preneurial energy had taken.[25] The Committee reviewed evidence that he had bought a plantation for himself, contrary to the Mission's explicit rules about the accumulation of private property. He ran this venture with the inden-tured labor of slaves whom he claimed to have "bought free," a practice that some of his more critical coworkers characterized as bond servitude, no dif-ferent in reality from outright slavery.[26] He meddled repeatedly in colonial and tribal politics and traded in gunpowder, flints, and brandy. He held the Committee in low regard and usurped its decision-making functions. He had

Akropong and Ussu, no. 2, January 13, 1845. Their concerns were acknowledged by the Committee, but without any decision being recorded, on May 14, 1845 (*KP* 18, p. 58).

24. The key letters that moved the Committee to action are preserved in BMA series D-1,2, Akropong and Ussu (1842-1848). The missionary Ernst Sebald's letter of May 16, 1845 (no. 13), comments in general terms about Riis's mistreatment of the West Indians. The missionary Johann Widmann wrote from Akropong on May 26, 1845, regarding Riis's mis-deeds and his own determination to quit or be reassigned if Riis were not removed from the scene. He also reported the desire of many West Indians to go back to Jamaica. Hermann Halleur wrote from Akropong to the inspector on November 1, 1843 (no. 9), say-ing that the West Indians cursed the day they first saw Riis. Other primary references that bear directly on Riis's behavior include letters from Halleur on June 7, 1844 (no. 10), from Sebald on May 16, 1845 (no. 13), from the West Indian settlers on January 13, 1845 (no. 2), and from Friedrich Schiedt, written from Accra on January 16, 1846 (no. 1). Schlatter covers the deterioration of Riis's relationship to the Gold Coast Mission community briefly but accurately (*Geschichte der Basler Mission*, 3:38-39). Committee discussions revealing awareness of and concern about Riis's offenses appear in *KP* 17 for October 23, 1844, p. 176, and November 13, 1844, pp. 184-85.

25. The Committee's deliberations during 1845 concerning Riis are recorded in de-tail in *KP* 18. Important discussions and decisions were recorded on May 14, p. 58; May 28, pp. 62-63; September 24, p. 106; October 15, p. 116; and October 22, pp. 119-20. His interro-gations by the Committee, including his replies to each of the charges brought against him, are documented in the minutes for November 26, 1845 (*KP* 18, pp. 130ff.); November 27, 1845 (*KP* 18, pp. 139ff.); and December 3, 1845 (*KP* 18, pp. 142ff.). A further discussion took place on February 11, 1846 (*KP* 18, pp. 167-68).

26. A report of Riis's dealings with slaves appears in Schiedt's letter of April 14, 1846 (no. 4 in D-1,2, 1842-1848), Akropong and Ussu.

extremely damaging relationships with fellow missionaries. He cheated the West Indian families of their contractual due in material goods (blankets, clothing, furnishings, tools) and disregarded their spiritual needs. Finally, on one notorious occasion, he ordered a beating for a West Indian settler who had aroused his disapproval by (so Riis charged) running away from the Mission community. Riis further insisted that this corporal punishment be administered by a "heathen," a decision that made the sentence especially humiliating in the eyes of the African Christian community. When the force of his blows caused the "heathen" to break his stick on the alleged miscreant's back, a witness said that Riis continued the "lesson" with his own boots and fists. That the Mission community on the Gold Coast was plunged into prolonged depression by this episode is an index of how unusual and unsettling it was.[27]

After all his years and accomplishments on the Gold Coast, Riis was not without defenders, some of whom testified before the Committee on his behalf,[28] but he could not answer the charges against him to the Committee's satisfaction and they reluctantly and quietly expelled him from the Mission.[29] A record in his personal file in the archive shows that he was paid a pension "in recognition of his accomplishments and his own suffering in Africa," with the payment continuing until he was able to settle into a new ministry in Norway.[30] The residue of the bitterness he caused among the missionaries and natives lingered for years, but with one exception (when his leaving the Mission was reported to influential supporters in Europe), only "impaired health" and a "disturbed frame of mind brought on by his heroic struggles" were given as the grounds for his inability to continue.[31]

27. This incident and the reactions of the Africans and other missionaries to it is described in graphic detail in Sebald's letter to the Committee of May 16, 1845, no. 13 in series D-1,2 (1842-1848), Akropong and Ussu.

28. Among them his nephew, H. N. Riis, who was also one of the Gold Coast missionaries at the time; see his letter to the Committee of December 29, 1845 (D-1,2 [1842-1848], Akropong and Ussu, no. 29). See also KP 18, p. 199, for a discussion by the Committee of a letter written by the nephew on January 13, 1846, in which he expressed disapproval of his uncle's manner but urged the Committee to follow a policy of "forgive and forget" in dealing with him. After Riis was dismissed, the Committee discussed, but did not accede to, a letter from Mission supporters in Hamburg suggesting that the dismissal was too harsh a response to his troubles (KP 19, August 9, 1846, p. 18).

29. The decision is recorded in Committee sessions of May 3 and 6, 1846 (in KP 18).

30. The file is numbered P124.

31. The language used to inform the community of Mission supporters of his departure was agreed upon in the session of May 6, 1846 (KP 18, p. 211). A request from a religious organization for information about Riis's dismissal was reported by a member of the

Years after Riis was dismissed this same cautious language reappeared in his obituary, which said:

> The arrival of the [West Indian] colonists on the Gold Coast and their settlement among their countrymen represents the greatest turning point in the history of the [Ghana] Mission. For although its beginning was very difficult it has continued from that point. . . . To be sure, Riis could not remain on the spot to share in the enjoyment of this development. A painful twist of circumstances made it necessary for him to return to Europe, never again to return to the land of his struggles and suffering. He felt much more the need to answer the Call to the far north of Norway. There he represented the Mission through preaching, traveling and other richly blessed activities [until his death].[32]

Riis was certainly atypical in many ways, but he was also in many ways a product of the Mission's own policies and decisions. It is crucial to point out that his troubles were not confined to a brief and "painful twist of circumstances" in his career. His time on the Gold Coast spanned the years from 1832 to 1845, and during that period his behavior repeatedly slipped outside the range of what was tolerated from others. It is remarkable that an organization virtually defined by its insistence on conformity tolerated his often egregious nonconformity for a dozen years. The surviving letters and Committee discussions show beyond any doubt that the details of his problematic behavior were known to the leadership throughout that time. They knew about the likelihood that the West Indian settlers would leave the Mission and demand to be returned to Jamaica, which they were contractually entitled to do. They knew also of the danger that many of the other missionaries would quit, as several had threatened to do, and of the possibility that colonial authorities and tribal leaders around the region would turn against the Mission. And there was a virtual certainty that natives otherwise attracted to the Mission would be alienated by his demeanor and avoid or leave the community. Given this knowledge, it is clear that expedient decisions were made again and again to absorb the *costs* of Riis's actions in order to reap their *benefits*. There was a delicate balance between the genuine need for his disobedient resourcefulness and the equally genuine danger posed by his disobedient volatility. Quite

---

Committee itself, and the request was honored ("Soll alles offen mitgetheilt"). This is the only recorded exception to the decision to keep the details of his troubles confidential (*KP* 18, June 24, 1846, p. 230).

32. See *Der Evangelische Heidenbote,* no. 10, October 1854, pp. 80-81.

simply, there was no one else at the time to do what he did for the organiza-tion. Decisive action was taken against him only when it became clear that his religious zeal and entrepreneurial energy could no longer be productively channeled by the existing authority structure. As the organization grew and depended less upon him, and as he became more visible and more eccentric in his behavior, it was apparent that to allow him to continue could bring the entire operation into public disrepute.

This precarious balance between moral dictates and practical exigencies is a leitmotif in the Mission. The reliance on a flexible moral calculus in such situations is further illustrated by Simon Süss and Johannes Zimmermann, two other strong-willed and talented missionaries who presented the Com-mittee with painful choices. Both were active in the 1850s, when the Mission's foothold on the Gold Coast had become somewhat more secure than it was in the time of Riis. The objective threat they represented to the larger undertak-ing was therefore probably less acute than in Riis's case, but their experiences show no less clearly the continuing moral and administrative dilemmas that such persons posed for the organization.

Simon Süss

From childhood, the Mission's official historian says, Simon Süss was a per-son who displayed great personal drive and vision but great single-minded-ness as well.[33] He was "insubordinate and stubborn" but at the same time "quiet and thoughtful"; he was a troublesome seminarian and an impatient subordinate, a person for whom rules had no relevance.[34] Soon after he was posted to a station in Akropong in 1851, he became restive under the restric-tions imposed on him. Schlatter describes his attitude: "The education of young natives through the schools and seminaries was not to his taste. He wanted to live among them, share everything with them, and intimately con-nect [religious] instruction to the work on the land. Everything possible he did on his own, throwing himself into practical projects, driving himself to pioneer labor, demanding that the collective life of the people be pressed to fruitfulness."[35] After two years of chafing under Mission authority, Süss set

33. Schlatter, *Geschichte der Basler Mission*, 3:69.
34. Schlatter, *Geschichte der Basler Mission*, 3:69. In German the description reads: "unbeugsam, starrsinnig und zugleich still und tiefsinnig. . . . Ein Mann für den keine Re-gel galt."
35. Schlatter, *Geschichte der Basler Mission*, 3:69. For a similar description, see the Committee's discussion of Süss's attitudes on January 28, 1863 (*KP* 34, p. 10).

out into the "bush" on his own, without prior permission from the Committee, in the hope of establishing self-sustaining congregations in remote regions as yet untouched by evangelism.[36] The Committee recognized his "honest nature" and respected the "courage and manliness" he showed in difficult circumstances. With considerable uneasiness and with one eye always on the possible dangers to the Mission's larger program in Africa, they also valued the inroads he made into previously unexplored territory, although they were not willing to guarantee financial support for his projects.

Over a ten-year period the Committee held frequent discussions of the troubles surrounding Süss. A conversation about his stubbornness and independence was recorded on June 29, 1853. Among the complaints discussed at that time were these: "He has a lot of self-confidence but little self-understanding; he has never learned to let his will be broken; he lets his cows graze everywhere and they have badly damaged the coffee trees and eaten up the arrow-root plants. He does not properly control his crops; he does not follow his written instructions, always starting something new before finishing the old; he does not cooperate with the others."[37]

One historian whose account of Süss's life is essentially sympathetic makes the point that his influence on the Mission was much greater than the organization was ever willing to acknowledge.[38] The example Süss provided of entrepreneurial initiative and economic independence on the part of remote mission outposts was particularly important. In the early days of his adventures the Committee allowed some of his long letters describing his experiences to be reprinted with approval in the reports the Mission circulated among its supporters.[39] In December 1856, however, he was actually dismissed because of his "excessive self-reliance,"[40] but was reinstated a little over a year later after he promised renewed obedience to Basel.[41] He was given limited recognition for the communities he had managed to establish or bring into the Mission's orbit, and he was cautiously allowed to affiliate them with the larger enterprise despite the unorthodox manner of their founding. One other missionary, a man named David Baum, was assigned to

---

36. Schlatter, *Geschichte der Basler Mission*, 3:69-72; Steiner, *Auf Einsamen Pfaden*, pp. 22ff.

37. *KP* 24, pp. 84-85. For similar discussions see *KP* 24, p. 141 (October 12, 1853) and p. 148 (November 16, 1853).

38. Steiner, *Auf Einsamen Pfaden*, p. 55.

39. *Der Evangelische Heidenbote*, no. 7, 1852, pp. 53ff., and no. 10, 1852, pp. 83ff.; no. 1, 1853, pp. 40ff.; *Missionsmagazin*, no. 4, April 24, 1856, p. 47.

40. *KP* 27, December 30, 1856, p. 150.

41. *KP* 29, February 3, 1858, pp. 18-19.

work with Süss, but beyond this, little in the way of material support was extended to his settlements. The understanding was that he and his congregations must make their way on their own, supporting themselves through agriculture, crafts, and trade.[42]

The Committee's continuing uneasiness about Süss is apparent in its discussions of him in its weekly meetings. More than once it was suggested that he would have to be dismissed (again) for his flagrant disobedience, but each time that possibility was discussed, a compromise was reached that rested on a principle that today might be called "deniability." By extending only limited material support and provisional recognition to his efforts, the Committee could benefit (on behalf of the Mission) from any successes that might come from his erratic excursions, but left itself in a position to dissociate itself from him quickly should one of his projects go hopelessly astray. In time, in fact, Süss became so prodigal and unpredictable in his behavior and so deeply embroiled in tribal disputes and colonial politics that much of what he did was eventually cut adrift or abandoned by the Mission.

Unlike Riis before him, Süss tried to close the distance between himself and the Africans among whom he worked. For this he earned credit from the Mission, however cautiously it was expressed.[43] Like Riis, however, he became involved in the munitions trade and accumulated private landholdings. Also like Riis, he was seen as publicly brutal in his treatment of members of his congregations whom he considered errant.[44] Physical punishment in the interest of discipline was not uncommon in the mission world (or indeed, in European families at the time), and in one episode Süss held a young boy hostage against a debt owed by the boy's father, chaining the youth to a tree until the father acceded to his demands.[45] He encouraged his subordinate, Baum,

42. Schlatter, *Geschichte der Basler Mission*, 3:69, 74; Steiner, *Auf Einsamen Pfaden*, pp. 26ff. Süss's letter to the Committee about this understanding was written from Akropong on January 27, 1857 (abstracted in D-12,2, p. 32).

43. In his quarterly report of October 26, 1859, Johannes Zimmermann expressed his grudging respect for Süss's willingness to pursue the Mission's ideal of life close to the level of the people it intended to serve. At the same time, he expressed doubt that Süss's eccentricities would ever fit into the Mission's larger program on the Gold Coast. Zimmermann, as we have already seen, was a persistent and influential voice in favor of narrowing the differences between the European and African ways of life. See also *KP* 26, April 18, 1855, pp. 34-35.

44. See the judgment in *KP* 30, June 8, 1859, p. 77, that his daily beating of an African under his charge exceeded what could be considered "necessary."

45. Letter from Baum to the Committee, August 9, 1856 (abstract in D-12,1,2); Committee discussion in *KP* 27, October 15, 1856, p. 123. See also Zimmermann's letter of October 26, 1859 (D-1,10, Odumase, no. 6).

to engage in similar actions, with near disastrous results.[46] Süss defended his own actions and insisted that they had been inaccurately reported to the Committee,[47] but in the end the complaints that came out of this incident threatened to embroil the Mission in a damaging, not to say embarrassing, legal proceeding with the British colonial authorities who controlled the region in which Süss and his assistant were active.

With the benefit of hindsight, it seems that relations between Süss and the Mission would have unavoidably reached a breaking point. "Unconditional obedience" matched by "fatherly guidance" in no way describes the relationship between him and the Committee. His assistant, Baum, was quickly expelled from the Mission in 1857 when the debacle he caused became known.[48] Süss himself, however, was allowed to go on for another five years before being recalled to Basel, interrogated, and forbidden to return to Africa. The discussion recorded in the Committee minutes at that time indicates that, rather than being subjected to the humiliation of being *entlassen,* or "defrocked," Süss was allowed to resign, but this was only because his offenses were considered less appalling than those of his assistant.[49] In the end, after several requests to be reinstated to the service of the Mission were denied, Süss moved to Texas to minister to the congregations of German immigrants who had settled there, and much of his work in Africa seems to have collapsed behind him.[50]

The Mission's ambivalence about Süss lingered long after the Committee decided to dismiss him. As with Riis at an earlier time, it is unlikely that the serious difficulties he brought to the Mission were ever widely known in Eu-

46. Baum held captive a husband and wife who were allegedly in debt to him; the woman was confined to the Baums' bedroom, where, she charged, he made unwanted sexual advances to her. See the details preserved in the personal file of David Baum (Personal File 347; hereafter PF); see also *KP* 28, 1857, October 12, pp. 139-40; October 14, pp. 140-41; October 28, p. 141; November 5, p. 144; and the minutes of a conference held at Akropong to discuss Baum's case, found in BMA D-1,2, Gjadam, no. 11.

47. Süss's own explanation of these events (*KP* 27, October 15, 1856, p. 123) stresses the commonness in Africa of holding a "hostage" against the payment of debts. His claim that the chief agreed to the arrangement casts his actions in a light much less damaging to himself.

48. *KP* 29, February 3, 1858, pp. 18-19.

49. The final dismissal of Süss was recorded in *KP* 34 for January 28, 1863, pp. 10-11. Other relevant discussions about the dismissal are to be found in *KP* 32, October 2, 1861, p. 140; *KP* 33, April 30, 1862, pp. 63-64, May 7, 1862, p. 75, December 30, 1862, p. 167; and *KP* 34, March 4, 1863, p. 32, March 18, 1863, p. 41, May 6, 1863, pp. 60-61, June 12, 1863, p. 75, September 30, 1863, p. 128, and October 7, 1863, p. 131. See also BMA D-1,16, 1864, nos. 4, 6.

50. His agreement to abandon his efforts to be reinstated are recorded on July 25, 1866 (*KP* 37, p. 94).

rope outside the closed meetings of the Committee. Those discussions were quite clear about him, but the minutes of the meetings were considered to be completely private. What was provided for the public record, in contrast, was very selective, displaying his accomplishments with approval while essentially shielding his less savory side from view. Over forty years after he left Africa, Steiner's laudatory account of his career, called, appropriately, *Auf Einsamen Pfaden (On Lonely Pathways)*, appeared in a didactic series published by the Mission called Mission Heroes *(Missionshelden)*. Schlatter's official history alluded circumspectly to the troubles surrounding him but did not mention any of the specific offenses with which he and his assistant were charged and which led to their dismissals.[51] Much more recently a pamphlet full of high praise, titled *Simon Süss: A Difficult Visionary,* was circulated for the edification of young Christians in Ghana, more than a century after Süss had left the Mission.[52] The choice of words in the title (he was "visionary" but also "difficult") shows some awareness of the dilemma he posed for the organization, but like the earlier accounts it provides no details about the distressing events in which he was involved.

Like Riis, Simon Süss remained on the Gold Coast for a decade after his first act of open challenge to the leadership and for years after engaging in activities that could (and did) cause other, less strategically promising missionaries to be summarily dismissed. In this the Committee's shrewd awareness of the potential benefits versus the costs of retaining him is evident, and so is the willingness to use a flexible moral calculus in weighing the balance between the two. It is significant that Süss's challenges to established procedures, like those of Zimmermann after him, came during the inspectorate of Joseph Josenhans, the one man among all the Mission's leaders who was most committed to obedience and conformity. Josenhans's ability to tolerate and eventually compromise with the departures of these men from the organizational law (rather than "smashing them down mercilessly") speaks loudly of the Mission's calculated use of "strategic deviants" to accomplish organizational goals. Had he felt the need to do so, Josenhans could have claimed that the flexibility he had shown was not entirely without theological precedent; for all Martin Luther's emphasis on unbending authority, he, too, left room for the "wise ruler" to balance the gains of obedience against its possible losses. "A person who can't wink at faults," Luther said, "doesn't know how to govern."[53]

51. Schlatter, *Geschichte der Basler Mission,* 3:69-72.
52. The author of this pamphlet, which is in English, is Atze van den Broek.
53. In Höpfl, ed., *Luther and Calvin,* p. 39.

Johannes Zimmermann

Johannes Zimmermann serves as the final illustration of the dilemma
caused by the personal initiatives taken by missionaries in the field. In two
critical respects Zimmermann was quite different from both Riis and Süss.
He enjoyed the respect and support of his colleagues in the field, and he finished his career in good favor. Indeed, his record is sufficient testimony that
not all the strategic nonconformists in the Mission displayed the disturbing
personalities and behavioral patterns of Riis and Süss. Like the other two
men, however, Zimmermann made important contributions to the work of
the Mission, particularly in his widely praised compilation of vernacular African dictionaries and in his translations of biblical texts into African languages.[54] It is ironic that the same professed love of Africa and respect for
African culture that he said motivated this linguistic work also brought him
into conflict with the hierarchy of the Mission. His ideas about the model
Christian community and the strengths of traditional African culture were
referred to briefly in chapter 3. In order to place those views in context and
understand why they brought Zimmermann into conflict with the Committee, it is necessary to look more closely at the Mission's "official" ideas about
African culture.

Europeans often referred to Africans as "descendants of Ham" and saw the
African way of life as a reflection of the spiritual darkness into which, in the
biblical story, those descendants had retreated. A letter to the Committee in
which the missionary Friedrich Schiedt describes a black coworker, Georg
Thompson, typifies that view.[55] Thompson was a West African who had been
taken to Basel as a child and educated by the Mission. He completed the
course of training in the Mission House and was posted to the Gold Coast as
a schoolteacher but not as an ordained missionary. Freely translated, this is
what Schiedt said about him:

[I do not believe that Thompson] is capable of contrition in the sense in
which we think of it there at home, for from my experience I cannot
help but believe that African contrition and European repentance are
essentially different from each other. That is the reason that we must
sigh and cry out to the Lord that He might give these poor folk this vital
contrition, because where deep and honest recognition of sin is missing

---

54. Schlatter, *Geschichte der Basler Mission*, 3:61; Vogelsanger, *Pietismus und
Afrikanische Kultur*, p. 119.
55. D-1,2, Christiansborg, 1847, no. 25, p. 2.

we will search in vain for evidence of true contrition. . . . If the Committee expects more than an African type of repentance from [Thompson] you will be disappointed.[56]

Schiedt's description of Thompson is not unlike the characterizations of Africans often offered by other missionaries. The missionary Johann Widmann, commenting on Thompson's ability as a teacher, said he lacked aptitude because "he is a black in the essential sense, with the exception that he thinks that he is a European."[57] Brother H. N. Riis, in the course of defending his uncle Andreas Riis (who had always been Thompson's severest critic and tormentor), told the Committee that Thompson caused irritation in the Europeans around him because he did not know his "place" and was always striving for something above himself.[58] In Africa, the older Riis remarked in the presence of others that Thompson should not be allowed into the same household as whites, should not be encouraged to expect the same treatment as Europeans, and that no white brother should have to suffer him at the same dinner table.[59]

Thompson complained directly and bitterly to the Committee about the racist treatment he received from the missionaries.[60] The message the Committee directed to him by way of reply is recorded in the minutes for April 2, 1845. It ratifies, indeed virtually repeats, Andreas Riis's judgment of Thompson: "With your thoughtlessness you brought these humiliating experiences upon yourself. . . . Learn to conduct yourself with more wisdom and humility and patiently accept it if the blacks are inferior to the whites. You do not have to suffer as much from the climate. Leave the complaints to God."[61]

Missionaries sent to Africa typically believed that their special calling was to guide the natives to salvation by teaching them a way of living radically different from what they had previously known. The new life would be centered on the villages, churches, and schools attached to the Mission's stations and outstations. Converts were expected to accept European names, dress, customs, and family forms and to assume positions in their new lives that were

56. D-1,2, Christiansborg, 1848, no. 25.

57. "[Thompson] ist auch ein Neger im eigentlichen Sinn mit der Ausnahme, dass er sich als Europäer betrachtet." D-1,2, no. 11, January 6, 1843.

58. See D-1,2, no. 29, December 29, 1845.

59. This was reported by Thompson and corroborated in a letter written by the missionary Halleur to his brother. The source is D-1,2, no. 4, April 31, 1844.

60. KP 18, January 2, 1845, pp. 1-2.

61. KP 18, p. 41.

subordinate to the missionaries in the Christian community.[62] As we have seen, Andreas Riis caused problems for the Mission because he enforced a separation between Africans and Europeans that was too absolute. Nevertheless, the missionaries in general were cautioned not to allow the personal separation between themselves and their African charges to become too narrow. In the Mission's view of things the natural hierarchy in the universe scaled downward from the Savior, to the Mission Committee, to the Inspector, to the missionaries, and finally, to the Africans. In other words, Christian Africans were to occupy the lowest position (excluding "heathens," of course) in a newly emergent social structure patterned along traditional (preindustrial) European lines. Note also that in this essentially imported social model, Africans were to be no less rigidly subordinated to the missionaries — socially, organizationally, religiously, and charismatically — than the latter were to their own superiors in the Mission.

This balance of authority would be thrown into disarray by social familiarity between Europeans and Africans in any form that suggested equality. This was the case even when the Africans involved were Christians. It was for this reason that true intimacy of any kind across racial lines was strongly discouraged. The prohibitions included being too friendly, adopting African customs or dress, exchanging gifts, or incurring or encouraging debts between Africans and Europeans. Despite the requirement that Christian converts take on European identities, theologies, and social norms, the Committee and many missionaries believed it was a mistake to "treat Africans too much like Europeans."

Zimmermann disagreed. He insisted that the paradigm for race relations that came out of this attitude forced a separation that was far too strict. He saw a glaring irony in imposing a "European social order" and then frowning on the treatment of Africans "like Europeans." He turned the problem on its head: it was racial *separation*, he testified, not *closeness* between Mission

---

62. The document "Ordnung für die evangelischen Gemeinden der Basler Mission in Ostindien und Westafrika" sets out these expectations in detail (BMA Q-9,11,8; 1859). In sections 121-137 (pp. 17-19), the proper conduct of life in the Christian household and in the larger community is defined, as is the duty of the Christian to obey secular authority. Nudity and half-nudity were prohibited for children and adults, as were "heathen" forms of body ornamentation, jewelry, and hairstyles. "The clothing of the Christians must be clean and dignified, but modest, for they are fleeing the lusts of the flesh and have turned away from the godless world" (p. 17). See also the letter from Inspector Josenhans to the Mission administrator (Präses) Widmann of December 12, 1871 (*Kopierbücher* no. 112, pp. 323-31), in which the reasoning used by the Mission to put European family structures in the place of traditional African extended family forms is most clearly stated.

agents and their charges that was too European. "So far as Christianity allows it," he said, "I would rather become a black in order to win over the blacks."[63] Taking this stand clearly threatened the hierarchical distance that the Committee thought was necessary for proper Christian order, but Zimmermann defended it by calling attention to the intrinsic worth of many African institutions, and by insisting that the preservation of some of those social arrangements was essential to the spiritual health of the people.[64] It was a mistake, he insisted, to introduce communities patterned too faithfully on the European experience if they were thereby also to include European vices but exclude the stronger features of the African communities that predated them. African communities in their unspoiled forms, by which he meant their pre–slave trade and precolonial state, were superior in many ways to contemporary European culture, he said, because they had not experienced the philosophical corruption of the Enlightenment, the corrosive radical ferment that came out of the French Revolution, or the socially destructive effects of the Industrial Revolution that was eroding the Lutheran agrarian ideal in Europe. In one of his quarterly reports to the Committee in 1852, Zimmermann wrote at length about the integrity of the traditional African families he had observed. Despite the cultural decay that was all around them, he noted, many families preserved a clear and stable patriarchal form, suggesting the presence of a strong Old Testament influence. This observation led him to join in the speculation that West Africans had ties to the ancient Christian communities in Ethiopia. Therefore, he reasoned, West Africans quite possibly represented a mixture of Semitic and Hamitic cultural and racial strains.[65]

Zimmermann first moved toward this position of respect for African institutions, so he told the Committee, when he was cured of a serious illness by a native practitioner after European medicine had failed to restore his health.[66] Africa, he said, had become his spiritual home, and to show his com-

---

63. "Mir is fast alles zu Europäisch, ich möchte mehr, soweits das Christentum erlaubt, Neger werden, um die Neger zu gewinnen" (Zimmermann to the Committee, July 29, 1850; D-1,3, Ussu, 1850, no. 10).

64. To understand the nature of Zimmermann's approval of African culture, see his letter of October 4, 1851 (D-1,3, 1849-1851, Ussu, no. 13). A carefully documented account of Zimmermann's arguments and actions in favor of the recognition of African culture is offered by Vogelsanger, *Pietismus und Afrikanische Kultur*, pp. 65-67, 123ff.

65. *Vierteljahresbericht* no. 10, Christiansborg, October 4, 1851, in D-1,3, 1849-1851. This theory of the "Semitic" origins of African culture was shared by the linguist Sigismund Koelle *(Grammar* and *African Native Literature).* See n. 2 above.

66. Cited by Vogelsanger, *Pietismus und Afrikanische Kultur*, p. 119. It is interesting that Riis had also spoken earlier of the transforming effect he experienced as the result of a native cure for a persistent illness. See Schlatter, *Geschichte der Basler Mission,* 3:27. Al-

mitment to it he offered to work without pay from the Mission, supporting himself and the congregations he served from the products of the labor they shared.[67] On two occasions his convictions and the social theories that were attractive to him forced the leadership to balance the value of his considerable evangelical contributions against the troublesome example (from their point of view) he set for other missionaries. The ultimate assessment in each case favored Zimmermann, but in one incident the result was a retreat on one of the Mission's most basic rules, a compromise that was later to cause the Committee considerable regret.

Zimmermann's first and most important offense, judging just from the Mission's reaction to it, was his marriage. To the Committee's great surprise and displeasure and despite the cautions of some of his superiors in the field, he married a black woman (see plate 24). His bride was Catherine Mulgrave, a resourceful and talented Christian schoolteacher who had come to the Gold Coast with the West Indian settlers recruited several years earlier by Andreas Riis. Her background, in fact, is a riveting one. She was born in Angola and kidnapped as a child by slave traders, whose ship was wrecked in a storm off the coast of Cuba. She survived and was educated and brought up as a Christian in the household of the British governor of the West Indies, whose name, Mulgrave, she was given. Zimmermann's union with her came to the Committee's attention as a fait accompli and caused them real consternation, first because it was a direct affront to the marriage rules (he married without permission) and second because of the sensation the members feared it would cause in the Pietist community in Europe (he married a black woman). Some members of the Committee insisted on Zimmermann's immediate expulsion, on the straightforward contractual grounds that he did not petition either for permission to marry or for prior approval of his intended mate. Others before him had been dismissed for far less consequential transgressions, and it was written into the definition of the missionary's status that any willful breach of the rules was, if the Committee cared to rule it so, tantamount to resignation, or summary dismissal, from the Mission community. The original marriage rules promulgated by Inspector Blumhardt in 1837 left little room for doubt concerning where Zimmermann stood: without definite prior permission from the Committee in Basel, no marriage — not even a tentative betrothal — could take place. Anyone who

---

though the two described the spiritual meaning of this experience in similar terms, they were obviously not led to similar personal attitudes toward Africans and African social realities.

67. *KP* 26, July 11, 1855, p. 68; and Schlatter, *Geschichte der Basler Mission,* 3:61, 87.

disagreed with the inspector was free to resign, but a person who went ahead and violated the rules was to be regarded as having been, in effect, dismissed.[68] Seminarians could be expelled, for example, if they simply admitted unsupervised contact or unapproved attractions to young women, and relationships between missionaries and native women were regulated with extreme strictness, increasingly so toward the end of the nineteenth century.[69] Given the Mission's disapproval of "too-familiar" social interaction between Africans and Europeans in general, its prohibition on interracial sexual contact and marriage was absolute.

Officially, then, the offense committed by the Zimmermanns was an egregious one. It was against all probability, therefore, that the Committee decided not to dismiss them. Instead, they reluctantly accepted the marriage, but with two strong stipulations: first, that Johannes was no longer to consider himself a European citizen, and second, that Catherine and their children must never expect to travel to Europe.[70] The usefulness to the Mission of Johannes Zimmermann's work played a key role in this relatively lenient decision, and so did the indispensability to the Mission of the woman he married. Indeed, the story of *his* challenge to the rules governing the conduct of missionaries could just as easily be read as the story of *her* challenge to racial separation and to the patriarchal principle that relegated women to subordinate and silent positions in the organization.[71] In one letter to the Committee, Zimmermann defended the marriage by pointing out that Catherine, who was a teacher in the Mission's school for girls, had considered leaving the Basel Mission and joining a rival Methodist mission.[72] By general consensus among the Gold Coast missionaries, she was an irreplaceable person in the Mission community, and it is interesting that the Committee members, like Johannes Zimmermann himself and those of his colleagues who defended

68. *KP* 14, December 27, 1837, p. 54; see also "Verordnungen über die persönliche Stellung der Missionare, Revidiert 1886" (BMA Q-9,21,7: section V).

69. The details of these policies appear in "Regeln für das Verhalten gegen das weibliche Geschlecht in Indien und Afrika (nach den Angaben erfahrener Brüder)" (BMA Q-9,3,10, June 1893).

70. *KP* 22, August 20, 1851, pp. 109-10, and August 27, 1851, p. 111. See also Schlatter, *Geschichte der Basler Mission*, 3:51.

71. See our discussion of this side of the episode in Predelli and Miller, "Piety and Patriarchy," and the collection of essays on similar topics in Huber and Lutkehaus, eds., *Gendered Missions*.

72. Zimmermann explained his marriage to the Committee in a letter on June 2, 1850 (D-1,3, no. 19), and again on September 10, 1850 (D-1,3, Ussu, no. 15). He did not hesitate to say in these letters that for the missionaries the marriage rules were very painful and threatened their trust for the Committee.

him, used the prospect of her loss to justify their decision to allow Zimmermann to remain a missionary despite the unauthorized marriage.[73]

In justifying their actions to the larger evangelical community, the Committee pointed to Catherine Mulgrave's importance and accomplishments as
evidence that Zimmermann had been concerned not with his own gratification but with the good of the Mission.[74] By marrying Mulgrave, Zimmermann kept her talent at the disposal of the Mission. It also says something
about class consciousness that the Committee members were swayed by the
fact that Mulgrave was not a recent convert or even a local African woman,
not, in their words, a "simple village girl." The Committee regarded her as significantly more "cultured" than the indigenous women of the West African
region. Despite their ability to construct these reassuring after-the-fact rationalizations, however, the compromise that the Committee reached was not an
easy one. It did not lead to a significant change in race relations in the Mission community in Africa or to the promulgation of a new and more permis-
sive marriage rule, any more than it resulted in meaningful change for other
women in the Mission community. Indeed, in the years to come the Mission's
resolve against interracial marriages hardened considerably,[75] and the precedent set by the Zimmermanns' special dispensation, because it looked like a
capitulation to personal initiative and personal choice, became a worrisome
example when other missionaries asked for the same consideration.

The second point of contention between Johannes Zimmermann and the
Committee involved his attitudes toward domestic slavery on the Gold
Coast.[76] The Basel Mission Committee took the abolitionist view common to
Pietism and by then to European religion in general, that all slavery was irre-
deemably evil, including not just the European-controlled international slave
trade but the indigenous forms it took within Africa as well.[77] In the early

73. Letters defending Zimmermann's marriage make his colleagues' opinions on this
matter clear. In BMA D-1,3, see no. 16 from Stanger dated June 1, 1850. In BMA D-1,4, see
the letters from Mader (no. 18, Ussu, June 2, 1851) and Stanger (no. 16, Ussu, June 2, 1851).
The report of a general conference on Zimmermann's marriage also stressed Mulgrave's
importance (D-1,4, Akropong, no. 20, June 2, 1851).

74. Schlatter, *Geschichte der Basler Mission,* 3:51.

75. When the scientific racism of nineteenth-century anthropology was added to
the biblical theory of the "curse of Ham," it contributed to this hardening of racial attitudes for many missionaries. For a focused discussion of this issue, see Gründer,
Christliche Mission und Deutscher Imperialismus, pp. 329ff.

76. I have relied heavily on Cornelia Vogelsanger's *(Pietismus und Afrikanische Kultur)* thorough treatment of the Mission's record on this question.

77. If Richard Gray (*Black Christians,* pp. 5-10) is right, there is a fascinating irony in
the fact that Christian abolitionism came to the fore in Europe because of elements of Af-

1850s the Committee decided that a person who remained a slave could be converted and embraced by the Mission but that neither a slave owner nor any person directly involved in the slave trade could be a part of the organization's activities.[78] For the Pietists the justification for abolition was straightforward: persons who owe complete obedience to an earthly master cannot truly give themselves up to serve a heavenly one. To be sure, slaves who are drawn to Christianity should not rebel actively against their lot, for it is not the place of Christians to overthrow worldly structures, even if they are evil. Rather, slaves must wait patiently for their liberation and salvation according to God's pace and plan. But a slave owner or slave trader is another matter altogether. They were answerable, by the rules of individual accountability, for placing a fellow human being in an untenable situation by taking away that person's God-given will. Slavery, in other words, destroys the balance in the formula for individual salvation. A sinner who has committed such an offense against the divine plan could never be considered a true Christian or be accepted as a part of the Mission community without first renouncing all ties to the practice.

Zimmermann considered the Mission's position to be ill informed and needlessly narrow. The same acceptance of African culture that led to his interracial marriage guided him into a position of opposition to the Committee on the slavery question. In his view the international slave trade was indeed an evil imposed by outsiders that should be immediately renounced, but a domestic form of slavery was part of the indigenous institutional structure of African society, and as such it provided a place for people who otherwise would have no community identity or role to play. To insist on its immediate eradication, as opposed to its inevitable but gradual erosion and displacement by Christian example, which he welcomed, would destabilize other aspects of that society and have far-reaching and undesirable results.

It is important to note that the controversy surrounding slavery and abolition was not just a moral issue. It also had a purely practical side. Colonial planters of the time opposed slavery because it removed eligible paid workers from the agricultural labor pool. Outwardly, at least, their position paralleled

---

rican religion, in particular the African notion of the eradication of evil, that were imported into Christianity. Gray tentatively traces the point of this importation to be the influence that an Afro-Brazilian priest named Lourenço da Silva had on the Roman Curia in the late seventeenth century. Gray says there is a direct line of development between those early abolitionist ideas and contemporary black theology (p. 7).

78. For the first comprehensive statement of the Mission's official position on slavery, see "Instruction zur Volziehung der die Sklavenfrage betreffenden Paragraphen der Gemeinde-Ordnung" (BMA D-9,1c,11c, 1861; also appears as Q-9,25,2c).

that of the Mission leadership.[79] Missionaries, however, were sufficiently alert to expectations of quantitatively measurable evangelical "success" that they worried about the number of persons, slave or free, who could be counted as members of the Mission community in Africa. To exclude everyone who had any connection with the domestic form of slavery could have a drastic effect in this regard. Schlatter cites the following revealing demographic breakdown of Africans in the Basel Mission community on the Gold Coast in 1861:

- Twelve African employees of the Mission were Christians but also slave-holders.
- Eleven other slaveholders were in practical terms part of the Mission community.
- Thirty-three Christian slaves had Christian masters.
- Two hundred nine heathen slaves had Christian masters.
- Five Christian slaves had heathen masters.[80]

Complete and immediate adherence to the Committee's hard position on slavery would have decimated the African community surrounding the Mission.

Other missionaries expressed views on slavery similar to those of Zimmermann, but his special threat to the organization on this issue really lay in his energy, his repeatedly demonstrated intellectual independence, and the unusual strength and persuasiveness of his views on this matter. This issue gradually escalated into the first direct *collective* questioning of the wisdom and hegemony of the Committee; at one point over half the missionaries had come around to Zimmermann's position. It was not without reason that the Committee saw him as the instigator of a frontal challenge to Mission authority.[81]

To guard against further displays of this obstinacy and to temper his threat to conformity in the organization, the Committee attempted to "resocialize" Zimmermann. By now, after all, he had openly flouted three mainstays of Mission discipline: first, the marriage rules in general and the

79. The alliance between Mission and planters on this issue was not deep. The Mission also opposed European-owned commercial plantations because they made proletarians of Africans and took them out of the orbit of the Mission community. See Gründer, *Christliche Mission und Deutscher Imperialismus* and "Die Basler Mission und die Land- und Arbeiterfrage am Kamerunberg"; Hallden, *Culture Policy*. See also Miller, "Missions, Social Change."

80. Schlatter, *Geschichte der Basler Mission*, 3:77ff.

81. Vogelsanger, *Pietismus und Afrikanische Kultur*, p. 120; Schlatter, *Geschichte der Basler Mission*, 3:81-82.

specific ban on intimate relations with Africans; second, the rules for hierarchical separation between Europeans and Africans; and third, the prohibition of attachments to all forms of slavery for all members of the Mission community. In the end the Committee's position on slavery prevailed,[82] and Zimmermann was called back to Basel in 1862 to be retrained in the norms of the Mission and recommitted to European values.[83] Unlike Riis and Süss, however, he was not dismissed or pressed to leave the Mission, and he went back to the Gold Coast and finished his career in the Mission in good repute. Eventually he was even able to break down the Committee's opposition to his marriage to the extent that his children were allowed to come to Basel for their educations, and Zimmermann himself, accompanied by his wife, was able to return to Germany in 1872, then retire there when his work in the Mission was done (see plate 24). The *Brüderverzeichnis* records that after his death in 1876 Catherine Zimmermann returned to Africa, where she died in 1891.

Although he won concessions for himself, Zimmermann's direct challenge to Mission policies did not expand the range of acceptable responses for others who disagreed with this or that part of the official line. Missionaries after Zimmermann who proposed marriages with Africans met more determined resistance than he had faced. I have found evidence of only three other interracial marriages in the nineteenth century, involving the missionaries Hermann Rottmann and Robert Spengler and an unordained *Handelsbruder* (a religiously trained tradesman in the employ of the Mission) named Jakob Isliker. Rottmann's bride was the mixed-race daughter of a Danish colonial official. His union, which took place in 1857, six years after that of Zimmermann, was accepted by the Committee with reluctance and he was not dismissed.[84] Nineteen years later, Spengler married the mixed-race daughter of Zimmermann and Mulgrave. He was pressed to "accept dismissal," but after he complied he was kept on as a contract employee and allowed to participate much as before in the life of the Mission community.[85] Isliker was summarily dismissed in 1887, even though he invoked the precedents set earlier by Zimmermann, Rottmann, and Spengler to justify his action.[86] It is of interest that

82. This episode over slavery is a clear example of what Wood (*Leadership in Voluntary Organizations*, pp. 11ff.) has called "organizational transcendence," i.e., the implementation of official objectives that run counter to the opinions of the ordinary members.

83. Schlatter, *Geschichte der Basler Mission*, 3:82.

84. See Rottmann's personal file (PF446) and *KP* 28, March 4, 1857, p. 35.

85. Spengler (*Brüderverzeichnis* 917) was discussed at length in *KP* 47, 1876, paras. 184, 289, 346, 377, and 645.

86. The details of Isliker's dismissal in 1887 are in his personal file, PF1142, and in *KP* 58, paras. 700 and 716.

his marriage, unlike all those before him, involved an alliance with a "simple village girl," and therefore was considered outside the range of compromise. He was not even allowed to be married in church.

Strategic Deviance in Perspective: Uncertainty, Charisma, and Nonconformity

The Mission careers of Riis, Süss, and Zimmermann say something important about how organizations absorb energy from the devotion of extraordinary individuals and about the risks that are involved when those individuals follow their own inspiration. Two theoretical points in particular call for elaboration, both having to do with the concept of charisma. Following common usage, I will use *institutional charisma* to refer to the claim to divine inspiration by the Mission leadership and *personal charisma* to describe the challenging behavior of the three "strategic deviants" in the field. The first point in need of discussion is the dialectical relationship between these two forms of charisma. The second concerns the way expressions of personal charisma were bound up with acts of individual rule breaking.

Ordinarily the loss of initiative and flexibility caused by the suppression of individuality would be viewed as "dysfunctional," but where an inordinately high priority is given to uniformity, the connection between strict organizational control and individual restraint is a vital principle that, far from being "corrected," needs to be safeguarded and put to effective use. In the Mission the stress on precisely this principle was legitimated by appeals to institutional charisma: in matters of governance the will of God was expressed only through the directives that issued from the divinely approved Committee. In situations of turbulence and uncertainty, however, measures taken to contain personal agency in furtherance of that principle could effectively block forward movement toward the accomplishment of organizational goals. The strategic deviants who through their personal initiative restored movement performed a function that was both necessary and potentially dangerous. Put simply, their individual charisma posed a direct challenge to the institutionalized charisma claimed by the leadership.

Charisma is often used interchangeably with persuasiveness and venerability, which in turn produce respect or adoration. An equally important dimension is audacity, by which I mean the willingness to bring definition to formless surroundings. This is often the key to worldly effectiveness. Abstractly, persuasiveness and venerability may be correlated with audacity; Andreas Riis and Simon Süss indicate, however, that the two sets of traits can be separated in reality. If we believe the letters that moved between West Africa and Basel, Riis in particular was not adored, and for many he was certainly not to be respected, but his audacity embodied many of the familiar traits of the classic charismatic character. He was an effective rule-breaker who moved forward resolutely in a time of uncertainty and inaction; he provided definition and exercised strong personal agency in the face of powerful normative and structural constraints.[87] He carried others along with him by the force of his energy, accomplishments, and ruthlessness, and not by the attractiveness of his person in the eyes of the other missionaries, West Indian repatriates, or African converts. His influence was exercised in spite of the fact that he alienated his fellow missionaries and came to be despised by the black Christians whose lives he often dominated. For their part, the leaders in Basel did not intend for such a person to become so critical to the Mission's programs, but they took advantage of his entrepreneur's energy and his willingness to confront potent external interests such as contending tribal groups and competing colonial powers on the Gold Coast. Because of this, Riis's idiosyncratic Pietist vision came to rival directly their own claims to revealed Pietist wisdom. His deviant personal charisma, in other words, challenged the Committee's authoritative institutional charisma, and his unacceptable disobedience was only thinly separated from his useful creativity.[88] Unlike the Committee, Riis was in the thick of the action in the field. The Committee was confronted with his exploits only at a great distance, both temporally and spatially. Their options were reduced to disowning him or trying to harness his energy for the organization. That he served on the Gold Coast for twelve years before being brought up short is an index of the mastery he achieved over the definition of his own role. Since the Committee controlled the organizational record, however, they could and must hold close the knowledge of what he had actually done in Africa and present a story for the Mission's European supporters that acknowledged neither his destructive actions nor the challenge he represented to their own hegemony. Because they were able to do this, the challenge to internal control was not compounded by a loss of control over the Mission's public face, and Riis's disobedience did not directly jeopardize the flow of funds and moral support in Europe. In the end, the Committee decided to remove Riis when the practical balance of his actions in Africa — the destructive versus the productive — tipped decisively to the

87. The elements of this definition of charisma are common to Max Weber (*Economy and Society,* vol. 2, chap. 14); Alan Dawe ("Theories of Social Action"); Michael Reed ("Problem of Human Agency"); and Gareth Morgan (*Images of Organization,* pp. 66ff.).

88. See Katz, "Deviance, Charisma," on the fine line that separates deviance from creativity.

negative side. They were only driven to do this when the critical mass of other missionaries on the Gold Coast had grown sufficiently large, first, to force the issue by their collective complaints about Riis and, second, to ensure the survival of the enterprise without him.

Süss and Zimmermann also had volatile relationships with the Mission, and they resembled Riis in their ability to avoid severe sanctions for their nonconformity until the balance between their contributions and their liabilities moved clearly in the wrong direction. But beyond these similarities the three men were very different. Süss removed himself from the company of other missionaries and pursued a solitary vision. Zimmermann was recognized in Basel for the respect he earned from his colleagues as well as for the threat represented by his ability to sway other, less dynamic missionaries to his own point of view; he was the only one of the three who combined the two sides of charisma, persuasion and audacity. It is interesting that he was also the only one of the three who survived in good standing in the Mission.

It would be wrong to conclude from the leaders' awareness and toleration of these three men that they were indifferent to disobedience or powerless to exercise control when they were challenged. After all, Riis and Süss were dismissed in the end. A number of other agents who caused even minor trouble without also making striking contributions to the Mission's objectives were simply fired, often summarily and almost always irrevocably, and sometimes disappeared practically without a trace from the Mission's records. For some, such a decision was reached within days of their arrival in Africa, so that they only touched African soil and then were carried immediately back to Europe in disgrace. Paradoxically, in this Pietist community small and quiet transgressions could lead to such immediate expulsion, while large and sometimes loud offenses could be, indeed must be, tolerated until the last measure of fugitive organizational benefit was extracted from them.

Through it all the official structure of discipline that depressed creativity among the rank and file was never relaxed, and the language in which that discipline was taught to the seminarians was not tempered. Strictness, imperative distance from native culture, and only selective awareness of the larger organizational picture continued to be integral to the training of the missionaries. When Inspector Wilhelm Hoffmann looked back on his own years of leadership between 1839 and 1850, he acknowledged the damaging effects of the structure he had helped to build: "It is undeniable that the seminary life with its constrained education and paternalism is not particularly favorable for the education of practical personalities, who suddenly have to leave a situation that is circumscribed and supervised from all sides and go into the most unconstrained life of an occupation that has so many arbitrary elements as missionary work."[89] Despite Hoffmann's insight, his successor, Joseph Josenhans, took it upon himself to tighten the regime still further. It was he, after all, who insisted that the initiative had to be entirely "smashed out" of the seminarians before they could be depended on to carry forward the programs of the organization.[90] Schlatter had this to say about the regime that resulted from Josenhans's attitude:

> Naturally, hardly a thought was given to individuality, and elements of the fortress [in the structure of the Mission] could not be avoided, [a fact that] gave concern to many friends of the Mission. But the preservation of the peace of the Mission House demanded that every inhabitant know his position exactly, and the yearlong subordination under a strict, all-encompassing order was valuable for the socialization of a dependable, well-disciplined fighting squad for the mission war. . . . It was not, to be sure, conducive to geniality, and a lot of good things were damaged by the strongly pronounced peculiarity [of the place]. But who could offer a better solution for the severe problems [the organization faced]?[91]

Surveillance and the Erosion of Solidarity

The contrast between the inhibition of the many and the impatient eccentricity of the few was not the only trouble the Mission faced because of the way it provided for social control. Its "solution" was not conducive to geniality, as the passage just cited indicates, but that, too, could be sacrificed to larger Pietist values. The "mutual watchfulness" woven into the social relations among the missionaries both presumed and created interpersonal estrangement. In the field the bitterness this caused sometimes made it impossible for the missionaries to work together productively and caused recurrent injury to the organization. This second organizational dilemma, like the first one to which it was closely tied, was widespread throughout the Mission's overseas operations. It was apparent in the Gold Coast project from the beginning to the end of the period of this study. I will draw upon the cases of two missionaries, Johannes Henke and Friedrich Schiedt, to illustrate the forms it took and the consequences it had.

89. W. Hoffmann, *Eilf Jahre in der Mission*, p. 78.
90. Hesse, *Joseph Josenhans*, pp. 212ff. See also Vogelsanger, *Pietismus und Afrikanische Kultur*, pp. 58-59.
91. Schlatter, *Geschichte der Basler Mission*, 3:243-44.

Johannes Henke

Henke was one of four missionaries in the first contingent sent to the Gold Coast in 1828. These men were embroiled in contention from the moment they left Basel, traveling first to Denmark for further training and official ordination before boarding a ship for the Gold Coast. Henke had been marked for attention by the "mutual watchfulness" of his fellow seminarians long before he was selected for service in Africa. His personal file and the Committee's minutes contain frequent references to the complaints his colleagues carried to their teachers, who in turn reported them to the Committee.[92] At different times he was suspected of theft, was thought to have an "unacceptably favorable attitude" toward Catholicism, and was accused of not participating fully in the Christian fellowship that should prevail in the Mission House. Serious thought was given to expelling him without giving him an overseas assignment, but because of a shortage of agents the Committee members decided instead to assign him to the new project they had in mind for the Gold Coast.

From intermediate points along the journey to Africa, a number of letters about Henke's comportment were posted to the Committee by his three co-workers and others he met on the way. The questions these letters raised about his character, his spirituality, and his competency show that mutual surveillance was as active and as divisive outside the seminary as it had been in Basel.[93] Soon after the four missionaries arrived in Africa, all of them fell victim to tropical illnesses, and in this situation their animosities further drained their failing energies. Inspector Blumhardt read their letters and described their quarreling to the Committee as "divisive arrogance, patronizing self-aggrandizement, masochistic severity, and childish gossiping."[94] Within

92. Key discussions appear in *KP* 10 in the minutes for September 13 (p. 74) and 20 (p. 76), 1826. Henke's personal file is PF55.

93. These letters, labeled "Briefe der Brüder Cappeler, Henke, Holzwarth, Riis, Salbach, J. G. Schmid," are in BMA D-10,3,2. For the Committee's discussion of the letters, see the minutes in *KP* 11 for August 29, 1827, p. 4; March 12, 1828, pp. 46-47; and April 9, 1828, p. 51.

94. This passage is quoted in Vogelsanger, *Pietismus und Afrikanische Kultur,* p. 57. In German, Blumhardt's words were "splitterrichterlicher Hochmut, bevormundende Eigenmächtigkeit, verdammungssüchtige Härte und kindische Klatschgeist." Vogelsanger follows the quotation with this perceptive comment: "The fact that complaining and arguing with colleagues, suspicions, criticisms, and gossip were reported faithfully over the ocean to the Inspector shines a light not only on the pitiful isolation and loneliness of the missionaries in the tropics, but also on the powerful position which the Inspector claimed in their existence."

months three of the men had died. Henke was the survivor, and he continued to write to Basel complaining of what he found when he searched through his colleagues' effects after their deaths. In a private diary, one of his companions (Johann Gottlieb Schmid) had confessed his "honest hatred" for Henke, of his own refusal even to pray with him, and the wretchedness he felt as a result of this violation of Christian fellowship.[95] When Henke found this remark, he said to the Committee: "I was always aware of [Schmid's] hostile attitudes toward me, as well as his hypocritical and dishonest nature; for this reason I could never stand him and it was necessary for me to bring this and his deficiency in character to his attention. . . . What do you think, Dearest Inspector, about these admissions [in Schmid's papers]? Are you still inclined to seek in me the causes for our alienated existence?"[96]

Despite the extensive discussions such revelations provoked in the meetings of the Committee, little of the turmoil that engulfed Henke and his coworkers was revealed to the seminarians in Basel or to the Mission's supporters in Europe. This protective insularity also characterized the second case, that of Friedrich Schiedt, whose even more convoluted troubles caused him to be the first Gold Coast missionary to be formally "defrocked" and expelled from the Mission.

Friedrich Schiedt

The events leading to Schiedt's expulsion took place in the late 1840s, but they are connected by a long thread of events to Henke's troubles twenty years earlier. Schiedt's difficulties in some ways form an interesting postscript to Henke's story. In broad outline the situation was as follows: over twenty years after Henke's death, Schiedt was caught up in the defense of the Mission teacher Georg Thompson, the Basel-educated African referred to earlier, who was facing dismissal for alcohol abuse and sexual transgressions that had been reported to superiors by his coworkers. In the course of the Thompson affair (itself a bitter episode traceable to the policy of mutual watching), Schiedt wrote a letter to Basel in which he repeated a rumor that Henke had kept a native mistress.[97] Again mutual watchfulness extended beyond the grave. Schiedt's hope was that Thompson would be spared the banishment

95. The diary is in Schmid's personal file (PF64) in the Mission archive.
96. These remarks are taken from a copy of the letter that survives in Henke's personal file (PF55). Much the same remark was also written by him in the margins of Schmid's diary.
97. The archive provides no corroborating evidence of this rumor.

and humiliation the Committee intended for him if it became known that European missionaries, too, fell prey to temptation in Africa. Privately the Committee expressed dismay over Schiedt's charge about Henke and wondered about the truth of it, but went ahead with Thompson's punishment without any outward acknowledgment of the additional accusation. Missionaries were, of course, vulnerable to rumors that questioned their unblemished moral character, and Schiedt was hardly a disinterested observer. His accusations are certainly revealing about interpersonal conflict, but in the absence of corroborating documentation they must be regarded cautiously.[98]

Adding another layer to the story, Schiedt himself was soon to come under suspicion for moral lapses that were alleged to his superiors in the field by *his* colleagues. A panel of senior missionaries looked into his behavior and transmitted a long list of charges against him to Basel.[99] Included were accusations of mismanagement of Mission property, associating with a "debauched" chaplain in the Danish settlement in Christiansborg, refusing legitimate orders from his superiors, and misappropriating the mail of his fellow missionaries, thus interfering with the lines of communication between the Committee and the field. Inadequate proof was produced for some of these charges, and the Committee considered others to be insufficiently grave to warrant dismissal. Yet the accusations from Schiedt's peers continued, and in time their accumulated weight was sufficient to bring his Mission career to an end. Their letters formed a grim litany: he used crude language; he was loud, insufficiently pious, ambitious, unkind, egotistical, dishonest, and unpunctual; he spread rumors about his coworkers, did not preach as often as the

98. Schiedt's letter (D-1,2, Akropong and Ussu, no. 13, December 13, 1846) about Henke's transgression included a similar charge about Andreas Riis. Before his marriage, Schiedt alleged, Riis, too, had "kept" an African woman with whom he had an illegitimate daughter, whose facial features, Schiedt said, were very much like those of Riis (*"völlig Riisisch"*). The letter was discussed by the Committee on March 24, 1847 (*KP* 19, pp. 107ff.): "Had we known about the behavior of Henke and Riis, we would have dismissed them" (p. 110). The index entry for "Riis" in that volume of the *Komiteeprotokol* refers to the *böse Gerüchte* (evil rumors) regarding him, a choice of language that hints that the Committee might have factored a measure of skepticism into its assessment of Schiedt's accusations.

99. D-1,2, Akropong, no. 17, which is the report of a conference held on June 28 and 29 and December 4, 1848. See also D-1,2, Akropong, no. 23a, dated December 4, 1848, which summarizes that report for the Committee. Individual complaints about Schiedt are found in letters from Widmann (D-1,2, no. 18, Akropong, July 6, 1848); Stanger and Meischel (D-1,2, no. 1, February 23, 1848); and Stanger (no. 15, February 25, 1848; D-1,3, May 2, 1850). The final judgment of his coworkers came in 1850, when the report of a conference in Ussu attended by Stanger, Dieterle, and Zimmermann concluded: "[W]e have to tell you ... that Schiedt must be dismissed!" This report appears in D-1,3, no. 13, October 7, 1850.

others, and threatened to become a Methodist (the Wesleyans had a parallel mission on the Gold Coast). Perhaps most telling, he was overheard expressing disrespect for the wisdom of the leadership, a direct affront to that legitimating charismatic pillar of the Committee's authority. The panel report concluded that he was a man guilty of "unbearable scoundelry, stubborn hostility, lying, and open betrayal" and opined that "[t]here at home [in Basel] one could not conceive of how far such people can go here [in Africa] once they abandon the way of the Lord and all honesty."[100]

At the same time that these complaints were making their way to Basel, Schiedt was relating equally bitter tales to the Committee about his accusers. He succeeded in undermining the careers of several of them.[101] Deep factions formed among the missionaries, and for two years the Committee's attention was consumed by the repercussions of their squabbling. The disciplinary panel on the Gold Coast that judged Schiedt finally packed him off to Basel to answer some twenty-five formal accusations that had been lodged against him. After a long investigation and interrogation, remarkable for its attention to formal process and legalistic detail,[102] he was dismissed and exiled, in effect, to America,[103] where he later found a position as a minister to several German-speaking Lutheran congregations.[104] Measured in demoralization, lost energy, and sacrificed resources, the effects of this interlude on the Mission were great. The storm around Schiedt embroiled every missionary then present on the Gold Coast and threatened the Mission's credibility in the eyes of the Africans who were by then within its circle of influence; Schiedt's allegations about Henke tarnished the Mission's collective memory of its earliest volunteers to the Gold Coast; both Schiedt and Georg Thompson, the man he defended, were expelled in disgrace; Andreas Riis, whose case I have already discussed, was also caught up in the events surrounding Schiedt, and this was one of many factors in his ultimate dismissal;[105] finally, two missionaries who were exhausted and depressed by the endless controversy simply resigned. One of them, Hermann Halleur, complained in a letter to his family that he had to leave the Mission "to save my own soul," and asked pointedly, "Is this the way we follow the law of brotherly love?"[106] It must not be overlooked

100. Excerpted from D-1,2, Akropong, no. 23a of December 4, 1848.
101. D-1,2, Christiansborg, no. 25, November 10, 1847, and no. 26, November 12, 1847.
102. *KP* 20, June 9, 1849, pp. 210-12; June 13, 1849, pp. 214-15; and June 20, 1849, p. 216.
103. *KP* 21, October 3, 1849, pp. 31-32.
104. *KP* 21, March 20, 1850, p. 125.
105. For years Riis had been the chief nemesis of Georg Thompson, whose defense by Schiedt seemed to be the trigger for many of Riis's troubles.
106. Halleur to the inspector, November 1, 1843 (D-1,2, 1842-1848, no. 10). See also D-

that each person lost to the Mission in this episode, whether by expulsion or resignation, represented a loss of five years of formal training and often of several years of hard-gained experience. These details show the impressive human and organizational price that was exacted when interpersonal support and trust were outweighed by the demand for mutual surveillance.

Despite its cost to the organization, the Mission never abandoned the policy of mutual watchfulness, any more than it gave up the emphasis on humility and conformity that gave rise to the complications associated with Riis, Süss, and Zimmermann. Both the damage caused by peer surveillance and the complications caused by strategic deviants were equally visible in the Mission's outposts in India and elsewhere. And according to Haas-Lill,[107] mutual watching and interpersonal estrangement eroded the sense of community among the women in the service of the Mission just as relentlessly as it did the fellowship among the men. Such a striking organizational ability to tolerate long-term social pain calls for careful explanation.

1,2, no. 4, April 31, 1844. In a letter written to his brother (D-1,2, no. 4, April 31, 1844), Halleur asked, "Is this the way we live according to Psalm 133?" (which reads, "How good it is and how pleasant / for brothers to live together in harmony"). See also Halleur's personal file (PF283) for letters to the Committee in 1844 (no month or day given) and to the inspector from Dobberan, August 13, 1845.

107. Haas-Lill, "Missionsgeschichte aus der Sicht der Frau," p. 24.

CHAPTER 5

Accounting for Organizational Persistence

Throughout this research, as I have sought to judge the balance between the Basel Mission's resources and its vulnerabilities, my curiosity has always come back to the simple fact of the organization's extraordinary persistence. The Deutsche Christentumsgesellschaft first met in Basel in 1780; the Mission itself was formed in 1815; and it has been more than 170 years since the first four Basel-trained missionaries went out to Ghana in 1828. For an observer present at any of those critical junctures, a confident prediction of endurance for the organization would have been hard to justify. How is it, then, that the Mission's members were able to bear the burdens that came with their work, and how is it that the organization was not pulled apart, either by the difficulties it faced in the field or by the troubles it brought upon itself because of the internal policies it chose to follow? In the earlier chapters I described how the preservation of Pietist beliefs often took priority over timely pragmatism and even over organizational peace. In complex chains of cause and effect, policies that the leadership regarded as religiously necessary caused inaction as well as protracted alienation and personal distress for many of the ordinary participants. As other researchers have often shown, the oral and written histories of the Christian missionary movement contain many stories of divisive interpersonal bickering of the sort I have described, even to the point of bitter estrangement among people who are passionately devoted to the same cause. Every mission also seems to have a stock of dramatic stories about creative moral entrepreneurs and troublesome eccentrics of both sexes. Often the same characters who populate the list of celebrated "mission heroes" also inhabit the much less publicized stories of "things gone awry" and "controversies overcome." In this respect the experiences of the Basel Mission, distinctive as it is in important respects, converge with those of many other missionary organizations.

It would be a mistake, of course, to extend an explanation of events in any one mission too readily or too literally to other missions. Writing as a sociologist, however, and not as a missiologist or historian, I would insist that it is equally mistaken not to be alert to commonalities that might help us account for the experiences of the larger category of missionary organizations. After all, missions in general, not just those of a Pietist persuasion, are both defined by their strongly held consensual values and bedeviled by the task of translating those values into coherent practice on the ground. How the Basel Mission confronted that task and managed to persist through time invites comparisons and suggests provocative questions for understanding the survival or demise of other organizations pursuing similar goals. In the Basel case, I submit, the key to survival was embedded in a process that at first appears hopelessly paradoxical. Authoritarian discipline and creative flexibility were often in a state of tension with each other, as were mutual watching and brotherly solidarity, but the organization could absorb those stresses — which really means it could persuade its members to "endure them patiently" — by wrapping them in a powerful and stable set of shared fundamental understandings and values. This is a complicated proposition that warrants more discussion. How far it can be generalized beyond the Basel experience is for students of other missions and similarly "value-drenched" organizations to determine.

Institutionalized Contradictions

"Contradiction," in the technical sense in which sociologists use this term, is the right word to describe the way the Committee's devotion to conformity and obedience led to a reliance on idiosyncratic and disobedient members to move the objectives of the Mission forward, even when those strong personalities at the same time threatened to undermine the authority of the center. In understanding how the leaders reached that awkward pass, it is not necessary to assume that conformists among the rank and file were always ineffectual and without imagination or that nonconformists were always creative, daring, and disruptive. To the contrary, there were compliant and uncontroversial missionaries with substantial accomplishments to their credit, just as there were "willful" members whose noncompliance took quite banal forms. Nevertheless, at several critical junctures in the history of the organization the leadership tolerated unbidden personal initiative because doing so pushed inertia aside and produced much-needed gains for the Mission. In those cases it had to be evident to the members of the Committee that the forces released by such initiative could spin off in threatening as well as useful directions. Riis, Süss, and Zimmermann, the three "strategic deviants" whose unexpected and zealous actions I have described at length, all illustrated that proposition.

"Contradiction" also describes the way mutual watching worked against supportive solidarity among the ordinary missionaries. Simple amity among the members was not always destroyed by the sort of complaining that isolated Johannes Henke from his coworkers or the sort of interpersonal acrimony that precipitated the dismissal of Friedrich Schiedt and others; firm friendships and cooperation survived and contributed vitally to the Mission's accomplishments.[1] But again, the weekly Committee records show that deep-seated hostilities tied to the policy of mutual surveillance occupied the attention of the leadership repeatedly over the years. Despite that record of turmoil, the policy of mutual watching was regularly reaffirmed throughout the period I have examined and well beyond it.

The Committee deliberated over those troubles privately and at length, and that fact alone provides strong clues about their hierarchy of values as well as the moral calculus that guided their management of zeal in the Mission. After all, there are problems in organizations that arise inadvertently and unforeseen, and there are those that, although in a strict sense unintended, are nevertheless expected and absorbed over long periods. It might be said of the latter that they are "discounted" in the interest of some higher value. The tribulations that were tangled up in the Mission's social control policies clearly fall into the latter category. To a great extent the problems that emerged in the Mission House and in Ghana were anticipated, and they had causes and consequences that were recognized by those in a position to shape organizational policy. Assessing the extent of this administrative anticipation and the clarity of this administrative recognition is one way to calibrate the strength of the organization's investment in its core values and policies. Three episodes provide a rough sort of gauge for this assessment.

The first episode involves a visit to Basel by William Jowett, a representative of the powerful London-based Church Missionary Society (CMS). Jowett's visit took place in October of 1829, a little less than a year after the mission's outreach to the Gold Coast began. He had been a CMS missionary

---

1. A good reference point here is Friedli Heinecken's autobiographical account of his life in the Mission toward the end of the nineteenth century: "When Grandfather Was a Young Man; or, A Missionary in the Making." Instances of conflict and controversy are not missing from his account, but he testifies persuasively to the friendship and cooperation he found there.

abroad and was now a central figure in the training and counseling of that organization's overseas agents. Jowett asked the Basel Mission's Inspector Blumhardt why so much emphasis was placed on "mutual watchfulness" when the unhappy effect of that practice on simple fellowship among the missionaries was so apparent. It will be recalled that the leaders of the CMS had good reason to be concerned about this policy because for several years they had contracted with the Basel seminary to train many of their own missionaries.[2] They were impressed by the toughness of these men but at the same time disturbed by the hostility they often displayed toward each other, which sometimes undermined their effectiveness as CMS missionaries. Here is what Jowett reported to London about his conversation with Blumhardt, in which he indicated to the inspector what he thought was the source of many of these difficulties:

> I noticed to [the inspector] an evil which I had seen result from the close intercourse to which [the seminarians] are subjected during the five years [in the Mission House]. They consequently acquire such an intimate knowledge of each other's tempers, habits, errors, and infirmities that when they meet together at the same Missionary station, they remember the disagreements of their younger days, and are in some danger of not sufficiently respecting one another. . . . This evil I have seen in operation among some of the [Basel-trained missionaries in the service of the CMS].

About the inspector's response, he continued,

> [T]here is only this answer [from the inspector]; that the evil [of estrangement and conflict] may happen, but that the benefit of mutual watching and reproof is too great to be foregone; through fear of this, however probable an evil, we must look also to the probability of confirmed Christian friendships being thus formed amongst some by the opportunity of earlier Christian intimacy. And for the evil itself, they must all be taught to anticipate its occurrence, and meet it with "Bear ye one another's burdens; and so fulfill the law of Christ."[3]

2. See Jenkins, "Church Missionary Society."

3. The reference for this document (which is in English) in the CMS archive in London is G/AC, 18/1, 1820-1834, 476ff. Jowett's visit took place between October 1 and November 1, 1829, and his report was received in the London headquarters of the CMS on January 8, 1830.

This was one of several such expressions of concern from the CMS. It is significant that such an open exchange about the unfortunate side effects of mutual watching took place at roughly the same time that the leadership in Basel was discussing privately the quarrels among the first four men sent to Ghana, namely, Johannes Henke and his colleagues. The problem and its consequences were very much in their consciousness. Yet, notwithstanding the risk of losing the more powerful organization's recognition, material support, and assistance in gaining entry to otherwise inaccessible mission fields (such as India), the inspector was not moved to alter Mission policy in any significant way or even to temporize about it in order to allay the misgivings of his English colleagues. In short, there can be no doubt about either the inspector's (and Committee's) awareness of the problem and its source or his determination to preserve the policy despite the troubles it caused.

Criticisms that originated closer to home provide the other two examples of the leadership's awareness of the consequences of Mission policies. In his history of the Mission, Schlatter recounts a dispute in the 1830s between the Committee and a prominent Basel University theologian named Tobias Beck.[4] Beck had been a strong contributor to the educational program of the seminary, but had gradually become disaffected. He took the Mission leadership repeatedly to task for its attempts to eliminate all forms of resistance to its policies and for stigmatizing as "unpious" any behavior that deviated from official doctrine. He was a strong advocate of mission evangelism and praised the seminarians for their industry, devotion, and courage. Yet he was increasingly sharp in his criticism of the system of discipline because he believed it left the missionaries almost no room for independent judgment, intellectual curiosity, or brotherly fellowship. Increasingly, Beck carried his criticisms into the public arena, subjecting the Mission's policies to just the kind of exposure among its supporters and potential supporters that the organization was determined to avoid. His importance to the Mission was well recognized; the records show that the organization did not want to lose his support or the imprimatur of his affiliation with the university. His objections were subjected to close discussion in the weekly executive meetings, but in the end his complaints led to no fundamental changes in policy. Seeing this, Beck eventually severed all ties with the Mission, and when he did so several students, influenced by his arguments, resigned from the seminary. He remained a vocal critic for years to come.

At about the same time as the disagreement with Beck, a seminarian in the Mission House named Christian Forchhammer was threatened with dis-

4. Schlatter, *Geschichte der Basler Mission*, 1:122ff.

missal for criticizing the atmosphere created by mutual watching.[5] Forchhammer insisted that a seminarian could be justified in refusing to give in to the "narrow, pious spirit"[6] that he said called for "unconditional and abject submission to [merely] human views and orders."[7] The constant mutual judging among the seminarians often proceeded without love and understanding, he believed, while at the same time truly open and honest souls suffered under the accusation of pride *(Hochmut)* and were likely to be seen as being "of an insubordinate demeanor" *(von ungebrochenem Sinn)* if they raised the slightest objection to Mission policies. Like the disagreement with Beck, Forchhammer's dissent was extensively but privately discussed by the Committee, but again produced no significant change in the regime of mutual watching.

In short, the demands of organizational discipline and the distress of interpersonal alienation were often related to each other as cause to effect. As we saw in chapter 4, these unsettling connections were certainly evident to the missionaries in the field, who had to deal with the consequences in their daily work. The examples just cited also reveal that these quandaries were equally evident to influential outsiders and seminarians in the Mission House. Whenever questions were raised about these troubles, there were Committee discussions about how to explain the policies, how to reaffirm their necessity, and how to overcome resistance to them, but I found little evidence of discussions aimed at altering them. From these and similar responses over the years, it is evident that those who guided the Mission calculated the costs of these practices against their gains and were not driven to

---

5. Forchhammer's remarks and the ensuing discussion of this incident by the Committee are preserved in Basel Mission Archive (BMA) *Komiteeprotokolle* (Committee Minutes; hereafter *KP*) 14, March 20, 1839, pp. 137-38, and April 4, 1839, p. 139. A young man named Schifterling, employed as a gardener, spoke out in agreement with Forchhammer's criticism of the discipline that prevailed in the Mission House and lost his job as a result. Forchhammer's complaint about life in the seminary was matched by expressions of distress by missionaries in the field. In chapter 4, I referred to the missionary Halleur's revelations about interpersonal strife among his fellows and his decision to leave the Mission. See Halleur to the inspector, November 1, 1843 (D-1,2, 1842-1848, no. 10; see also D-1,2, no. 4, April 31, 1844).

6. In German the phrase was "sich jenem engherzigen, frömmelnden Geiste [nicht] zu unterwerfen."

7. In his words, "unbedingtes und willenloses Schmiegen unter menschlichen Ansichten und Gebote." I have appended "merely" to the word "human" because Forchhammer's point clearly was that the narrow, pious spirit he observed did not have a divine origin. That opinion was what made his challenge to the Committee such a fundamental one.

adopt fundamental structural change in order to avoid the stress that these troublesome dilemmas caused for the organization. Inspector Josenhans's call for the smashing of any resistance to discipline, which I have cited several times, makes this point with special force.[8]

This harsh policy demanded considerable forbearance from the missionaries over a long period of time. In fact, the zone of what they could tolerate emotionally and ideologically was quite broad, broad enough, it turns out, to encompass the contradictions they had to deal with in their work. As Inspector Blumhardt explained it, the missionaries had to be taught to anticipate the "evils" of mutual watching, and they had to be ready to bear those difficulties as a matter of their Christian duty. To express the same idea in sociological terms, the contradictions in the Mission were "institutionalized," by which I mean that they (1) emerged from deliberate and calculated decisions; (2) were attached to a predictable set of policies and practices; and (3) were wrapped in an effective religious explanation that made them tolerable to the rank and file. But when sociologists theorize about irreconcilable contradictions, they usually expect them to produce conflict between groups that are widely separated in power (conflict, in the usual case, between the group that imposes and derives benefit from a practice and the group whose activities are shaped and whose interests are circumscribed by the practice), and that confrontation in turn is expected either to pull an organization apart or precipitate radical changes in its structure.[9] In this view, to speak of "institutionalized contradiction" as I have defined it here appears oxymoronic, almost nonsensical. But institutionalization of contradictory policies is exactly what happened in the Mission. The problems I have described did not precipitate a wholesale withdrawal of commitment by the ordinary members, nor did the visible costs of the organization's troubles trigger a fundamental restructuring of its more worrisome practices. This, I believe, may be the key to how ideologically or religiously motivated organizations — those driven forward by zeal — are able to survive difficulties that can destroy more instrumentally driven groups. They are by no means free of basic dilemmas just because they display a strong consensus on core values, and indeed the policies attached to those consensual values can exact a high price in interpersonal conflict among their members when they undermine the solidarity that would ordinarily unite them. But such predicaments, no matter how excruciating they sometimes are, do not necessarily form a fault line that will irrevocably separate the decision makers from the rank and file. The ability to tolerate the

8. Quoted by Hesse, *Joseph Josenhans,* pp. 212ff.
9. Dahrendorf, *Class and Class Conflict,* chap. 6; Benson, "Organizations."

strain of contradictory policies, in short, is perhaps the best single index of the strength of an organization's core philosophy.

Again in sociological terms, what this means is that the connection between organizational contradiction and significant structural change is contingent, not direct, and the most important contingency in the equation is the emotional centrality for individuals of shared core beliefs. Examining the force of those beliefs in the lives of the Mission's members suggests a two-part explanation for their remarkable perseverance. In the first place, the missionaries' *reasons* for enduring in a difficult course of action had to do with the all-important symbolism of the Mission's public identity as a Pietist organization. In the second place, their psychological *ability* to persevere, which is quite a different matter, was tied to the logic of moral responsibility in the organization; this logic, I will argue, insulated the decision makers from accountability for many of their decisions and at the same time provided the members with a kind of "social anesthesia" against the "social pain" that the Mission's troubles caused for them. I will address the question of Pietist identity first and then turn to the matter of Pietist logic.

Ordnung Muss Sein! Fulfilling the Law of Christ

The admonition "There must be order!" was deeply embedded in the Pietist identity of the Mission's participants. As I explained in chapter 3, their commitment to individual and collective discipline was a central feature of the Pietists' reputation among other missions of the time, and it was meant to be the cornerstone of the communities they set out to establish in West Africa. In other words, it was very high in their hierarchy of values. For the Committee, therefore, it would have been a betrayal of their calling in the deepest philosophical and theological sense if they had compromised this moral imperative by making visible changes in policy, simply in the interest of quick organizational expediency (to reassure the CMS, for example) or in order to achieve temporal harmony (among quarreling missionaries). Moreover, with the discipline taken away, much less that was *distinctively* Pietist would have remained, either to attract truly convicted missionaries, the authenticity of whose conversion was gauged to a significant degree by their acceptance of the Pietist concept of order, or to offer to the "heathens" abroad. In the Baslers' eyes the latter in particular were struggling in misery precisely because they lacked the redeeming social arrangements, above all discipline in family, vocation, and religion, that could be sustained only by internalizing the Christian view of (divine) law and (worldly) order.

Within their own protected circle, however, removed from public view, it was sometimes a different story. There the Committee often fashioned expedient private adjustments to trouble in the organization and then resolved to conceal the internal controversies that had necessitated those adjustments from the scrutiny of interested observers in Europe. This is precisely what they did in the three cases of strategic deviance I described. But it was unthinkable for the Committee to allow itself to be *seen* to be relaxing the official disciplinary regime *in order* to prevent trouble and controversy. Simply to replace mutual watching and central authority with other, less trying or less confining principles of governance, which they might have done if their rational bureaucratic instincts had prevailed, was just not an option. This was not because different ways of doing things were unknown to them; indeed, other prominent missions provided examples of less confining practices, as did organizations outside the evangelical movement, including in some cases their own business enterprises. Rather, faith in central authority, obedience, and alertness to the weaknesses of self and others were core values beyond question for the Pietists. These were not just instrumental means to an end, but were passionately embraced and relentlessly pursued for their own sakes.[10] Therefore, when it came to a choice, Pietist identity had to weigh more heavily than organizational peace or efficiency, however high the costs of this choice might be. As we have seen, the rules were preserved for the vast majority of the ordinary rank and file, even if it meant that the Mission would have to tolerate interpersonal hostility and personal alienation among the members and even if it made the organization dependent upon the unpredictable actions of nonconformists. It is an irony worth noting that, from time to time, deviation from the rules that occurred further down the moral stream (that is, out in the field, out of view of Mission supporters in Europe) was countenanced because it could be shielded from scrutiny and eventually reinterpreted in a favorable light for dissemination to the public. All of this was in the interest of preserving the appearance of moral orthodoxy closer to the Pietist source.

To rephrase this in Max Weber's terminology, when matters close to the Mission's moral core were involved, "instrumental rationality," the central feature of modern bureaucratic reasoning, had to yield to "value rationality," which is a more compelling imperative in traditional or charismatically driven undertakings.[11] The tenets of Pietist discipline had to be preserved

---

10. Fulbrook, *Piety and Politics*; Lehmann, *Pietismus und Weltliche Ordnung*; Troeltsch, *Social Teaching*, vol. 2.

11. Weber, *Economy and Society*, 1:24-25; see also Willer, "Weber's Missing Authority Type."

even at the cost of severe organizational troubles at the point where the actual work of the Mission was being carried out. It is useful to digress briefly and note that it is not just organizations built on religious or ideological zeal that continue with troublesome policies when the only alternative is to abandon their goals and their identity. Barry Staw and Jerry Ross offer an impressive catalogue of other reasons for organizations to display such persistence, including simple inertia, saving face, trying to protect "sunk costs," and being trapped by their own historical definition of themselves.[12] Most of the examples they give are taken from contemporary organizations involved in the secular marketplace of goods and services, but the likelihood of being pulled into this syndrome is particularly great, I submit, for organizations that are defined by their ideological commitment to a cause and carried forward by the emotional energy of their members. For the latter category of groups, and for religious ones especially, the subjective sense of organizational uniqueness and personal worth comes from the claim to "specialness," that is, from the sense that the organization exists in a moral space quite separate from, different from, and superior to that of mundane organizations engaged in the practicalities of ordinary life. For the Pietists this sense of specialness meant nothing less than a divine call to "save the heathen" by giving them a complete plan for personal and collective salvation. The inspiration of that plan and its practical outlines on the ground were the hallmarks that set the Mission and its members apart as morally different from the common run, even from other Protestant missions. When such badges of specialness are lost, the motivation of the members of an organization can be fatally undermined. This loss is most likely to happen at that delicate boundary between the insular inner world that can be controlled more or less as values dictate (for example, in the Committee, in the seminary, or within the immediate circle of missionaries) and the outer "real" world that can never be fully predicted or managed. It was at this critical boundary that the creative energies of Riis, Süss, and Zimmermann came into play, and it was there that the struggle to preserve evangelical momentum — attracting converts, building communities, dealing with the politics of a colonial setting — while preserving the outward marks of religious orthodoxy was most apparent.

This organizational struggle around religious identity is not at all peculiar to the Basel Mission. Helen Ebaugh has shown that some contemporary Western orders of Catholic nuns, quite remote from the Basel Mission in time, place, and religious philosophy, are mortally threatened in much the same way and reflect the quandary of lost uniqueness in a particularly sharp

12. Staw and Ross, "Behavior in Escalation Situations."

form.[13] In dealing with the redefinitions imposed on the Catholic world by Vatican II in the 1960s, she explains, some orders relinquished the marks of their separation from the larger society, such as their distinctive dress and their cloistered isolation, in order to be more effective in their dealings with the external world, only to find that they had undermined the resolution of those members who had been attracted to that very uniqueness. What does it mean to be a nun if one dresses, works, and lives much like those in the secular world? If the moral "capitulations to the world" that lead to such losses of identity for conservative insiders become visible to key conservative supporters outside an organization, the support of the latter group can be threatened as well. In the Mission, concern not to succumb to such "weaknesses" increased the Committee's resistance to compromise in the areas of religious rhetoric and official policy (witness the exchange with William Jowett of the CMS over the policy of mutual watching), even though change in those areas may have led in the short term to greater practical effectiveness and internal harmony. That same concern to be seen as not capitulating to necessity reinforced their determination to control the flow of news about the Mission to the outside world.

Of course, there is another side of this issue that sharpens the dilemma for religious organizations. By emphasizing specialness and separation in order to retain their conservative members, such orders risk alienating the less conservative ones, namely, those drawn to the idea that the barriers between the religious movement and the rest of the world can and should be minimized. Those more practical members may well be the ones who are best at dealing with the realities of that outside world. To lean toward the mandate to be "special," in other words, may be to jeopardize worldly efficacy, whereas to lean toward worldly efficacy is to jeopardize the appeal of the movement for those drawn to orthodoxy. Again, in Ebaugh's study, Catholic religious orders resistant to change lost their more progressive members and those orders ready to embrace change lost their conservative members. Some orders tried to erase the contradiction, as it were, by investing their worldly activities with special religious legitimacy, that is, by breaking down the identification of *specialness* with social and physical *separation*. Religious organizations that succeed in such a redefinition would no doubt reject the idea that they are actually on the horns of a dilemma. The overall decline of women's orders, however, would suggest that few manage this successful reframing of their identity. In her more recent work on this subject, Ebaugh has placed the quandary facing religious orders into a comparative and historical frame-

13. Ebaugh, *Out of the Cloister.*

work.[14] The dilemma that has resulted in declining memberships, she has proposed, is most acute in economically advanced nations where opportunities for women outside the cloister (and along with those opportunities, the pressures to adjust to the external world) are increasing, and least acute in economically underdeveloped regions where opportunities for women are few and acceptance by a religious order still represents a mark of family honor and an avenue of social mobility.

At the opening of the twenty-first century, the Basel Mission presents itself as an eclectic, ecumenical, and pragmatic organization, one that does not derive its identity from a commitment to a distinctively rigorous system of authority and orthodoxy. These days it may well be in a category that escapes the dilemma I have been describing here. But in the Basel Mission of the 1800s, and in general in organizations that are identified by their doctrine and discipline and can be described as to some extent separatist, this philosophical redefinition was not available. To be sure, Riis, Süss, and Zimmermann represented radical and (up to a point) tolerated departures from the prescribed way, but inside the organization they were treated as carefully rationalized exceptions or, perhaps more aptly put, as "mysteries." Not only does God work his will in mysterious ways, so the belief seemed to go, he communicates that will through the voice of the anointed leadership. For the Committee it was a question of balancing the gravity of the more audacious *violations* that Riis, Süss, and Zimmermann committed against the equally real *accomplishments* that also came out of those same infractions. As long as this ratio tipped clearly toward the favorable side, the accomplishments were publicly celebrated and the violations were screened from the view of important support groups in Switzerland and Germany. Indeed, each of the three men was at one time or another held up to the Pietist community in Europe as a model of missionary success.

From the decision makers' point of view, the stratagem at work here seems fairly straightforward: they tolerated, rationalized, and selectively packaged for public consumption the behavior of the deviant few whose actions, on balance, were useful as well as innovative, but they punished, even summarily expelled, the deviant few whose actions did not produce clear gains for the Mission. In taking this approach the errant gains of the first group of violators (the ones I have called "strategic") were captured for the Mission, while the quick and quite visible descent from favor of the second group (the ordinary transgressors) served to remind those in the compliant majority of the continuing sanctity and force of the official Pietist rules.

14. Ebaugh, "Growth and Decline."

Again a theoretical digression may be helpful: in his discussion of the social dynamics of transgression and punishment, Emile Durkheim said a certain minimum rate of deviance (obviously, below a critical threshold) is actually *necessary* in a community, paradoxically, because without periodic violations followed by visible punishment there is little reason for the group's rules to be reviewed and reaffirmed, and therefore they start to lose their force. When this happens, the stability of the group itself is threatened.[15] I agree that transgressions provide opportunities for reaffirming the rules, but see little need for the nebulous assumption that transgressions are "functionally necessary." More to the point in a process that is essentially political (in the sense of "internal organizational politics") is whether a given forbidden act advances or impedes the agenda of those in control. The Committee in charge of the Basel Mission provides an excellent case in point. These men had the power to decree what was and was not nonconformity as well as the power to apply or not apply public sanctions. In purely practical terms, this discretion enabled them to capture gains for the cause as they saw it, whatever the source of those gains may have been, that is, whether they were accomplished by conformists or deviants. Clearly forbidden activities were tolerated and shielded from public awareness, while far less confrontational personal misdemeanors were singled out for display and public sanction. Riis, for example, who could have been dismissed in an instant if the rules had been as strictly applied as the Mission's rhetoric would clearly seem to demand, was tolerated for over a decade. Lesser figures than he, in contrast, were sometimes defrocked and sent home even before they had time to adjust to the climate in West Africa. It was these dispensable small fry who were used to "set an example" and reassert the rules of the Mission. The stronger swimmers like Riis had more important uses.[16]

Accountability and the "Freedom to Obey"

What the foregoing discussion suggests is that threats to the Mission's identity and to its external support in the community provided ample reason for

15. Durkheim, *Rules of Sociological Method*, p. 67.

16. The search for the reasons why some actors are marked as violators and others are not is part of the labeling approach to the study of deviance; see Gove, "The Labelling Perspective." To my knowledge that approach has not looked specifically at how the application versus withholding of a deviant label is tied either to the prospect for advancing the long-term moral agenda of those in power or to the balance of productive versus destructive violations in the profile of a given offender.

the leadership to cling to its official policies despite the difficulties that came to be associated with them. But that motivation at the top does not by itself explain the organization's ability, especially at the level of the ordinary members, to persist in the face of its predicaments. Most observers would judge an organization's chances of simple survival to be low and the likelihood of real success to be even more remote if they knew the organization faced challenges like those that nineteenth-century missions set for themselves and especially if it also harbored internal complications of the sort I have described in the Basel Mission. To understand how the Mission ultimately overcame those odds — which is to say, how it came to have a history at all — we must look beneath the level of executive policy making and "impression management" and pay closer attention to the capacity of the ordinary missionaries to endure the difficulties they faced. Down at their level, after all, abstract contradictions of the sort I have described became personal experiences, in some cases personal catastrophes. It was they who had to come to terms with those complications on a day-to-day basis if they were going to continue to fuel the organization with their energies. To discover the key to their ability to do this, it is necessary to probe more deeply into the social psychology of their religious and ideological commitment.

In discussing Mission discipline in chapter 3, I explained how Pietist beliefs guided the development of the Mission's distinctive organizational profile. Charismatic, traditional, and bureaucratic justifications for compliance were woven into the broader Pietist moral framework in a way that provided an array of decision strategies for the Mission's officers to use as circumstances dictated. That shared framework strengthened the resolve of the rank and file and predisposed them to obedience, but at the same time it insulated the leaders from direct accountability for the organizational judgments they had to make. No matter what they decided or what form one of their rulings might take, they could claim and their subordinates were ready to believe that it conformed to a higher moral mandate. If a measure that was pursued in the interest of that larger morality proved to be uncomfortable for subordinates, and even if it had counterproductive outcomes (and we have seen that this was often the case), the legitimacy of the leadership was not directly called into question. James Wood has described how this sharing of core values can enable leaders of religious organizations to press ahead with specific actions that are not actually supported by the majority of the membership.[17] In chapter 4, I pointed to the dispute over domestic slavery in Africa as an example of this. An equal challenge, however, is to understand how such a consensus

17. Wood, *Leadership in Voluntary Organizations.*

could actually enable the members of the Mission community to endure the acute social distress they sometimes experienced in their own daily lives.

To decipher the logic at work here for individuals, it is necessary to look again, from a slightly different angle, at the connection the Pietists made between (personal) freedom and (social) order. The reasoning implicit in their thinking provides a useful clue to the way individualism, or "personal agency," can be reconciled with social constraint in other conservative religious systems. This excerpt from a larger passage in the *Hausordnung* quoted in chapter 3 is revealing: "[When seminarians] enter . . . into the realm of unlimited evangelical freedom, . . . [they] have to give account only to their invisible Lord and Master for their daily behavior. . . . [W]hoever . . . is in need of the . . . crutch of orders and prohibitions, entreaties and threats of punishment . . . excludes himself from our circle."[18] "Unlimited evangelical freedom" may await the truly committed members, but it was abundantly clear that those same true Christians would never elect to question duly constituted authority as a way of expressing their spiritual freedom. If they did so, their arrogance or, turned at a slightly different angle, their weakness would offend God and violate the law of Christ. This was a heavy charge to bear. Persons who came under scrutiny or were openly sanctioned by the hierarchy for some supposed misdeed would be led by their own faith in revealed authority, and by the converse of that faith, their own self-doubt, to look inward to private failure for the sources of their difficulty rather than outward to organizational structures, administrative policies, or the actions of peers or superiors. In other words, those whom authorities found reason to label as nonconformists would presume themselves and be presumed by others to have used their precious personal freedom to make wrong spiritual or worldly choices. By weakness in thought or by thoughtlessness in action they would have *called down God's wrath upon themselves.* This concept of blame and guilt is altogether different from the belief that they had been "subjected to sanctions by their organizational superiors." If we take the concept one logical step further, punishment was ultimately self-inflicted, and the language of the Committee often described it in precisely those terms. Administrators, to be sure, were responsible for promulgating the rules that had been revealed to them and then applying the sanctions that were religiously necessary for the enforcement of those rules. But they, too, were only subordinate deputies in the larger Christian enterprise, not the authors of that divine process.

If at a given moment a brother or sister in the Mission community were relatively secure in his or her own blamelessness, that inner security would

18. Blumhardt, *Hausordnung*, p. 4.

provide a measure of anesthesia against the pain the person had to endure in following the Christian law. It would give the person the strength, for example, to bear the burden of estrangement that might come from being watched or watching over and reporting on the shortcomings of fellows ("This watching fulfills the law of Christ"). When the information he or she provided to the Committee about a colleague triggered some corrective discipline against that person, it would also veil the reasons for that administrative action, including his or her own part in precipitating it, from his or her critical penetration ("The will of God is evident in the will of the Committee"). In principle, a true nonoffender against the rules, that is, a Christian whose conversion is of a "mature kind," would not feel oppressed by such mutual scrutiny, nor would there be reason for such a person to fear the constant presence of the machinery of punishment. Yet even such a theoretically blameless individual must patiently bear — and learn to gain validation from bearing — the social stress that accompanied the functioning of that machinery when others, by their own weaknesses, put themselves in its path.

To look at the other half of the picture, a person inclined to insecurity and self-blame (a description that would apply to every Pietist at least part of the time) would ordinarily take a reprimand from above as a signal of the immaturity of his or her own conversion and of the superior wisdom of the Committee. For that individual, the response might well be to devote even greater effort to the Pietist cause in order to atone for personal lapses or reestablish a sense of personal worthiness. This assumes that the violation in question was not one of those offenses regarded as so basic that it could lead to summary expulsion, an outcome that would obviously eliminate the need for any very complex rationalizations. Forchhammer, the dissenting seminarian, learned that questioning the very need for subordination and mutual watching could be just such an offense.

As Harro Höpfl has pointed out, Protestant political theory, which I construe broadly here to include organizational philosophy, has turned on the opening three verses in the thirteenth chapter of Romans: "Let every soul be subject unto the higher powers. For there is no power but of God: the powers that be are ordained of God. Whosoever therefore resisteth the power, resisteth the ordinance of God: and they that resist shall receive to themselves damnation. For rulers are not a terror to good works, but to the evil."[19] Close reading of the Bible was a defining feature of Pietist practice, and true to this passage, Pietists were conditioned to recognize the will of God at work

19. Höpfl, ed., *Luther and Calvin*, pp. xv-xvi. The passage is from the King James Version.

whether they were being punished, escaping punishment, causing others to be punished, or simply witnessing the punishment of others. They accepted a logic that said the application of a sanction was by itself sufficient evidence of the commission of an offense. They were not alone among Christian movements in embracing this reasoning. An instructive parallel can be seen in Kai Erikson's description of the way personal agency, blame, and punishment were seen by the early New England Puritans, another group distinguished by their commitment to strict religious discipline.[20] The Puritans, like the Basel Pietists, stressed individual moral freedom, but to look on the darker side of that principle, they too held individuals responsible for their own state of religious virtue and insisted upon unceasing self-examination and mutual watchfulness as the means of assessing the thoroughness of a person's conversion. Departure from divinely revealed norms was taken as an abuse of choice, a surrender to temptation, and an affront to the religious order. Following one's own impulses through life was a sign of irresolution or weakness, but confining one's behavior to the limited pathway to virtue required great strength of character. Willfulness, in other words, equaled weakness, while submission equaled strength. It is not a long logical reach from this principle to the general distrust of individual initiative and creativity.

From an organizational perspective, the crucial similarity between the Puritan and Mission communities lies in the insistence by leaders in New England that *they* had not formulated the array of sanctions, including a fiery death for some offenses, out of their own desire for severity. Nor did they use those sanctions to express their own moral disapproval or anger. To the contrary, in Puritan as in Pietist belief God revealed the need for those measures. Leaders chosen by God to receive this message merely erected the necessary worldly structures of punishment, in order that he could then use them to express his divine judgment about the failings of individual sinners. This logic, like that of the Pietists, reconciled the rhetoric of personal freedom with the realities of constraint and personal inhibition.

By this reasoning the leaders of Puritan and Pietist organizations alike were exonerated from blame for the harshness of their decisions; for the ordinary communicant the same reasoning rationalized the anguish that came from following the norm of mutual watching and explained the way punishment was exercised in the community of believers. A witness to any act of nonconformity must report it, no matter how much personal distress or interpersonal strain was caused by doing so. Taking this action against a religious colleague might bring sadness, but it need not carry guilt or the stigma

---

20. Erikson, *Wayward Puritans,* pp. 50-54, 185ff.

of betrayal, because it conformed to a higher spiritual loyalty. In theory, both leaders and followers in these communities were servants of a higher discipline whose origins and logic lay outside their control and whose intrinsic value buffered it from practical criticism.[21] This doctrine rationalized mutual watching and informing on peers by rendering those practices moral and reasonable for those who ordered them as well as for those who carried them out.

As the Mission's *Hausordnung* put it, the one who strays from the rules "is in danger of destroying the walls of Zion instead of building them up."[22] Such a danger could not go unremarked by any witness who wished to remain in the spiritual community. By transgressing, however covertly, the offender had already excluded herself or himself from the favor of God, and the sign of God's displeasure with such abuses of freedom became manifest when the machinery of sanctions was switched into motion. The responsibility of the faithful was to the larger religious cause and to the community of belief, not to any particular individual and certainly not to one accused of a moral violation. This understanding subordinates interpersonal solidarity to religious necessity. Elevating such an understanding to the status of an organizational decree prevented seminarians and missionaries from supporting each other in ways that could produce collective complaints about shared grievances ("The Mission is not a republic!"). They were taught to accept the alienation from their fellows that came from this lack of solidarity as a further test of their individual faith. In that acceptance, of course, they were often robbed of the brotherly support and trust they needed to do their practical work as missionaries. The "contradiction" that I have described penetrated their lives at both the most intimate and the most practical levels.

Commonalities with Other Organizations

Such contradictions that roiled beneath the surface of the Mission and from time to time were visible to the outside observer remained to the end of the period I have examined and well beyond it. They did not pull the organization apart or even substantially alter the outlines of its system of discipline. They were not often unveiled to the members as contradictions at all, and the psychological and social costs they entailed were absorbed by the participants as the price of their membership in the select circle of God's messengers. The

21. Weber, *Economy and Society*, 1:24-25.
22. Blumhardt, *Hausordnung*, p. 4.

religious language of control used by those at the top of the hierarchy was faithfully replicated in the religious language of consent used by those at the base. The result was a true hegemony that wove themes of religious and organizational orthodoxy, spiritual freedom, mutual surveillance, interpersonal estrangement, and Christian brotherhood into a single fabric. At the expense of frequent alienation in the relations among the lower participants, this ideological consensus preserved the vital trust between them and their leaders.[23] The ethical insulation that shielded the leaders from the negative repercussions of their own decisions also freed them to go on making those hard religious choices and holding to the hard Pietist necessities that created difficulty for the Mission and had visibly agonizing consequences for their subordinates. It is important to note that the power they wielded also allowed them the discretion to make occasional exceptions to their own policies and to rationalize or, if necessary, conceal those exceptions in a way that left their legitimacy intact. The energy unleashed by those strategic exceptions provided the momentum that kept the Mission from sinking into failure.

Subordinates, in their turn, reinforced this structure every time they censured each other or blamed their own weaknesses for their quandaries rather than the structure, the inspector, or the Committee. Their participation in this process reduced the likelihood that the stress they experienced in their work, which was socially caused but individually experienced, would crystallize into collective resentment and precipitate a united challenge to the legitimacy of the administration. The rank-and-file members took satisfaction from their ability to absorb adversity because it validated their pious strength and devotion. Even knowing in advance about the interpersonal turbulence they would face along with the difficulty and danger of the assignment to the Gold Coast, seminarians continued to volunteer for that assignment and argued "with one voice" against its abandonment.[24]

In addition to the resemblances referred to earlier between Basel Mission Pietism and the New England Puritanism of an earlier generation, other likenesses in the history of missions and other religious movements should be examined. Like any organization, the Basel Mission was assembled from the cultural resources available to its members; its structure and the path it followed were not just like any others that will be encountered in the mission literature or in the broader field of organization studies. Weber was right to characterize

23. Giddens, *The Constitution of Society*, pp. 51ff.; Blau, *Exchange and Power*, pp. 91ff.

24. Schlatter, *Geschichte der Basler Mission*, 3:41-42. For other discussions of organizational loyalty in the face of stress, see Hirschmann, *Exit, Voice, and Loyalty*, and Wood, *Leadership in Voluntary Organizations*, pp. 91ff.

such specific configurations as "historical accidents," meaning they do not reflect any single, invariant developmental pattern, even one that prevails just within a given broad organizational type. But to rule out an invariant pattern or master template does not mean that simple commonalities among missions do not exist. If properly displayed against the backdrop of its own distinctive features, the experiences of any one mission can raise questions to be asked about other missions and for the larger class of commitment organizations and social movements that share some of the same internal logic.

Beneath all the differences among nineteenth-century missions, for example, it can be noted that they shared many evangelical priorities and communicated with each other about those interests. They faced similar obstacles at home and abroad, and they worked, often competitively but sometimes cooperatively, with comparable human and material resources toward generally similar objectives. These commonalities help to account for the similarities in official charter that are apparent among them. In some cases the isomorphism between one and another could be described as derivative or even imitative.[25] Most, for example, had something like the division of labor between the "home board" (directors) and the "secretary" (executive officer) in Britain's CMS.[26] The distinction between the Committee and the inspector in the Basel Mission directly mirrored that separation. In part this was because the CMS was well connected politically and quick to establish itself as a strong evangelical presence, and thus it was visible as a model for other missions. It was also because the direct support and counsel of the CMS were vital to the Baslers in the formative stages of their own undertaking. It was prudent, therefore, to display an organizational outline that looked sensible to those in the more prominent organization.

The example set by Basel in turn guided some of the missions that followed it. Organizers of the Norwegian Missionary Society (NMS), who embraced many of the same Pietist values concerning authority and conformity as the leaders of the Basel Mission, consulted directly with the Baslers and patterned the structure of the NMS directly after the Basel model. Given the contradictory elements in that model, it is not surprising that the Norwegians also experienced some of the same internal problems, including, significantly, the suppression of creativity, a lack of openness to new ideas and cultures, and chronic internal disharmony.[27]

---

25. DiMaggio and Powell, "The Iron Cage Revisited."
26. This pattern was established even earlier in the Baptist Missionary Society (founded in 1792) and the London Missionary Society (1795).
27. Simensen with Gynnild, "Norwegian Missionaries."

Such similarities as these, where the exchanges between missions were direct, come readily to mind. But at a higher level of abstraction, even quite different missions that are widely separated in time, place, and auspices can display significant similarities. Robert Burns made this point when he described two missions in very disparate historical settings, one an Islamic venture in thirteenth-century Valencia and the other a Catholic mission on the American northwest frontier in the nineteenth century.[28] The philosophies, structures, and cultural and historical circumstances of those two undertakings were widely different, but Burns demonstrated that some of their problems were remarkably alike. In both organizations policies that were ill suited to the realities of the missionary task and dissonant with the cultural surroundings in the field were sustained because they conformed to religious beliefs that took precedence over practical organizational exigencies. "Given the external situation and the respective psychologies of the actors in each case, neither set of actors had options other than those they followed."[29] The similarity to the Basel Mission's commitment to its Pietist identity is obvious. Parallels between Basel and the two missions Burns studied are also evident in their lasting long-term impact on their Islamic and Native American subjects despite their short-term difficulties.

The China Inland Mission (CIM), a nineteenth-century British group that attracted Max Weber's interest, offers another revealing example. As Weber pointed out, there were many variations on the Protestant themes of individual responsibility, divine intervention, and the path to salvation, and they could produce strikingly different evangelical and organizational strategies.[30] I have explained why the Pietists in the Basel Mission, motivated by a Lutheran conception of the ideal social order, believed in sending couples and teams of missionaries into an area, where they would pursue verified and lasting conversions and try to create permanent Christian settlements in the "heathen world." The Baslers were not content until a new community of belief and a new way of life had been established. Individual natives may profess Christianity, but they were not considered fully integrated into that community and style of life until they had achieved the state of "mature" conversion, which was gauged not just by the claim to a spiritual "rebirth" but also by the acceptance of Christian names, dress, comportment, occupations, and social institutions. In contrast, the model embraced by the CIM called for agents

28. Burns, "The Missionary Syndrome."
29. Burns, "The Missionary Syndrome," p. 281.
30. Weber, *Protestant Ethic,* p. 225 n. 34. For a related and more contemporary discussion, see Heise, "Prefatory Findings."

working alone to simply make the gospel known, "announcing the Word" or "broadcasting the seed," as it were, and moving on. Being exposed to the Word was sufficient to give individuals a religious "choice" about the shape of their lives from that point forward. Once that revelatory contact had been made, it was up to those individuals to reject the gospel or take it in as a part of their own spiritual life.

Weber's account of the CIM captures the logic of this doctrine: "Whether [the] heathen should [actually] be converted to Christianity and thus attain salvation, even whether they could understand the language in which the missionary preached, was a matter of small importance and could be left to God, Who alone could control such things."[31] The parable of the weeds (Matt. 13:24-30, 36-43), which is the evangelical model that guided this group, counsels that it is in God's province, not that of man, to separate the truly saved (the healthy plants that have issued from the broadcast seed) from the multitudes who remained untouched by the gospel (the weeds). By one calculation the CIM determined that if a thousand missionaries pursued this broadcast approach, each one could reach, say, fifty families a day; in this way all fifty million Chinese families could be "touched" in three years. William Bainbridge visited the CIM in a world tour of missions he made during the late 1870s and early 1880s, and his description confirms Weber's characterization of the group.[32] The missionaries showed little concern, Bainbridge said, about becoming proficient in the local languages and were indifferent to matters of organization. "[T]hey retain perfect liberty to roam over the country at pleasure, or rather it is claimed, as they may feel led from day to day by providence. Their dress and style of living is conformed to that of the natives."[33]

The organizational implications of such a doctrine are dramatically different from those attached to the Pietist worldview. In the broadcast view the responsibility of the individual missionary was to "touch" the families by speaking the gospel in their presence — and little else. Compared with the Basel Mission, organizations embracing this interpretation paid far less direct attention to the attitudes and actions of individuals, and creating separate communities of converts was not as high on their agendas. Moreover, because the CIM took this view, they allowed their missionaries to move about independently, spreading the Word over wide territories. This led to such an open reliance on individual initiative that firm hierarchical authority over their evangelists could not be exercised, just the opposite of the situation in the Basel Mission.

---

31. Weber, *Protestant Ethic*, p. 225 n. 34.
32. Bainbridge, *Around the World Tour*, pp. 221-28.
33. Bainbridge, *Around the World Tour*, p. 222.

Little discipline or direction was provided for individuals, and often the result was dissipated resources, erratic communication, and slack coordination.

Organizationally the stories of the CIM and the Basel Mission are quite at odds with each other, and these two missions in turn are very different from the medieval and frontier missions studied by Burns. Abstractly, however, a common thread runs through all four cases. In each of them basic beliefs shaped organizational strategies, limited structural choices, and caused the persistence of burdensome arrangements far beyond their practical utility. A generalization of sorts emerges, then, that I believe has wide applicability in the study of missionary movements: *depending on the organizational feature being examined, there will be specific differences as well as broad similarities among missions, but the variations — in structure, internal problems, and patterns of change and stability — will be influenced by beliefs and worldviews as much as by practical precedents, external environments, the availability of resources, and the complexity of tasks.* A challenge for organizational sociology and for the study of social movements is to see how far this proposition can be extended beyond purely religious organizations.

Conclusion

Zeal, as I said in the first sentence of this book, is a powerful but volatile resource for social action. What is interesting about this emotionally charged energy is how different organizations manage to channel it, or fail to do so as the case may be, into coherent and sustainable social action. In chapter 1, I located the Basel Mission in its historical context in Europe and briefly recounted its impact on Ghanaian society as seen by historians and missionaries, insiders and outsiders, Europeans and Africans. Chapter 2 looked closely at the social origins of the participants, explored the secular gains experienced by generations of families as a result of their taking part in the missionary movement, and called attention to some of the differences in the experiences of women and men in the Mission. In chapter 3, I concentrated on matters of structure, examining the ways in which beliefs, historical circumstances, and cultural and material resources shaped the Mission's organizational outlines. Chapter 4 described the contradictions inherent in that structure and called attention to the human consequences of imposing rigid constraints on duties that had to be carried out in a world of turbulence and uncertainty. The first part of the present chapter has asked how the Mission survived those troubles, finding important clues in the Pietists' beliefs about individual responsibility and in their ideas about organizational legitimacy and appropriate strategies of social control.

Many missionary undertakings in the nineteenth century were clear failures and had to be abandoned, often at great cost to their members and their sponsoring organizations. Many more, however, continued for a very long time in an ambiguous condition somewhere between clear success and unmistakable failure. Marshall Meyer and Lynne Zucker have offered a useful discussion of what they call "permanently failing organizations," by which they mean those characterized by "high persistence" and "low performance."[34] There is much in the history of evangelical missions, and in the Basel Mission in particular, that brings their analysis to mind. The troubles the members endured on the Gold Coast must have seemed endless, and I have pointed out that for decades the record of success, measured just by the number of converts, can only be called meager. The same could be said about many other evangelical missions. In the final analysis, however, given their objectives, the Baslers did not fail, either in their own terms or by any objective assessment of their eventual impact on Ghanaian culture. Perhaps the final irony lies in the fact that it was their refusal to adapt to recurring internal and external pressures by changing either their philosophy or their structure that was one of the key reasons for their survival. In a recurrent theme, the missionaries often used *hartnäckig,* meaning "obstinate" or "stubborn," to describe each other. On that same theme, I would suggest that "organizational stubbornness" (or Gareth Morgan's evocative term with the same meaning, "organizational egocentrism")[35] is a better description of their record than "organizational failure." The missionaries were always able to find the energy and determination to press ahead as long as new recruits and material resources were available. The record they left behind shows quite plainly how troubled they were by the dilemmas they faced ("Is this the way we follow the law of brotherly love?"), and some of them threatened to resign if their concerns were not addressed. For the most part, however, they were undeterred by the problems they had to live with. On their side, the leaders knew the case that could be made for fundamental change in their practices, but they for the most part were unmoved by such admonitions. "Bear ye one another's burdens," they intoned, "and so fulfill the law of Christ." For over a generation there were few converts to mark the missionaries' labors in the field, yet they were still "on the ground" and ready to settle into the structural niche that opened up for them when in increasing numbers the people of the Gold Coast began to seek the practical benefits they had to offer. Again the concept of "elective affinity" comes into play, this time to characterize the eventual alignment of African and European beliefs, interests, and cir-

34. Meyer and Zucker, *Permanently Failing Organizations,* p. 19.
35. Morgan, *Images of Organization,* p. 243.

cumstances. Once that point of convergence was reached, the place of the Basel Mission in the institutional history of Ghana was assured.

In bringing this narrative to a close, it is useful to pull together briefly some of the theoretical conclusions and paradoxes that have emerged from the Mission's history and to call attention to some pressing questions that I could not resolve here. These remarks fall into four categories: first, I will address some effects that I believe the missionary movement had on the larger social order, including specifically the class dynamics and patterns of social mobility that were emerging for both men and women in the nineteenth century; after that I will comment on the similarities and dissimilarities in the organizational forms that missions adopted; third, I will summarize the relationship between consensus and conflict in enterprises such as missions; and finally, I will review the part that I think missions played as agents of social change abroad. It is my hope that these comments will stimulate further curiosity about missions, but also about the intricate tension between emotional zeal and institutional control in the considerably broader category of value-driven organizations.

Missions and the Social Order

No mission with which I am familiar defined itself specifically as a class-based organization, and missions in general certainly did not embrace the restructuring of class relations at home as one of their critical objectives. Nevertheless, the structures and the activities of these organizations were affected by the class origins of their participants, and they required enduring cooperation across class lines that were usually quite clearly marked. In time this collaboration contributed to the blurring of those same class boundaries because of the social mobility that many missions offered to their lower participants, especially the men. All of these — the collaboration, the "social betterment," and the differences between the experiences of women and men — merit a few final words.

Class Collaboration

Karl Marx[36] and Max Weber[37] are preeminent among the theorists who explored the complexity and fluidity of the modern class dynamics that were

36. Marx, "Class Struggles in France" and "Eighteenth Brumaire." See also Lichtheim, *Marxism*, pp. 86ff.
37. Weber, *Economy and Society*, 2:926ff.

emerging in nineteenth-century Europe. Their descriptions of class relations are at many points at odds with each other, but both noted how, for reasons conditioned by the time and cultural context, similarly situated groups, such as adjacent classes or even factions within the same class, might pursue very different courses of action. Despite their closeness, the contention between them was often much more evident than any joint antagonism to groups from which they were both widely separated. Conversely, improbable bridges of cooperation between the members of widely separated strata evolved when there were points where their interests converged. It was just such an unlikely but durable collaboration that developed between the sophisticated urban "aristocrats" who created the Basel Mission and the Württemberg villagers who became the Mission's most common recruits. Notwithstanding the profound differences between these two groups, there were strong resonances in their beliefs, interests, and experiences. I examined those affinities against the background of the social changes that were taking place in Switzerland and Germany in the nineteenth century. In other places and times, other religious, economic, and political realities would have to be brought into the picture, but in most of the missions whose stories I have read, shared efforts that reached across class lines were more the rule than the exception.

An aspect of this picture that has not been satisfactorily explained, however, is the relative absence of members of the emerging urban proletariat among the recruits to the missionary movement. The class collaboration I have described in Basel simply did not include them. South German villagers were simultaneously sought out by the Basel Mission and drawn to it by their own circumstances; but urban industrial workers, in contrast, were neither recruited by nor, apparently, attracted to the Pietist missionary movement, in the latter case quite possibly because they were increasingly alienated from the churches. In the Basel Mission, their numbers were quite small throughout the nineteenth century, and a similar pattern of exclusion, whether intended or inadvertent, is apparent in some of the other notable missions of the time. Closer study of more missionary organizations will clarify the extent to which this proletarian exclusion took place and why. Research addressed to this topic should yield new insight into the patterns of interclass relations in the larger social order.

Social Mobility and Change in the Class Structure

Insight of a closely related kind is provided by the evidence of social mobility among the Basel missionaries. The collaboration across class lines into which the seminarians were drawn provided tangible rewards for them in the form of visible gains in their social standing and economic well-being. The Basel organization is not unique in this regard. I have not found other archives with the same richness of cross-generational family information that was available to me in Basel, but substantial returns in "cultural capital" for the ordinary male members (evident in such things as education, occupational advancement, material rewards, social honor, and favorable marriage alliances) are part of the collective memory of most nineteenth-century missions. Unlike the Baslers, who discouraged the discussion of "social betterment" and deplored the popular glorification that some missionaries enjoyed, other organizations openly acknowledged these advantages and used the prospect of social advancement as an attraction in recruiting suitable members.

I have not directly shown how widespread this pattern of upward social mobility was, but if my conjecture is correct, its accumulating impact on the larger social structure must have been substantial. Crucially, however, it was a largely unintended outcome. The separate missions of the time communicated with each other, to be sure, but I doubt that they were more than dimly aware that, together, over an extended period, they were sending thousands of educated families — those established by the children of missionary parents — into the modern division of labor that was emerging around them. When those largely unwitting but multiplicative, secular effects on the class structure at home are added to the intended and unintended transformations that the missions brought about in their overseas ventures, little doubt can remain about their role as agents of social change domestically and internationally. What is needed to firm up the impression of their domestic impact is a systematic reconstruction, across many evangelical societies, of the social origins and ultimate class destinations of missionaries and their children. This will make it possible to gauge more conclusively the cumulative impact of the missionary movement on the larger social structure and to compare that impact with other, better known secular forces that were also shaping modern class structures.

Women and Men in the Missionary Movement

In all this discussion it must be kept in mind that most of what I have reported concerns the experiences of men. At the beginning of my account I described Juliane von Krüdener's influence during the formative years of the Mission, and later on I described how, at a crucial time in the struggle for stability in Ghana, Catherine Mulgrave commanded considerable regard and (together with Johannes Zimmermann, her resourceful husband) extracted some important concessions from the Committee because of the role she played. Both von Krüdener and Mulgrave left their mark on the organizational record, but the experiences of women in the Basel Mission were not systematically examined in any depth until Waltraud Haas took on this task in her important book, *Erlitten und Erstritten: Der Befreiungsweg von Frauen in der Basler Mission 1816-1966,* followed a few years later by Dagmar Konrad's *Missionsbräute.* Elsewhere, looking at other missions, Dana Robert's *American Women in Mission* stands out among recent scholarship on this part of the story, as do *Gendered Missions,* an anthropological, sociological, and historical collection assembled by Mary Huber and Nancy Lutkehaus, and *Women and Missions,* edited by Fiona Bowie and others. It is clear that the missionary movement was male-dominated, indeed self-consciously patriarchal, in the realm of organizational control, but it is inaccurate to describe the movement as one in which the labor of men was ever predominant, let alone sufficient. Whatever their founders may have intended, missions of the era soon learned that they must rely heavily on the energy and personal commitments of women in all that they did. In this connection Jane Hunter has written of the "feminization of the mission force" which took place in the United States in the late nineteenth century, and Ruth Brouwer, looking at Canada, has found that "well before the turn of the century, single women missionaries and missionary wives outnumbered their male colleagues in many overseas fields."[38] In Great Britain and Scandinavia, too, as Susan Thorne and Line Predelli, respectively, have shown, the women's missionary movement was the largest social movement of women in the nineteenth century.[39]

Unlike what was commonly the case for men, however, women's hierarchical subordination in missions was not likely to be balanced by an accumulation of "cultural capital" that substantially improved their social standing. The marriage patterns I described in chapter 2 are the best example of this. In the Basel organization the men courted or were assigned to brides from a social station somewhat higher than their own, but the reverse of the coin is that for many women, a missionary spouse meant they had married *beneath* their station, and the common notion that individuals were attracted to the prospect of "social betterment," while true for men, is not persuasive as an explanation of women's participation.[40] Women's religious commitment and

---

38. J. Hunter, *The Gospel of Gentility,* p. 14; Brouwer, *New Women for God,* p. 5. See also Hill, *The World Their Household,* p. 2, and Mitchison, "Canadian Women," p. 58.

39. Thorne, "Missionary-Imperial Feminism"; Thorne, *Congregational Missions;* Predelli, "Contested Patriarchy."

40. Helen Ebaugh's recent research ("Growth and Decline") indicates that social opportunity is part of the dynamic of participation in Catholic women's orders, but the intergenerational transmission of those gains is not part of the picture, any more than it is with the men attracted to the priesthood.

energy matched that of the men, but the configuration of beliefs, interests, and circumstances — the balance of "pushes" and "pulls," as it were — that accounts for their involvement in mission has yet to be discovered. The Basel Mission was not unusual in this regard; indeed, I regard the widespread divergence of men's and women's experiences, *given the indispensability and resources of the women,* as one of the greatest remaining puzzles that mission scholarship still needs to solve.

The Convergence (or Divergence) of Organizational Forms

Other organizations, including other missions such as those in Britain, provided administrative precedents for the Basel Mission to follow. This accounts for the similarities that are apparent in some of the structural features of the Basel Mission, the CMS, and other evangelical organizations. The structure created in Basel, however, was not intended to be a mere duplicate of anything that had gone before. In building an effective administration, the members of the Committee were influenced by elements of theology and philosophy taken from Pietist, Lutheran, and Calvinist sources. At the same time, they brought together in one place strains of modern individualism and aristocratic privilege, and they mingled democratic rhetoric with themes of theocracy and patriarchy. There was a struggle to reconcile remembered agrarian virtues with emerging urban realities. In the distinctive synthesis that was created from all these diverse elements, decision-making principles rooted in charisma, tradition, and rational-legalism converged to form an unusually powerful structure of imperative control, one with a broad base of legitimacy for those at the top of the structure and an equally broad zone of acceptance for those in subordinate positions. No part of this organizational configuration could be understood without knowing about the historical circumstances that prevailed in Basel and the convictions, expectations, and capabilities of the participants at all levels.

The assembling of this structure demonstrates in a concrete way what Weber strongly implied about the evolution of organizational authority; that is, that there is no single, transcendent logic of organizational development that is waiting for us to discover it. What participants are ready to accept as consistent and sensible among available moral axioms and organizing premises varies with time, place, and culture. Similarities in mission structure appeared where circumstances and beliefs were similar; for example, wherever the missionary movement cut across class lines (there may be exceptions, but I have not found them), governing committees drawn from the ranks of the relatively privileged emerged to lead missionaries who came from considerably more modest origins. Similarities also appeared when the lines of influence between one organization and another were so strong that one would be motivated to imitate the other. At the same time, however, profound variations in the details of day-to-day operations could proceed from differences as (seemingly) small as the interpretation of a key biblical passage. The move to centralization or decentralization of operations in the field, as a case in point, could be influenced by whether evangelical priority was given to "broadcasting the seed" or "creating communities of belief." We have hardly begun to explore the effects of these variations on the courses of action followed by different missionary organizations, and similar questions need to be asked about the effects of doctrinal beliefs on the histories of other social movements and other sorts of commitment organizations. Interpretive case studies are well suited to this kind of investigation.

Consensus, Conflict, and Change

Paradoxically, the really important conflicts in the Basel Mission were linked more directly to the members' *consensus* on basic beliefs than to philosophical disagreements, incompatible class interests, or struggles between the levels of the organizational hierarchy. The members lived in a structure that relied strongly on vertical differences in rank and honor, but because they were united by shared religious convictions, the participants were able to bridge over the differences in their class origins. Conflict along those lines, therefore, was infrequent, and in the final accounting they were able to carry on jointly in an impressive array of culture-transforming activities abroad. But this description of the unifying effects of consensus, though accurate, must immediately be qualified. The atmosphere of moral certitude and the concentration of extraordinary power in the hands of the Committee also produced serious dilemmas for the Mission's activities in the outside world. It was demanded of the missionaries that they validate an administrative structure and a set of social control practices that constantly tested their interpersonal bonds. In providing that validation the ordinary members reinforced the same regime that, while it neutralized the independence of most of them, sometimes extended autonomy to those who showed the *least* commitment to established procedures.

Consensus, therefore, may actually be causally linked to intractable contradictions, and through those contradictions it can be the source of divisive controversies and conflicts. Contrary to a neat "dialectical" formulation, however, these contradictory strains may not be the cause of either fundamental structural instability or productive change in the organization. The stresses that were a feature of daily life in the Mission, I have shown, were absorbed by the missionaries for generations, and during that time basic structural alterations in the organization are hard to detect. As we have seen, the beliefs that were the source of many of the Baslers' troubles also made those ordeals themselves appear ordained and rendered them understandable and tolerable to the participants. This justification of travail produced renewed energy as often as resignation, and it culminated in renewed devotion to the Pietist cause far more often than it precipitated fundamental rebellion. In the end the organization always absorbed the gains and withstood the damage caused by energetic-but-eccentric members who pursued their own agendas, just as it always got past the turmoil that resulted from the periodic breakdown of interpersonal harmony. *The often-assumed connection between "system contradiction" and "system instability" is clearly in need of more scrutiny.* Troubles that are institutionalized can be borne by an organization's participants for a very long time.

Missions as Agents of Change and Resistance in the Colonial World

Much of my attention here has been directed toward the implications of the research for organizational sociology and the sociology of religion. The questions I began with and the archival information I drew upon contributed to this focus. Missions set out to change the world, however, and I will conclude as I began by pointing to their importance as agents of change and resistance in the colonial and postcolonial world.

The present-day Presbyterian Church of Ghana is one concrete result of the Mission's role in the transformation of the colonial Gold Coast into the modern nation of Ghana. But the Mission's impact on that country goes well beyond the establishment of a church and the promulgation of a set of religious beliefs. Both Europeans and Ghanaians close to the mission movement (including members of the present Ghanaian governmental elite) have testified that the Baslers helped to fashion the infrastructure, especially the educational underpinning, for a modern division of labor in that region. It will be fruitful to ask about the extent to which missions in general, not just this one, served in this way to provide the organizational experience, perhaps even the organizational blueprints, for emerging institutions in former colonial dependencies. In the final accounting the objective significance of missions may lie as much in this role as in the success or failure of their more exclusively religious claims. What has been true for the Basel Mission in Ghana may well be true for other missions in other areas.

Beyond their formal education and technical training, the Africans who passed through the Mission community on their way to important positions in the colonial regime were also learning about modern organizational realities. A large part of that lesson, if only by example, involved dealing with contradictions, conflicts, and alienation. The troubles I have described in this book were part of the experience of African Christians just as they were of the German and Swiss missionaries, and they must receive more attention in future research. The experience of Africans in the Mission also included exposure to much of the instrumental reasoning and contractual language of Western bureaucracy, as well as daily object lessons about the use of organizations as tools for managing relationships with a contemporary political economy. If we judge by the way the Presbyterian Church of Ghana has in recent years handled its relations with the secular government of that country, these lessons appear to have been learned very well by the African heirs to the Basel Mission's legacy.

Moving such topics closer to the center of the research agenda means paying closer attention to the effects that missions had on the places in which their evangelical activities were carried out. It also means paying closer attention to the way they were received and used by the people in those places. One important line of influence, as I have just suggested, radiates from missions to the emerging structures of organizational control in colonial and post-colonial societies. Also included in an expanded research agenda, however, must be the part that missions played as a source of resistance to established colonial and postcolonial authority. More than once the core values of the Basel Mission placed the organization in direct opposition to colonial policies. A striking instance of this contrariness took place not in Ghana but in Cameroon, where the Baslers formed a hard knot of opposition to the confiscatory land-ownership policies of the German colonial government. With that episode in mind, a hypothesis that I have advanced elsewhere is that missions committed to community building were the ones most likely to be pulled into such conflicts with their fellow Europeans.[41] The reason for this is that commitment to community (an especially strong theme in the Pietist/Lutheran worldview) carried with it a determination to create an infrastructure in which stable vocations in stable villages built around stable patterns of

41. Miller, "Missions, Social Change." See also Wolf, ed., *Religious Regimes*, and Comaroff and Comaroff, *Of Revelation and Revolution*, vol. 1.

land usage could develop. The participants in such an effort naturally become spiritual as well as material stakeholders in those institutional arrangements. This model of stability and self-sufficiency was and continues to be in diametric contrast to extractive and exploitative, Western-controlled production and labor systems. Missions devoted to the "broadcast the Word and move on" strategy had, in my view, little need for concern with such matters, and they were therefore far less likely to be pulled into such controversies.

*   *   *

These tentative conclusions and suggestive hypotheses reach far beyond the single case history that has occupied my attention here. The message of this concluding section, and for that matter the thrust of this entire analysis, has been that the mission legacy has been mixed indeed. As organizations, missions defy simplification. As a way to close this investigation, I would suggest that of all the intriguing features of the Basel Mission that could be singled out, it is the refusal to relinquish its basic identity that comes closest to accounting both for its troubles and for its persistence as a structure of social discipline and instrument of social change. Whatever value judgment one attaches to the Mission's activities, the same "organizational stubbornness" that accounts for the readiness to impose a new social order on its convert communities also explains the willingness to oppose some of the harsher policies associated with colonial rule. The only simple truth about evangelical missions is that there is no simple truth about evangelical missions.

The Basel Mission, the Presbyterian Church, and Ghana since 1918

PAUL JENKINS

Jon Miller's analysis of the nineteenth-century Basel Mission might appear at first sight to be about an era which is dead and gone, buried under the changes brought about by two world wars and the end of the colonial empires. But the past in Africa is never dead — or perhaps one should write that sensing which parts of the past get forgotten when, and which parts live on mentally now, should be a major part of the task of historians considering any of Africa's changing traditions and identities. Certainly the conversations and speeches triggered in contemporary Ghana by the two words "Basel Mission" — or the single Twi word *basilfo*,[1] still widely used to refer to members

___

1. I.e., "Basel people." A strong and often repeated oral tradition in Basel Mission circles in Basel recalls how a president of the church in Basel was being helped by an immigration official in Accra to fill in his forms on arrival at the airport in the 1960s. The official asked, "Where have you come from today?" The Swiss churchman replied, "Basel." The official repeated his question and the churchman his answer until the frustrated official said

___

Author's note: In this Afterword, I follow Jon Miller's convention of using "Gold Coast" to refer to the colony and "Ghana" to the independent state. Equally the abbreviation PCGC denotes the Presbyterian Church of the Gold Coast, and PCG the Presbyterian Church of Ghana. For the sake of simplicity and style, however, the name Ghana in the title above and the section headings on pp. 200 and 209 also refers to the Gold Coast from 1918 on. I would like to express particular thanks to Rev. Peter Kodjo, chairman of the Ga Presbytery PCG, for stimulating discussions when this text was in the planning stage. Veit Arlt read an early version of the manuscript with critical attention. Samuel Prempeh, the current moderator of PCG, made his 1977 Edinburgh Ph.D. dissertation available to me — "The Basel and Bremen Missions in the Gold Coast and Togoland, 1914-1926: A Study in Protestant Missions and the First World War."

of the Presbyterian Church of Ghana — are long and lively.[2] There are thus serious contemporary grounds for attempting to build a bridge between Jon Miller's analysis of the nineteenth-century Basel Mission and the place the Basel Mission holds in Ghanaian consciousness now.

In relation to the Basel Mission as a European institution, there are also serious grounds for attempting to follow Jon Miller's lines of analysis through the twentieth century. Miller points out that missionary societies' "influence as agents of change was substantial. . . . These effects belie the notion that missions in general, and the Basel Mission in particular, were peripheral players whose traces in the colonial drama will be faint."[3] Tom McCaskie makes a similar point when he observes that modern research has neglected the study of this "formidable research enterprise" — i.e., the Basel Mission of the era Miller studied.[4] There must, indeed, be a general interest in looking at the way this notable nongovernmental organization has been involved in the vexed and tragic history of the German-speaking peoples in the twentieth century. At the opening of the twenty-first century the Basel Mission is still a substantial movement, many of whose members have been waiting for years for something like Miller's study to appear — a critical analysis of the classical Basel Mission from an innovative point of view not dominated by the wish to force it into an ideological framework. Their interest is also acute in an attempt to show how Miller's analysis can be linked with the development of the postcolonial and ecumenical organization they themselves know.

Jon Miller's analysis of the classical Basel Mission ends with the outbreak of the First World War. This is not surprising. The First World War is undeniably the pivotal episode in the history of the Basel Mission in Ghana, after which nothing was ever the same again. In Europe, too, the First World War begins the decades of crisis and confusion out of which, eventually, the modern Basel Mission emerged in the 1950s. The logic of studying the pre-1914 Basel Mission as a unity with a stable structure was clear. But in order to build

---

angrily: "No, I don't want to know your religion, I want to know which town you left this morning to come here."

2. The current Swiss ambassador to Ghana related, in a presentation in the Mission House, Basel, on August 28, 2000, how for him the Basel Mission had remained a shadowy and unimportant entity — even though he had grown up in a Protestant family in German-speaking Switzerland — until he was posted to Accra, where public interest forced him to realize what major dimensions are hidden behind the name Basel Mission. His recent publication documents his personal discovery in Ghana of this Swiss institution: Schweizer, *Survivors*.

3. See above, p. 33.

4. McCaskie, "Asante and Ga," p. 144.

a bridge to the start of the twenty-first century, it is necessary to survey the many dimensions of the changes which the war forced on the organization and its work in Ghana.

If one takes Jon Miller's analysis of the Basel Mission as a history of its operations on the Gold Coast before the outbreak of the First World War, it is clear that this was, over all, a period of sustained and impressive progress and development. This progress was achieved not without years of almost permanent crisis and at what the organization rightly considered a high cost, not least in human lives. But progress it was, by any standards, not least if one uses the criteria which will have been in the mind of the Basel Mission itself in those years — the stability of the Mission's presence on the Gold Coast, the sustained responses elicited in the population of the area in which it was working, and the integrity of the organization and discipline flowing from its leadership in Basel.

Early on a small group of missionaries had been living almost cut off from Europe and severely endangered by illness and death. As Miller's study clearly shows, at the beginning of their work their physical viability as a group was anything but assured.[5] From about 1870, however, the Basel Mission had maintained a mission staff of between fifty and seventy people on the Gold Coast.[6] The development of transport services and cable communication to West Africa gave them increasingly close and reliable contacts with their European base. And following the identification of the malaria parasite in the 1890s and the development of effective means of prophylaxis, the death rate among missionaries at last dropped to something like normal standards.[7]

In the early decades of mission work it must also have seemed touch and go whether significant numbers of indigenous people would become Basel Mission Christians. As Miller himself points out, after twenty-three years on the Gold Coast less than fifty Africans could be counted in the Basel Mission community, of whom more than half were ex-slave repatriates the Mission had itself brought back from the West Indies.[8] But by 1900 the total "Basel

5. See above, pp. 21-22.

6. This figure includes both men and women. In particular it *includes* missionaries' wives. Source (as with the other statistics quoted in these paragraphs) is the lists of personnel in the printed annual Basel Mission *Jahresberichte*.

7. F. H. Fischer, *Der Missionsarzt Rudolf Fisch;* see especially the statistics on life expectancy among members of the Basel Mission, 1828-1914, on p. 559.

8. See above, p. 23. Kwaku Sae, the first head of a family to be baptized in Akropong, twenty years after the missionaries' arrival, was given the promising name of Abraham, but was in fact a polygamist and baptized with his two wives, so eager were the missionaries to secure at least a small number of converts who were, in traditional terms, socially well situated. See Haenger, *Slaves and Slave-Holders*, pp. 36-37.

Mission Christian Community" was about 25,000 people,[9] and in towns like Akropong the relations between traditional state and church had reached a maturity in which many influential people had a foot in both camps. This plateau of mutual tolerance had, of course, a lot to do with the rapid spread of colonial authority on the Gold Coast after the subjection of Asante in 1896-1900 and the wide acceptance of the idea that the colony's future lay with the British Empire and the adoption of British and European models of life and organization.[10]

In this general picture of progress the Basel Mission's educational efforts were also important. By the last quarter of the nineteenth century the Basel Mission church had a competent cadre of indigenous pastors, teachers, and catechists in its employment, numbering, in the 1890s, something like two hundred individuals.[11] And the educational system the Basel Mission had pioneered on the Gold Coast — primary schools, middle schools, a seminary for teachers and pastors, but also education in practical trades — was widely admired as an unusually effective instrument of social and economic development in West Africa.[12]

Last but not least, when mapping the favorable situation for the Basel Mission on the Gold Coast just before the outbreak of the First World War, we should not forget the Basel Mission Trading Company, at this stage still very closely linked to the missionary society. This company was riding high on the tide of the cocoa boom, which had started in the 1890s. From the beginning the Basel Mission and its trading company had been trying to promote prosperous indigenous rural communities — so it was "in on the ground floor" when the cocoa boom began. It continued to offer inspired and

9. The printed *Jahresberichte* of the Basel Mission give statistics of congregational membership. This particular figure includes children as well as adults.

10. In 1914 the southern parts of the Ivory Coast and Ghana were just on the point of experiencing the first great wave of mass conversions in their history — those linked to the names of Prophet Harris, John Swatson, and Samson Oppong. Harris and Swatson worked farther west, but Oppong spent much of his time in the Basel Mission area of Asante, and was based in the Presbyterian congregation in Bompata for a time. How far the pre-1918 Basel missionaries, who deeply distrusted the phenomenon of mass conversion, sensed that this massive acceptance of Christian teachings (as perceived in local terms) was just around the corner is hard to establish. For Samson Oppong see McCaskie, "Social Rebellion," and Jenkins, "A Comment."

11. The annually printed Basel Mission *Jahresberichte* sometimes contain lists of the names of such indigenous employees.

12. Prempeh, "Basel and Bremen Missions," pp. 69-71, gathers a number of testimonials to the quality of Basel Mission education. See also Fred Agyemang's testimony cited above, p. 29.

innovative services to rural communities: for instance, the trading company was probably the major importer of motor lorries into the Gold Coast in the years before 1914 (see plate 25).

But then catastrophe struck. The First World War broke out. Although the local British authorities' early reactions did not threaten the Basel Mission on the Gold Coast, by 1916-17 unambiguous instructions were being received from London hostile to the German-speaking presence in the colony.[13] By the end of March 1918 all the Basel missionaries and Basel Mission Trading Company expatriates, whatever their nationality, had been expelled or interned, and the two organizations and their assets handed over, temporarily as it turned out, to British bodies. On the church side the Basel missionaries were replaced by a small staff of Free Church of Scotland missionaries who had been serving in Calabar. These immediately (in 1918) set up the structures of a national Presbyterian church with an indigenous synod, synod committee, synod clerk, and moderator. Basel missionaries were allowed back on the Gold Coast only at the end of 1925.[14] They never reached the same numerical strength as they had before 1914 (with the exception, as we shall see, of a time during the development enthusiasm of the 1950s and 1960s). As a result, the kind of authoritarian control from Basel which Miller analyzes could never function again. And this was not only a matter of numbers: since 1925 there has never been a time when the Presbyterian church had only one source of European assistance, or only one European partner.

Nineteen eighteen marks, in other words, a sudden and unexpected change, and at least on the Basel Mission side the beginning of a real crisis of consciousness. The organization was fully unprepared, theologically and morally, for what happened. No doubt it had seen its success up to 1914 as evidence of the particular blessing God was giving to a mission which was pleasing him especially, and more than its rivals. In this framework the war could only be seen as a — severe — setback caused by the evil in the world. It cer-

---

13. The best published account of the fate of the Basel Mission on the Gold Coast during the First World War is in Schlatter, *Geschichte der Basler Mission,* 4:162-95. The parallel publication on the history of the Basel Mission Trading Company is Wanner, *Die Basler Handels-Gesellschaft 1859-1959,* pp. 315-17. Prempeh, "Basel and Bremen Missions," pp. 63-132, confirms, broadly, a picture of local government sympathy with Basel missionaries everyone knew being gradually overridden by a higher authority for whom all Germans were the enemy. Prempeh does, however, indicate that there was some dirty work at the Dog and Whistle, so to speak, going on on the Gold Coast — agents of British trading firms in competition with the Mission Trading Company being suspiciously ready to urge and justify measures against their German-speaking rivals (pp. 78, 104-7).

14. Witschi, *Geschichte der Basler Mission,* 5:304-5.

tainly took a generation before the Basel Mission was able to divest itself of a majority belief that nationalism and an almost unconditional loyalty to the "powers that be" were Christian virtues, and to find the ecumenical orientation which guided it in the second half of the twentieth century.

What happened in 1918 in what became the Presbyterian Church of the Gold Coast? It is tempting to see a situation at the end of the war in which the organization broke out of the missionary-imposed carapace and started to spread its wings as an indigenous church. But, as we shall see, defining what changes happened when in the former Basel Mission church on the Gold Coast is not easy. It is, in any case, important, in attempting to trace the implications of Jon Miller's study for the later history of Christianity on the Gold Coast and in Ghana, not to set too narrow a chronological framework. Seeing the dilution of Basel Mission significance as a linear development starting in 1918 would be a mistake. If the heroic period of Basel Mission work on the Gold Coast, a time when the organization played a unique role in the development of this part of West Africa, ends abruptly with the First World War, the *idea* of that classical Basel Mission is, as we have seen, still part of the Ghanaian scene now and needs to be treated as a historical phenomenon deserving definition and discussion. This afterword begins, thus, with a narrative summary covering the period between 1918 and the year 2000, before tackling in a more analytical way the separate questions of how Basel Mission organizational forms have changed, in Ghana and in Europe, over this same period.

Narrative Summary: The Basel Mission and Ghana, 1914-1999

As noted above, the last Basel missionaries on the Gold Coast during the First World War were expelled in March 1918. Only a brief handing over was possible from the last Basel Mission *Präses* (field chairman, Rev. G. Zürcher) to the leader of the Free Church of Scotland party (Dr. A. W. Wilkie). Within months the Scottish missionaries had set up an early example of mission-church relationships in a third-world country: the indigenous church had the full — in this case Presbyterian — panoply of church organization under indigenous leadership, and power was shared in practice between the church and a missionary council. Is "shared" the operative word, however, or merely diplomatic theory? The official history of the Basel Mission[15] does express the belief (though without citing any sources) that the indigenous church leaders

---

15. Schlatter, *Geschichte der Basler Mission*, 4:195.

refused to have special constitutional arrangements made for missionaries in the structure of their newly independent church. After decades of mission tutelage they were asserting their independence. And in any case, the number of Scottish missionaries in Ghana in the years after the end of the war was tiny. There must have been wide areas of decision and administration in Ghanaian hands.[16]

One interesting episode awaits a final analysis — a movement which developed among laypeople on the Gold Coast in these years which was highly critical of the Scottish missionaries, and was pressing for the return of the Basel Mission. As a result of this pressure, a referendum of adult church members was held in 1922 in which they apparently voted two to one for future cooperation between the Basel and Free Church of Scotland missionaries (rather than the 100 percent return of the church to the responsibility of the Basel Mission). Even an insider like Samuel Prempeh finds it difficult to assess what was really going on in the church as a whole when the question was posed about the Basel Mission's return, but it seems very plausible that the officeholders who had gained independent status through the new church constitution were not keen on returning to the tutelage of the years before 1914 and they did insist, in one moment of sharp conflict in 1922, that the discussion of the future of the church must be carried on within the new Presbyterian constitution and not by self-appointed advocates of Basel interests writing independently to Basel.[17]

---

16. My main source here is Prempeh, "Basel and Bremen Missions," pp. 203-91 and 362-434. We do not yet have a thorough investigation of the organization instituted with the founding of the synod in 1918. This is a point where reflective reading of sources is especially important — it looks as if the promulgators of the 1918 church constitution were keen to use the *language* of continuity while in fact creating the organizational basis for a sharp change in that a certain independence was invested in the church structures.

17. For Prempeh's very provisional judgment about what was going on, see "Basel and Bremen Missions," esp. pp. 399-402. One touching point is that public subscription on the Gold Coast brought together a sum of £1,022 to be sent to relieve ex-Ghana missionaries suffering as a result of the war in Europe (p. 273). The referendum is discussed on pp. 402-15, and the official results are tabulated on p. 529. The acute conflict among Ghanaians when the indigenous church leadership insisted on the authority of the new formal church constitution is noted on p. 385. Veit Arlt is convinced after his reading of archival materials in Basel that African pride and self-assertion was a serious issue in relations between the Mission leadership and its indigenous employees before 1914, so that the likelihood of indigenous opposition to the full-scale return to pre-1914 forms of organization in the church is high. However, the conflicts unleashed by the movement to get the Basel Mission back to Ghana after 1918 can be seen both in the specific context of the church and in the general context of the history of the colony — two rather different arenas of action — and promise rich pickings for a sensitive analysis.

Noel Smith, whose history of the church is very much still worth reading,[18] certainly depicts a Ghanaian leadership with a steadily developing profile, pointing to the adoption in the 1926 Synod of the name Presbyterian Church of the Gold Coast[19] as an important innovation. A further important step in this consolidation of church structures lay in the promulgation in the Synod of 1929 of revised regulations for the church (the famous "Regulations, Practice and Procedure") developed from, but not identical to, the Basel Mission *Verordnungen* ("Regulations") in force at the outbreak of the war. In the following year the church took over trusteeship for property. Beyond this the church leadership began, more and more, over the years, using a term propagated by the ecumenical movement, to assert their status over against European missionary societies: "partnership."[20]

Meanwhile Basel missionaries had been welcomed back in small numbers to the Gold Coast in 1925, though initially under conditions imposed by the colonial authorities that confined their work to Asante and what is now Brong-Ahafo and put it under the clear control and responsibility of the Free Church of Scotland field secretary and the new church leadership.[21] An event of great symbolic significance occurred in 1928. The centenary of the Basel missionaries' first arrival on the Gold Coast was celebrated with a Basel delegation present, though the Basel Mission did not have the role of master of ceremonies. Simultaneously the new buildings for the Teachers' Seminary in Akropong were dedicated. This was a project of the Scottish mission (if financed by the government and to an interesting extent by public subscription).[22] The college was on a much larger scale than anything the Basel Mission had put up before 1914, and was far more "official" in its architectural style. Very soon afterward, however, building began on what is still the leading Presbyterian hospital in Ghana, at Agogo. This was Basel-financed and Basel-staffed. The leadership of PCGC must have realized at this point, if not

18. Smith, *Presbyterian Church of Ghana*, pp. 155-64.

19. I.e., neither Basel Mission Church, nor, as seems to have been the usage at the beginning of the 1920s, Scottish Mission Church.

20. The term "partnership" amounts to the declaration of independence of third-world churches, the declaration that when meeting with, for example, first-world missionary societies, they demand and receive the status of equal "partners."

21. The Basel Mission's return to Ghana in 1925 was linked to an agreement that there would be a full separation from the trading company, which had been allowed back onto the Gold Coast much sooner — 1921 — but under a new name: the Union Trading Company (UTC); see Wanner, *Die Basler Handels-Gesellschaft*, pp. 431-38. Although informal relations between Basel missionaries and UTC staff remained close, the separation between the two organizations seems to have been very real.

22. Smith, *Presbyterian Church of Ghana*, pp. 178-79.

before, that being linked to two missionary societies in a state of implicit rivalry could very well work out to their advantage.

In 1931-32 a newly appointed director of the Basel Mission, Karl Hartenstein, made an extended visit to the Gold Coast. His reflections on this experience were published in *Anibue*, a 125-page text which would still be worth putting out in English as a historical document.[23] As we shall see, it was culturally very conservative. But Hartenstein — who had a distinguished career as a soldier during the First World War — expressed himself in very laudatory tones about British colonial policy on the Gold Coast. At the time of his visit the restrictions on the Basel Mission presence were being lifted. Basel missionaries could — and did — work anywhere on the Gold Coast. Basel Mission initiatives broadened, especially in relation to women. In Agogo a Women's Teacher Training College was opened with Basel Mission staff. The first steps were also taken to build up a professionally led "women's work" in Asante.[24]

The return of the Basel Mission to the Gold Coast was not, however, problem-free. Tensions and conflicts between Basel and Scottish colleagues were frequent. It is probably not enough simply to point to the evident causes for this tension — latent nationalistic antagonism between the British and the Germans, or the Basel missionaries' dislike of an organization which was reaping where their ancestors had sown. One suspects the tension was partly because the missionaries came from such different worlds, and students of European Christian cultures might find much to interest them in relations between two such pieties forced into close and operational contact in a non-European setting. The Free Church of Scotland mission had seemed, at first sight, to be a very appropriate organization to take over the Basel Mission work. After all, many members of the Basel Mission were Reformed in background, like the Scots. The Scottish mission was also the United *Free* Church of Scotland Mission when it took over in 1918. At first sight the Free Church of Scotland might appear, like the Pietists of the Basel Mission, to be one of the rereforming movements in the nineteenth century concerned with building up pure Christian subsections in society, and convinced that the whole of a society can never be "properly" Christian. But the Free Church as a body was never committed to pure voluntarist principles, and by 1918 the Free

23. Hartenstein, *Anibue, die 'Neue Zeit' auf der Goldküste und unsere Missionsaufgabe.*

24. It is a strange paradox that women from a European tradition which was, especially in Switzerland, very slow indeed to accede to their demand for formal equality, seem to have played a major role in triggering, in the 1940s, the dynamic women's movement in the PCGC/PCG — a movement among women whose traditional position, at least, included major rights and powers. See Haas-Lill, *Erlitten und Erstritten,* and Gewecke et al., *Women Carry More.*

Church of Scotland was moving back toward membership of the established *Volkskirche,* the Church of Scotland.[25] If the Scottish missionaries in Ghana were at all motivated toward developing a kind of colonial *Volkskirche,* their Basel colleagues did still believe they were building up a church of an elect minority. This may have been one cause of tension between the Basel and the Scottish missionaries. If it was, it would have frequently spilled over into central questions in their joint operations. The Basel Mission was strong in education, for example, but Basel Mission education had always been close to the soil, orientated to building up a rural Pietist intelligentsia, and far removed from the general intellectual milieu of the German university tradition. The Scottish missionaries were often university graduates. Their emphasis on education seems to have been integrated into a much broader liberal context — and this may have been a point of tension. Furthermore, the Basel Mission policy of separating Christians from the general community had always been a thorn in the eye of traditional authorities in Ghana (as we shall see), and if the Scottish missionaries or the pastors nearest to them in the church hierarchy were trying to loosen this aspect of church discipline, the potential for conflict between the two sides will have been substantial.

It is not easy, from a desk in Basel, to assess the quality of the Scottish missionaries' work. And assessing the quality of the leadership provided by the indigenous church is even more difficult. One can say that the generation which had grown up with the Basel Mission seems to have moved smoothly into office in 1918. But two events should be mentioned which remain well known in Ghana to this day. They both indicate that the indigenous leadership of PCGC held to the culturally conservative course of their old Basel Mission mentors. In 1933 a young music teacher, Ephraim Amu, was dismissed from the teaching staff of the Presbyterian Teachers' Training College in Akropong for not adhering to the line of separation customary between Christian and traditional culture. He had preached wearing native dress, and had written motets for singing bands in an adapted local musical idiom.[26]

---

25. The Free Church of Scotland, formed by the Disruption of 1843 in protest against civil control of patronage, claimed to be the authentic national Church of Scotland. It united in 1900 with the United Presbyterian Church to form the United Free Church of Scotland. In 1929 reunion took place between the United Free Church and the Church of Scotland on a basis which reconciled establishment with spiritual independence.

26. The best account of this incident is in Agyemang, *Amu the African,* esp. pp. 73-102. Addo, in *Kwame Nkrumah,* also devotes an appendix to documenting this event — pp. 209-14. I owe this reference to Patricia Purtschert. E. O. Addo is a pastor of PCG working in the USA. Ephraim Amu's *Twenty-Five African Songs in the Twi Language,* which included music intended for use in church, was published by Sheldon Press in London in 1932.

Then in 1941 Ofori Atta I, king of Akyem Abuakwa and one of the key and influential traditional leaders on the Gold Coast, presented a long and serious memorandum to the synod of the PCGC when it met in his state capital, demanding a substantial relaxation in PCGC rules about Christians participating in traditional state practices. The conservative reply was drafted by a small group whose secretary was a rising young Protestant theologian on the Gold Coast, Christian Baëta.[27] In later life Baëta would make no bones about saying that the church had missed an important opportunity to forward inculturation — and indeed, to legitimate what was already happening at the grass roots — by responding negatively to Ofori Atta's memorandum.[28]

By 1940, however, catastrophe had already broken out over Europe again. But this time the Mission in Basel had decided what its national identification was, and had taken careful steps to ensure that when war broke out the organization would be in a good position to claim neutral (i.e., Swiss) status. All German members of its leadership in Basel retired at the outbreak of war. A "Basel Mission (German Branch)" was to take charge of the organization's assets and obligations in Germany. Control of overseas operations was firmly in the hands of the Basel Mission in Switzerland. But even so, the Basel Mission presence on the Gold Coast was substantially weakened. German members of the staff who happened to be on the Gold Coast at the outbreak of war were interned. Many Swiss missionaries were marooned by the war on leave in Europe. British measures against the Basel Mission on the Gold Coast were much more moderate than they had been in 1916-18. But there were some grounds for British worries about pro-Nazi attitudes on the part of anyone from Germany. Support for the Nazi government was very widespread among patriotic Protestants at home and abroad. Although the Basel Mission was linked through its leadership to the German church opposition, individual missionaries could take a pronouncedly pro-Nazi stand. One photograph published in Stuttgart in 1941 shows a flag with a swastika flying over the Agogo hospital compound.[29] It is conceivable that it had been "touched in" for publication in Germany. Even if this were so, it would still indicate that not all Basel Mission personnel were behaving in a neutral or anti-Nazi way as Europe moved once again into war.

In many ways the post-1945 world in which the Basel Mission gradually

---

27. A copy of this memorandum and the church's reply is held in the Basel Mission Archive (BMA), ref. no. D-10,1,15.

28. Baëta, interviewed by Paul Jenkins, Accra, October 14, 1988. See also Arends, "One Piece of Firewood," BMA ref. no. D-10,62,3.

29. The frontispiece in Gminder, *Arzt im Busch und Steppe*. Gminder was a Basel Mission doctor in Agogo, 1936-38.

returned to the Gold Coast in greater strength was very different from what it had been in 1939. Independence was evidently just round the corner — on the Gold Coast the 1948 riots were the writing on the wall. Young mission employees were now often idealistic about the handover of political authority to indigenous leaders. At the same time, missions in countries such as the Gold Coast/Ghana were soon taken up into the effort to achieve accelerated development to back up the foundation of the independent states.

This development happened in the years in which, in Europe, the impact of the Marshall Plan and the German currency reform of 1948 had once more given the Mission the economic muscle to expand its operations. So in Ghana the Mission saw a brief golden age in a postcolonial world in which, from the mid-1950s to about 1970, the mission staff reached the same size it had before 1914.[30] With Basel Mission support, PCG's medical work was extended to run three hospitals, not just one. The Mission was also involved in a strong further push in the field of education (for instance, the first principal of the new Government Women's Teacher Training College in Tamale was an experienced Basel Mission lady teacher seconded to government service).[31] Above all, the Basel Mission, like other missions elsewhere, was in the forefront of innovation. In Ghana no organization was quicker to try to apply the ideas of E. F. Schumacher ("small is beautiful," and the idea of appropriate technology) in grassroots agricultural work and in building up primary health care (including cooperation with traditional healers and midwives) around the three PCG hospitals.[32]

Even in recent years, many stories have been told by Basel Mission people about the competence and charisma of the Ghanaian leadership of PCG in

30. Statistics taken from the Basel Mission's annual printed *Jahresberichte*. The Basel Mission personnel in this period were, of course, very different from the decades before 1914. They were not products of a five-year mission seminary course, nor were they nationally and culturally homogenous — in particular, in addition to people from Switzerland and Germany there were large numbers from Holland, following an agreement on staffing between the Basel Mission and the main Dutch Protestant mission agency based at Oegstgeest near Leiden. And although some members of the Basel Mission were, at this stage, still working for decades in Ghana, the majority were there for much shorter periods.

31. Berinyuu, ed., *History*, pp. 183-87.

32. E. F. Schumacher (1911-77) was one of the great prophets of alternative forms of organization and production. His concept of "appropriate technology" (i.e., technology which could be usefully developed in specific cultural and ecological settings without damaging the environment or creating economic dependence) was extremely influential among grassroots development activists in the 1960s and 1970s; see his book *Small Is Beautiful*.

the decades after the Second World War. Fritz Raaflaub, himself an extremely energetic and authoritative Africa secretary for the Basel Mission from 1950 to 1976, loved to tell the story about who had the key influence in the decision that PCG should develop a Northern [Ghana] Mission Field in 1954: it was the then synod clerk, C. H. Clerk, a man who impressed even Raaflaub with his incisiveness.[33]

This short golden age of missionary activism was also, however, a kind of Indian summer. By the early 1970s four major developments were causing fundamental changes in the relationships between the Basel Mission and its home base, on the one side, and PCG on the other.

First, the educational effort of the Ghanaian church and of many Ghanaian families meant that the need for highly trained European specialists, which had fed the call for large numbers of mission personnel in the 1950s and 1960s, declined sharply after 1970. So, therefore, did the number of Basel missionaries. These were now, incidentally, termed "fraternal workers" and were mainly requested for work in especially remote regions like Upper East, or for innovative tasks like building up the Tema Industrial Mission. In a moment of great historical significance the last Basel Mission field secretary, Ernst Peyer, returned home in 1971, and his responsibilities were taken over by a Ghanaian member of the church administration, the secretary of the Interchurch and Ecumenical Relations Committee (ICER).[34] In the future all fraternal workers would have a local superior officer, and only the rights and duties of any other employee of the PCG.

Secondly, structural changes were happening in the world of mission in Europe. The Basel Mission and its European constituency were very sensitive to the call made by the World Council of Churches at its Third General Assembly in New Delhi in 1961, that mission should be seen as part of the church and be integrated into church structures. In a complicated maneuver which had different organizational characteristics in Switzerland and south-

33. See Fritz Raaflaub, "Mission in Northern Ghana: A Basel Mission Perspective of How It All Began," in Berinyuu, ed., *History,* pp. 11-22. C. H. Clerk was a Ghanaian pastor and direct descendant of the black Christians and freed slaves whom the Basel Mission had brought from the West Indies to support the establishment of their work in the 1840s.

34. To make this point quite specifically: the head of the Basel Mission in Ghana had, up to 1914, been designated the *Präses,* which may be translated "field chairman," or perhaps even "field superintendent." At some stage after the First World War the head Basel missionary on the Gold Coast had come to be designated "field secretary," but this office was clearly the direct lineal descendant of the *Präses.* So when Ernst Peyer returned to Switzerland and was not replaced, this was a major event, recognized as such by PCG, whose then synod clerk, A. H. Kwansa, took over the post of secretary of the ICER as Peyer's successor.

west Germany, the Basel Mission became part of two overarching bodies linking a small group of missionary societies (of which it was in both cases by far the largest) and the regional established Reformed or Lutheran churches. The separation between Switzerland and Germany was necessary because the legal basis of the churches did not allow them, in budgeting matters, to be part of a two-nation European organization. In a decision calculated to divide the responsibility for overseas territories which had previously been concentrated in Basel, the German body EMS[35] was made responsible for carrying on Basel Mission work in the Mission's two oldest and best-established fields, Ghana and southwest India. Formally the Basel Mission is a member of EMS and has delegated its work in these two areas on a permanent basis to EMS, so that it is not correct to say that the Basel Mission is no longer present in Ghana. But both in Switzerland and in Ghana many people have found it difficult to understand why the major official linking the world of German-speaking Protestantism with the Presbyterian Church of Ghana should be the Africa secretary of EMS with his office in Stuttgart, rather than the Africa secretary of the Basel Mission with his office in Basel.

Thirdly, the model one can frequently meet in the non-Western world, of a single missionary society still exerting great influence as the major overseas partner of a church it claimed to have founded,[36] already decisively weakened, in the case of PCG, by the First World War, became less and less appropriate as a way of understanding this church. In a development which has become formalized since the 1970s, when PCG sits around a table — as it does every year — with its first-world partners, not just one or two organizations are represented, but up to ten, including people representing missions of a Presbyterian/Reformed character in the USA, Scotland, England, Holland, and Germany/Switzerland, and several specialist church bodies for development cooperation.

Finally, the balance between first- and third-world organizations in the German-speaking world has been changed by a systematic policy of having people from overseas partner churches like PCG working in Europe, and creating as the top bodies in EMS and the Basel Mission, mission councils in which all partners, including those overseas, are represented. EMS's international Mission Council and the Basel Mission's Joint Planning Council are still new. But Ghanaian "fraternal workers" (missionaries) have been working

35. EMS is the abbreviated form of the name Evangelisches Missionswerk Südwestdeutschland, known in English as the Association of Missions and Churches in South-West Germany.
36. In fact, of course, no African church was "founded" only by expatriates.

in southwest Germany and Switzerland since the early 1970s, characteristically on five-year contracts (which allows time for people to become fluent in German). And for some years a member of the Executive Committee which takes daily responsibility for EMS work (the ecumenical secretary) was also a PCG pastor, Peter Kodjo.

This narrative summary should close with the remark that, of course, the context of EMS/Basel Mission relations with PCG is very different now from what it was in the relatively prosperous 1950s and 1960s. Ghana suffered a major economic crisis in the years around 1980, recovered by following painful World Bank prescriptions for economic policy, and is still very much dependent on external loans and the money transferred back to their relations at home by Ghanaians holding down professional jobs in Europe and North America. Various factors stopped PCG's first-world partners being drawn into ever growing responsibility for the PCG budget during the crisis years, however — not least the ideology firmly held on both sides that the church is independent and self-supporting. The visitor to PCG finds, indeed, nowadays, a lively church refreshingly independent at all sorts of levels, and one with a multiplicity of international contacts.[37] The same factors that created a colorful Ghanaian diaspora in many parts of the world have also helped to create and maintain a number of local and regional partnerships in which, characteristically, church districts in Ghana maintain direct relationships with church districts in the first world — for instance, the relationship which exists between Kwahu in Ghana and the Upper Rhine Deanery of the Protestant church in Baden, Germany. This was impressively displayed by a delegation from Kwahu (along with half a dozen other delegations from other parts of the world) at the Mission Festival for the year 2000 in the small Schwarzwald town of Schopfheim.

The Influence of Nineteenth-Century Basel Mission Forms of Organization in Ghana since 1918

Miller's analysis of organization and authority in the pre-1914 Basel Mission prompts one to attempt more than merely a summary narrative of the eighty years of Presbyterian presence on the Gold Coast and in Ghana since the First World War. What happened to this oligarchic, not to say absolutist, way of

---

37. In Paul Gifford's *African Christianity*, p. 62, the PCG is reported as having the highest rate of growth among mainline Protestant churches in Ghana in a survey carried out recently by the Ghana Evangelisation Committee.

running a human community once the single focus on the authority of the Basel Mission Committee had been fractured? The answer to this question needs two separate geographical parts. One refers to Europe, and is chronologically posterior to the other, since in the Basel Mission in Europe the First World War and what followed will have been seen, at the beginning, primarily as a setback, not demanding radical change. More dramatic were the immediate changes on the Gold Coast in 1917-18 where, as we have seen, not only were the missionaries, the source of local authority, expelled. They were replaced by a much smaller group of missionaries from a different culture who surely did not intend to exercise Basel Mission–type authority, even if they had the numbers to do so, and who immediately set up the formal structures of an independent church. At first sight we are looking at something like a revolution.

The question of the radicality of the change in 1917-18 is, indeed, evidently more than merely rhetorical. Jon Miller makes clear how strict and hierarchical the Basel Mission organization had been, and we can assume without risk of contradiction that it was still operating on these lines at the moment of the outbreak of the war. So the removal of Basel authority must have been dramatic indeed. It is true that his subject was the organization of the *Mission*, and not of the indigenous church and its congregations. Nevertheless, we can also be sure that the Basel Committee's control over all its employees, European and African — amply documented by the various questions in personnel administration which had to be referred back to Basel — was amplified and consolidated by the missionaries' attempt to reproduce in relations between them and their Gold Coast employees the relations which existed between the Basel Committee and they themselves. A more extended analysis of this pre-1914 hierarchical parallel between the Basel Mission Committee and the missionaries, and between the missionaries and their Gold Coast staff and congregations, confirms this point. But it also suggests that our approach to what happened after 1918 must be somewhat more sophisticated than the word "revolution" at first sight implies.

First, looking at their pre-1914 relations, the missionaries evidently felt the same kind of worried skepticism about the abilities and reliability of their Gold Coast staff as inspired the Basel Committee's attitudes to them. This is most evident in a point mentioned, a little shamefacedly, by Wilhelm Schlatter in his official history of the Basel Mission and its fields during the First World War. When the missionaries were expelled, they were only beginning to consider the possibility of handing over responsibility for local congregational finances to local leadership — under appropriate safeguards, of course.[38] Key

---

38. Schlatter, *Geschichte der Basler Mission,* 4:191.

power, in other words, still lay in missionary hands, and having been a senior member of the Basel Mission's indigenous staff on the Gold Coast in the years before war broke out was no preparation, at least in a straightforward sense, for self-government afterward.

So, just as the Basel Committee did not trust the judgment of the people it had itself trained (i.e., the missionaries) and insisted on close control of their activities, so the missionaries did not trust the judgment of the people who had gone through their schools and seminaries on the Gold Coast. It is true that, probably from the 1880s, regular synods were held by the Basel Mission at a district level — the Twi Synod and the Ga Synod — and it is equally true that none of us have looked to see what the proceedings of these synods were like. But the likelihood is that only in a very limited sense were these allowed to be an exercise of power and authority by indigenous people. To begin with, they were only *district* synods and not national ones. They met much less frequently than the annual main conferences of the missionaries. And the existence of a synod is no guarantee of even a dawning wish to delegate power and act more democratically. Even in the 1980s and 1990s in Basel, it was possible to hear conservative voices saying loudly and clearly that the organization's own European synod was primarily an organ through which the leadership could inform the masses about mission policy. If this kind of approach — reminiscent of the theories in Russian government circles about the nineteenth-century Duma — was prominent in Basel in the late twentieth century, how much more will it have characterized missionary attitudes to synods in Africa a century before?

Second, an acute paradox has to be seen in the Basel Mission's famous attention to language[39] and the massive reporting required of its missionaries about situations on the Gold Coast on the one hand, and the fact that the Mission's Basel leadership before 1914 had scarcely ever traveled beyond the limits of the European grand tour on the other. The message of this fundamental characteristic of the organization of the Basel Mission must have been that, in order to set the Mission's policy and pronounce judgment on its work, it was not necessary to know much about particular situations or cultures. The clarity and purity of theological thinking were what counted — an attitude which could be immediately taken over, without adjustment, by a Gold Coast church leadership.[40]

39. Most recently considered by Bearth, "J. G. Christaller."
40. Ulrike Sill pointed out, when reading an early draft of this paper, that more intensive study of the Basel leadership's responses to reporting from the Gold Coast in the period analyzed by Jon Miller could be very suggestive. Certainly the volume of the docu-

Third, however, there was a serious contrast in one respect between the Basel Mission as an organization of Europeans and its indigenous church on the Gold Coast. The Basel Mission could maintain organizational integrity at a very high level on the Gold Coast because it had almost complete control over its white employees. Indeed, the only Europeans resident on the Gold Coast and exercising influence over the Basel Mission were the Mission's Basel-trained employees.[41] The situation of the indigenous church was different. There was a very large wastage rate in the ranks of young teachers and catechists. Various infringements of church rules led to their dismissals, all linked to the Basel Mission's attempt to ban aspects of popular or traditional social practice from its church — in relations between the sexes and patterns of family life, for instance, or in participation in traditional festivals (including, of course, dancing at them). Dismissed ex-teachers remained in the communities around the mission stations (though not in the Salems) and, if they had the right gifts, became people of general influence with increasing age. Indeed, there are clear indications that such people, with their literacy and their knowledge of European ways, were becoming preferred candidates for chieftaincy, for instance in Akwapim, already in 1900. And my suspicion is, too, that they played a leading role in the spread of cocoa farming.[42] Their opposition to Basel Mission rules was making for considerable difficulty well before 1914. So that maintaining the kind of organizational integrity which Jon Miller describes in relation to Europeans was impossible in the indigenous church on the Gold Coast.[43]

---

ments sent to Basel from Ghana from 1828 to 1914 (Archive series D-1) is five or six times larger than the volume of letters sent by the Basel leadership to Ghana. How did the leadership choose which documents from Ghana to discuss and respond to? And what did members of the staff on the Gold Coast feel if, over years, as often seems to have been the case, they received no personal response to what they had written?

41. As far as I know, only Simon Süss and Jakob Isliker stayed on the Gold Coast after being dismissed from the service of the Basel Mission, and Süss emigrated eventually to the USA (see index to this volume, under Süss and Isliker). Of course, colonial officers were usually also "Europeans resident on the Gold Coast and exercising influence over the Basel Mission," but this was at a very different level, and only on rare occasions a threat to the Basel Mission's own internal authority.

42. One of the weaknesses of the literature on the development of cocoa growing in Ghana is that the role of people who had been trained in Basel Mission schools or had been Basel Mission employees is not discussed in any extended way. But it is surely no coincidence that the home areas of the first generation of migrant cocoa farmers were almost exclusively areas with a strong Basel Mission presence.

43. When working on the history of the Anglican Church in Ghana at the beginning of the twentieth century, I realized that, in a sense, Anglican congregations acted as a flexible African church in Basel Mission areas, gathering up people under church discipline in

All of this points, at first sight, to the years after 1917 seeing a considerable revolution in the Basel Mission's former church. The exercise of power from Basel which must have penetrated way down into the life even of isolated rural outstations[44] disappeared in the course of a few months. The Scottish missionaries were neither numerous enough to take over the old Basel Mission role nor, one suspects, had the intention of so doing. Leadership had to be taken over, in the framework of the new synod and its organs, by indigenous pastors and church elders.

But did the new Gold Coast leadership work differently from the Basel missionaries, or develop new ways of thinking or acting? The easiest hypothesis to formulate and discuss is the idea that after 1917 the PCGC leadership attempted to maintain the authority previously exerted by the Basel missionaries as well as the tradition that leadership was concerned essentially with theological purity and not with creative adjustments to local problems caused by local styles of life and local culture. Various straws in the wind suggest that this happened. One refers to long-term continuities. More than one senior pastor of PCG has remarked, on hearing or reading Miller's expositions of Basel Mission organizational principles, that one or the other point which has been puzzling him in PCG organizational models has been cleared up — for example, the very centralized, not to say military, way in which PCG pastors are posted to new congregations by headquarters' decision clearly goes back to the all-important centrally steered allocation of missionaries to their posts in the Basel Mission period. The incidents involving the dismissal of Ephraim Amu and the broad refusal to negotiate with Ofori Atta I (see above) also point in the same direction: when challenged frontally to adjust PCGC regulations to greater flexibility in relations to indigenous culture, the church leadership refused.

This would indicate that something very much less than a revolution happened. But this view can easily turn out to be Eurocentric. The only in-depth study of actual congregational life in its local cultural setting which we can consult — John Middleton's study of Akropong in the 1970s — offers us an intriguing view of continuing encounter and negotiation between the traditional and the Christian communities in the town, and asserts that the pro-

---

the Basel Mission. They, like Methodist congregations in Basel Mission areas, thus threatened the integrity of Basel Mission discipline. Indeed, because of this, not a few early Anglican priests and teachers were Basel Mission trained and originated from towns like Larteh — see Jenkins, "Anglican Church," esp. pp. 23-39.

44. The major new exploration of the nineteenth-century Basel Mission Committee's ambition to control aspects of the lives of remote families in rural areas of the Gold Coast is Haenger, *Slaves and Slave-Holders*, chaps. 2 and 3.

cess of achieving mutual accommodation between the two goes back to the last quarter of the nineteenth century.[45] Michelle Gilbert's more recent anthropological essays on Akwapim, though not primarily focused on the church, also frequently portray relations between church and "tradition" in which tradition plays a very strong role.[46] How far did the removal of Basel missionaries from positions of authority facilitate the search for mutual accommodation at an informal, local level? And did the new indigenous church leadership implicitly approach this question with new values, and new intentions?

The more one reflects on this kind of issue, the more it becomes apparent that a simple question posed at the level of organizational orthodoxy misses the drama of the "reception" of the classical Basel Mission's model of organization and morality and its long-term impact on Christian consciousness in Ghana. Indeed, the case of Ephraim Amu reveals some strange features when one examines matters in detail. Amu is widely, and often passionately, depicted as a victim of alienating discipline, which indeed at the beginning of the 1930s he was. But in fact, from then on his music swept through the Presbyterian and other churches, passed on orally from singing band to singing band, and thus really did achieve, as Agyemang puts it, with a twinkle in his eye, a "quiet revolution." Amu himself died an internationally respected musician and composer and an active and recognized church leader in his district of southeastern Ghana, while the church leaders who dismissed him have been forgotten.[47] So why, sixty or seventy years later, is it the story of his dismissal in 1933 which is so dominant, and not the history of his musical revolution? We are forced here into a kind of discourse analysis, with all its subjectivity, when trying to explain this phenomenon. This analysis seems to indicate that, beyond the more lapidary question of the Basel Mission's influence on organization, its place in people's consciousness in Ghana —

45. Middleton, "One Hundred and Fifty Years."

46. For an example of early, close, if conflict-ridden, relations between church and traditional state, see the essay in which Michelle Gilbert reminds us that a pastor's wife was virtually queen mother of Akwapim for a time early in the twentieth century; Gilbert, "Cimmerian Darkness." Gilbert also depicts the dilemmas of a family in recent decades which was closely connected to the PCG but wanted at all costs to maintain its right to an important traditional office; see Gilbert, "The Christian Executioner."

47. The relationships between Ephraim Amu and Christian Baëta and the PCGC/PCG are complicated, because both were really members of the Evangelical Presbyterian Church (the former Bremen Mission Church). The links between the two churches were close, however. Baëta himself received his main theological training in the Basel Mission House, and Amu also received part of his postprimary training in Basel Mission/Presbyterian Church institutions on the Gold Coast.

linked to the strength of its organization in the decades before 1914 and the quality of the demands this made on Ghanaians — is rather extraordinary.[48]

The story of Amu's dismissal fitted perfectly into the common nationalist and academic discourse about the Basel Mission which I experienced in the 1960s in Ghana. It was difficult, in those heady nationalistic days, to hear praise for anything colonial at these levels of Ghanaian life. But the Basel Mission was the target of a particularly bitter critique. Its Salems, its Christian villages, had uprooted Ghanaians from their culture, it was argued, and separated them from their traditional loyalties. The separation achieved was depicted as complete. Kings and chiefs lost their subjects, families their members, when they converted and joined the Basel Mission church. The Amu story appeared to make the critique unanswerable. The church had been prepared to sacrifice its relations to a very talented young man, who was known for his upstanding character and puritanism, on the altar of a laughable refusal to let quite innocent aspects of traditional culture into its activities. This attitude had its roots in the old Basel Mission's insistence on pushing through a dichotomous view of Christianity and heathenism.

It is true that even as this very nationalistic discourse was being conducted in academic and political circles, one could participate in discourse of a different nature at another level. As we have seen, John Middleton provides us with the best printed access to the complex story of the role of local church elders in the give-and-take between Christian and traditional community,[49] in which the boundaries of acceptable Christian behavior were being constantly revised "outward." Faced with Middleton's findings — which, one has to say, are still not very much integrated into modern Ghanaian discussion about the church — the idea of a deep gulf between Christian and traditional communities needs immediate adjustment.[50] But the conduct of relations be-

48. Ebenezer Obiri Addo is part of the phenomenon I am discussing here, since he refers to Amu's dismissal in 1933 to elucidate conflicts between the Ghana Christian Council and Nkrumah which took place thirty years later (Addo, *Kwame Nkrumah*, p. 135). He does this without referring to the actual impact Amu has had in the Ghanaian churches — or, indeed, asking what Amu's attitude to Nkrumah was. Interestingly enough, neither Addo nor Agyemang write about Amu's position in the independence struggle or in the cultural tensions between the churches and the Convention People's Party.

49. See the printed and translated version of an elder's history of the Presbyterian Church in Bompata, which begins with the history of the origins of the town and thus indicates how the coming of the church is linked to the very heart of traditional identity: M. P. Frempong, "A History of the Presbyterian Church at Bompata in Asante Akyem . . . Translated by E. A. Kyerematen," *Ghana Notes and Queries* 12 (1972): 20-23.

50. The challenge posed by such findings to the theory of a complete separation *in practice* between Christian and traditional community is frequently confirmed when peo-

tween Christianity and tradition which Middleton observed draws a lot of its dynamic and seriousness from people's clear knowledge in Akropong of the intransigent position adopted by the old missionaries and still — so it would seem — regarded, by various groups, as possessing powerful legitimacy.

More recently the word "discipline" has dominated in the conversations I have had about the classical Basel Mission in Ghana. Miller notices this discourse even in Ghanaian daily papers and in convictions expressed by President Rawlings.[51] This discourse goes on at two levels. It is certainly possible to hear people talking for whom "discipline" means, quite crudely, being beaten. In their years as pupils in rural schools, such people had suffered at the hands of teachers trained by pre-1914 Basel missionaries, or claiming to continue their ethos. Certainly the stick was an important part of family and school pedagogics in nineteenth-century Europe and was applied in Pietist families in Pietist ways. It would be very surprising if it was not exported, by hand of missionary, to African schools and ideas of Christian upbringing in Ghana.[52]

There is, however, a second strand in the discourse about the Basel Mission and discipline. This insists that there was more to discipline than merely imposing one's will, as an adult, on children, by the resort to violence. In this

---

ple study the nineteenth-century Ghana archive in Basel in depth. In my opinion the area where "traditional practice" and the Basel Mission congregations overlapped should be a priority for attempts to research the nineteenth-century situation, not least because it bears directly on the position of the many chiefs who are sincerely Christian but under church discipline in PCG for participating in rites of ancestor veneration.

51. See above, pp. 30-31. In 1981 I was assigned to act as Basel Mission *okyeame* (spokesman) during the only visit yet paid to the Basel Mission House by a current head of state — the then president of Ghana, Hilla Limann. I was asked to speak first, and *inter alia* apologized on behalf of the Basel Mission for our ancestors' refusal to engage in dialogue about appropriate forms of Christian behavior within Ghanaian cultures. President Limann had a prepared speech with a simple message and made no reference to what I had said. The Basel Mission had brought discipline and education, and contemporary Ghana needed both. He seemed to be offering back to the Basel Mission its old status as a major provider of schools. But the institution was — sadly? — deaf in that ear.

52. This could be a serious theme for someone looking for a research topic. Were all European cultures really equally reactionary about corporal punishment in, say, 1900? When and why did corporal punishment decline as an instrument of mission? Interestingly enough, Veit Arlt's impression is that Basel Mission discipline became more rigid and more violent among the last generations of missionaries before 1914. One should also note that the *locus classicus* for these questions in the Basel Mission is the life of Hermann Hesse, son and grandson of Basel missionaries, with his touching memories of a community of two parents and their children in which an intensive and attractive family life was constantly being cut across by the parents' perceived need to mete out punishment according to norms in their environing society which they shared only halfheartedly.

kind of discussion discipline is seen as a general education in modern kinds of organization. Discipline meant, for instance, having a clearly planned day, divided into periods, signaled by the school bell. Sanctions here might be less directly violent: the person who did not turn up at the right time for a meal would have to go hungry. Evidently we are in contact here with a Ghanaian discourse like that on early factory discipline during the Industrial Revolution in Europe — the development of forms of cooperation which linked large numbers of people in complicated activities carried out to an accurate time plan. The Basel Mission was, in this view, not simply propagating puritan discipline but offering the classical Protestant religious and organizational preparation for people's involvement with modern forms of production.

Discourse analysis *à distance* is a risky and subjective matter. But so many straws in the wind seem to indicate that the unusually strong organization and discipline of the pre-1914 Basel Mission remain a powerful point of attraction or repulsion, and a powerful point of orientation, in Ghanaian historical consciousness. It looks as if the memory of the old Basel Mission has become a powerful "other" when Ghanaians think about the past, about progress, and about the good life. But if this is the case, it is also an "other" which can hamper modern initiatives, and about which there is considerable ambivalence. John Middleton remembers meeting the feeling in Akropong that the time of real heroes, of greater reality even, lies in the past, in the age of the pre-1914 Basel missionaries.[53] There are good reasons why people no longer follow Basel Mission rules nowadays, but it is indeed not hard to find the sentiment that the period of really effective progress and development lay with the missionaries and those indigenous people who seconded them. And I remember, too, Swiss development workers operating in two localities, and wondering why in one Presbyterian church a free development of liturgy and spirituality was taking place in response to people's intellectual and emotional needs, while in the other an old, sober Basel Mission tradition was being maintained which seemed to have little to do with people's daily lives. The explanation they had worked out for themselves was that the first congregation was unburdened by a local history with Basel missionaries while the second was an old Basel Mission station, and it was even said there that a Basel missionary was buried under the communion table.[54]

53. Personal communication.
54. This is almost certainly incorrect. There is a well-tended Basel Mission graveyard. But, as Veit Arlt has pointed out, family elders *were* traditionally buried in their compounds, so the idea that a missionary is buried under the altar has clear traditional roots.

Change in the Post-1918 Basel Mission in Europe

Whereas the former Basel Mission church on the Gold Coast had to adjust quickly to the absence of Basel missionaries, the Mission itself was not forced into rapid change. This seems paradoxical, since the impact of the war on the Mission in Europe was grave. It was expelled from all its overseas mission fields other than China. Many of its young German men in training were killed in action. The war and the general economic and political difficulties which followed it in Germany seriously weakened its financial basis. And to cap it all there was an attempt, backed, it seems, by "perfidious Albion," to promote a new missionary society in Protestant Switzerland untainted by the link to Germany. This, it was hoped, would ease the Basel Mission out of its dominant position both in Switzerland and in relation to mission work in southwestern India.[55] Nevertheless, there was clearly enough conservative stubbornness to keep a minimal Basel Mission organization ticking over at home until the time came when the Mission could return to normal. By 1930 the scale of the conservative reconstruction of the organization was becoming visible on the Gold Coast. The old Basel Mission had been led — both in terms of committee membership and recruitment to its leading executive offices — by people who had not experienced mission work overseas, but who expected to exercise their authority in the organization by virtue of their social positions and their superior training and knowledge. In 1930 this was still the case, and the faith in the authority of the center was so pronounced that the new director (who, as we have seen, visited the Gold Coast in 1931-32) and the new Africa *Inspektor* who was appointed in 1932 were both young men who had not worked overseas.

The old Basel Mission had also been convinced of the correctness of its own "only-one-way" spirituality and ethic. Politics had forced the Mission to share its work on the Gold Coast with another missionary body whose spirituality and ethics were different. But the Basel Mission, at the time of Hartenstein's visit in 1931-32, was claiming a special calling and responsibility to set the theological tone in PCGC. It was, at the same time, sending out three pre-1914 missionaries as *Seelsorger* — i.e., with a specific responsibility for the cure of souls — to promote revival and evangelization among the nominal and falling-away Christians of its oldest station areas. Hartenstein's

---

55. This is a reference to the short-lived Kanarese Mission; see Jenkins, "Die Basler Mission im kolonialen Spannungsfeld Indien." Samuel Prempeh has also found traces of British attempts to encourage a purely Swiss Protestant mission which would take over the Basel Mission's work on the Gold Coast; Prempeh, "Basel and Bremen Missions," pp. 92-97.

Anibue expressed deep conservatism about true Christian ethics. He refused to accept any compromise at all between the "Christian" nuclear family in Europe and the possibility of a Christian extended family on the Gold Coast. He was horrified at even the most minimal rhythmic movements on the part of church choirs or singing bands. When one puts these points together, one sees a mission evidently bidding to reset traditional standards of belief and behavior truly pleasing to God, and to reestablish structures which would allow it to promote these standards by moral pressure and personal influence, even if the clear "command" structures which characterized its work before 1914 were no longer possible.

The decades in which a Basel Mission Committee could exercise the full panoply of authority as analyzed by Jon Miller were past, however. A brief look at one Basel Mission field chairman, Hermann Henking, makes this clear. At an annual conference of the Basel Mission staff on the Gold Coast in 1936, Henking gave a keynote lecture under the strident title *Führer an die Front,* which, roughly translated, means "The real leaders must go into the trenches."[56] This demanded a more decentralized form of organization in the Basel Mission, with more powers in the hands of missionaries "in the field" and far fewer questions reserved to the decision of the Committee in Basel. The problems arising from the triangular partnership with the indigenous church and the Scottish missionaries had brought Henking to the point where he saw a great weakness in the need to refer so many decisions to Basel which, on the Scottish side, were being decided by the missionaries themselves on the spot. Getting a decision from Basel might take a couple months, and the answer, formulated in the rarefied middle air of a European mission headquarters, might well then turn out to be evidently inadequate compared with decisions evolved on the spot.[57]

The mission leadership in Basel did not approve of Henking's suggestion. But "straws in the wind" — memories of younger missionaries, or Henking's son's own estimate of how his father coped with being caught between relatively streamlined Scottish procedures and the slow elaborate procedures of his own

56. BMA, reference D-4,5,3a.

57. A. W. Wilkie had a professional profile and a reputation far beyond anything the Basel Mission could put into the field in the interwar period. He was a member of the Phelps-Stokes Commission, and eventually left the Gold Coast in 1931 to take over the leadership of the Lovedale institutions in South Africa. It would also be interesting to know if the famous first headmaster of Achimota, A. G. Fraser, who was from Scotland and had been a missionary in Ceylon (though with the CMS), had a hand in Scottish mission deliberations on the Gold Coast. If he did, this will have emphasized the weakness of the Basel Mission's cadre.

mission — indicate how the Mission's workers on the Gold Coast began to cope with the situation. Information and queries sent to Basel came to be filtered, in order to maintain a degree of necessary operational independence.[58]

This tactic — though no doubt attempted before 1914 — was soon brought to naught in those generations by the mechanisms of mutual surveillance which Miller describes. But in the 1930s these were heavily diluted since, at a fundamental level, the Mission had to adjust its policies on the Gold Coast to the wishes of its Ghanaian and Scottish partners, and the negotiations necessary to do this took place on the Gold Coast and not in Basel. The relatively simple bilateral relations of the decades before 1914 between mission staff on the Gold Coast and mission leadership in Basel had been replaced by a complex situation in which policy was undoubtedly being made on the Gold Coast in more or less formal tripartite consultations between the "men on the spot."

Nevertheless, in the 1930s the leadership of the Mission in Basel retained its ambition to direct and control in the pre-1914 spirit. The orientation to that pre-1914 past in the mission and in its German Pietist background was too strong, and the conviction that the First World War had been a setback which would be overcome by God's help was too pronounced. The years of the Second World War appear to have been the crucial period of transition in Basel when the determination to change the inner structures of the Basel Mission matured under the presidentship of Alphonse Koechlin.[59] He was a major figure in the ecumenical movement, a patriarch of the first order in his instincts, yet someone who clearly insisted, after the war, that the key area secretary posts in Basel should be held by people with field experience, and one who saw that the Mission could not continue its mission seminary in Basel. Already during the war recruitment was being reoriented to taking people into the Mission who had completed a normal professional training and

58. In an important statement of memory about Hermann Henking's missionary attitudes, his son Karl Henking — himself a professor of anthropology emeritus of the University of Zurich — asserted, in a conversation at which I was present in 1997, that his father had equipped himself with an umbrella and umbrella-carrier, a stool and stool-carrier, and a linguist/*okyeame* so that, as Basel Mission local chairman, he could approach Ghanaian chiefs in a way appropriate to their and his status. He went on to say that this, as a contravention of what had become the Basel Mission's general attitude to culture, was never reported to Basel. Furthermore, since his father's papers were lost in a U-boat attack during the Second World War, our only source of this information was the family oral tradition with which he was acquainting us.

59. Alphonse Koechlin was a member of an elite Basel family, the leading Swiss Protestant church leader during the Second World War, a key figure in founding the World Council of Churches, and president of the Basel Mission from the mid-1930s till 1959.

would probably return to this profession on completion of some years in service overseas. The social hierarchy which had characterized the old Basel Mission lay in rapid dissolution. In the future the same kind of people, sociologically defined, would be working for the Mission abroad as held the key positions in its leadership at home.[60] And indeed, people in the leadership at home had often experienced a change in their own characters and attitudes caused by the experiences of a substantial period of work in the context of a non-Western culture.

It was, thus, only after 1945 that the Basel Mission finally reconstructed itself. At the same time it came to be convinced that the ecumenical view of mission, summed up in the terms "partnership," "dialogue," and "justice," had to be the compass guiding its policies in the postwar world. This reorientation was not simply an internal matter but a response to the two metachanges which had happened in its environment between 1945 and 1950. German nationalism collapsed in circumstances so disgraceful as to demand a new spirituality purged of even implicit national special pleading. Moreover, the rapid achievement of colonial independence (plus the trauma of the Chinese Revolution) meant a radical change in the status of peoples which up to then had mainly been seen as objects of mission work. It was not only that the Mission no longer possessed the kind of socially deferential staff overseas which had fostered the exercise of authority in Basel. In a world in which racial equality was being propagated forcefully and Christianity was losing its privileged status, people in Basel might have views about mission policy, but the natural authority of the people-on-the-spot meant that the Mission House in Basel was becoming primarily a recipient, rather than a purveyor, of wisdom.

Conclusion

A missionary society articulates the responses of active Christians of one or more related pieties in a "sending" region to their contact with people living in radically different cultures, or practicing other religions. The nineteenth-century Basel Mission indicates that this definition is neutral in respect of democracy — the authoritarian structure Jon Miller describes flourished be-

60. Dubach-Vischer, *Mit Boot und Stethoskop,* is an account of the life of her parents as Basel missionaries in Kalimantan in the 1930s and early 1940s. The tensions between her father, a doctor, and one of the very few members of an elite Basel family to work overseas in the mission before 1945, and the missionaries who had been trained in the Basel Seminary were often acute, and can count as a good example of the problems which the traditional social hierarchy in the organization were still causing in the interwar period.

cause, as he shows, through an innovative communications network people of two social classes were brought into cooperation to support an institution which needed both to survive. The question of how such an organization, with its supporting movement reaching right out into most villages with a Protestant population in southwestern Germany and German-speaking Switzerland, could come to reorient itself so radically to an open internationalist and democratic ecumenism, is no mere footnote in the history of the twentieth century. It seems to indicate that those articulating a broad popular movement in mission can indeed respond to experience, and are not necessarily tied by neofundamentalism to continue the structures and practices of a bygone age.

A Presbyterian Church of Ghana is no less tightly bound to a broad population, again reaching out to remote farming villages, especially throughout southeastern Ghana and Asante. It reflects all the complexities of Ghana's relationships with the process of modernization and Westernization, energized not only by the wish to appropriate the fruits of industrialization, but also to explore the solutions offered by Basel (and Scottish) Christianity to the cosmological and social problems set by southern Ghanaian societies. As with the Mission at home, questions of continuity, of the proper respect for truths which seemed unchallenged generations ago, are very present, and this applies not only to the future of traditional Basel Mission piety. It applies to the future of local tradition, and the not-to-be-forgotten problem of the hundreds of Christian chiefs in contemporary Ghana who, by performing the traditional rites of ancestor veneration, are put automatically under church discipline in a fellowship like the Presbyterian church.

A mere human — as opposed to a recording angel — easily becomes giddy when assessing as one linked set of related developments the kinds of changes the Basel Mission and the Presbyterian Church of Ghana have experienced since, say, 1850. But this complex task for a historian reflects the complexity of the task faced by the two institutions — articulating change as sovereign institutions in each one's own quite distinct situation without losing touch with the long-standing partner. Jon Miller has shown how far innovative research can enrich our view of one side of this relationship, in one of the two or three major periods into which their 170 years of contact can be divided. I have tried to sketch in this essay how rewarding an equally intensive study of one side and its links to the other could be for the twentieth century. Social histories which arch between the grass roots in two continents as different as Europe and Africa — and which study the pursuit of ideals and fellowship — surely deserve such sustained and ever deepening attention.

Methodological Appendix

Archival Sources

I first became aware of the potential for research in the Basel Mission from Paul Jenkins, the social historian who administers the Mission's archives. He knew of my interest in organizational sociology and suggested that I would find the record preserved by the Mission to be one of extraordinary extent and richness. At his invitation I visited Basel to take a close look at the archive's holdings. Based on what I learned during that visit, I was able to persuade the Faculty Research and Innovation Fund at the University of Southern California to support a second trip to compile more complete documentation on specific aspects of the organizational structure of the Mission. The result of that visit, which lasted several weeks, was a successful research proposal to the National Science Foundation that provided the support for most of the work that appears here. Before the first edition of this book appeared in 1994, I made more than a dozen trips of varying duration to Switzerland. Altogether these visits added up to about a year in the Basel Mission Archive.

The members of the Basel Mission community today, particularly those who work in the library and archives, are determined to preserve the record of their past but also to understand their history in order to build upon it. An open-archive policy is followed, and the holdings are catalogued and administered in a way that facilitates their accessibility to serious researchers. I should point out that "serious" here includes facility with German and the willingness to learn to read the nineteenth-century Gothic handwriting used in most of the Mission's early documents. Given the nature of my project, I did not need to see individual records from the recent past and was not hindered by the archive's thirty-year rule on confidentiality. I was not asked to use pseudonyms for the individuals whose careers I have described. My accounts and interpretations of their actions can therefore be evaluated and compared with accounts by other researchers who have worked with the same documentation.

The Mission allowed the archivist Waltraud Haas-Lill to work with me under a subcontract arrangement. Her contributions included searching out and abstracting documents, providing assistance with translations and transcriptions of key materials, conducting interviews with knowledgeable informants, carrying out research of a demographic sort in the civil records of Switzerland and Germany, and, not least, sharing with me her own extensive knowledge of the organization's past and present. Her work on women in the Mission is the most comprehensive to date, and I have drawn on it at several points in my own analysis.

In the archive I most frequently consulted five categories of documents. The *Brüderverzeichnis* (literally translated, "list of brethren") is the organization's central personnel register. In this record are listed the names and vital statistics of the hundreds of men who have worked for the Mission since it opened its seminary in 1815. Included are places of origin, dates of birth and death, and the occupations of each of the missionaries and their fathers. Also listed are the names of the witnesses who attested to each individual's religious conversion and the dates of major events and accomplishments in the missionary's career, such as ordination, postings to various field stations, marriages, births of children, honors, and promotions. Unless otherwise indicated, this document is the source of any basic background information I cite about the individual missionaries. Only men could be ordained as Basel missionaries, and, except for missionaries' wives, women were sent out in comparatively small numbers in the period covered by my research, usually as teachers or nurses. Information about these women is preserved in a smaller and less extensive companion record called the *Schwesternverzeichnis*.

The *Komiteeprotokolle* (Committee Minutes) contain the records of the weekly decision-making meetings of the Mission Committee. These minutes are extensively indexed by the topics discussed in a given meeting, the mission regions involved, and often the individuals who were the subjects of the discussions. The participants in each meeting are identified, and their points of view and the information upon which these views were based are often summarized. The decisions reached are recorded, and, of major importance to the researcher, cross-references are given to supporting documents elsewhere in the archive that bear on the matter at hand. This record, which is unbroken for the entire period covered by my study, was kept only for the reference and benefit of the Committee itself. It was closed to anyone not in the ruling circle of the Mission. Until very recently the minutes were kept in a large safe devoted just to their safekeeping. Because these records were both meticulous and confidential, I have relied very heavily upon them for purposes of reconstructing not only decision making in the organization but the debates and reasoning that lay behind those decisions. In my documentation I have provided the volume number, the date, and the page number (or paragraph number in some of the later volumes that do not show page numbers). With this information the cited passages can be found quickly and reliably.

The *Hausordnung* (House Rules) is a formal document that, in its several editions, sets out the basic organizational constitution of the Mission and its seminary. This charter serves as the best single source on the evolution of official policies, administrative structure, division of labor, rules, and contractual agreements. The first version was written in 1816 by the first Mission inspector, Christian Gottlieb Blumhardt, and is referenced in the normal bibliographic way under his name. Periodic revisions and updates of the *Hausordnung* appeared until the 1950s; when one of these later editions is cited, the reference given in the notes locates the document in the Q-9 series (Rules and Regulations) in the archive.

For each member of the mission community there is a *Personalfasikel* (Personal File) that adds more extensive vital facts, social background data, and autobiographical information to what is recorded in the limited entries of the *Brüderverzeichnis* (with which it shares its numbering sequence). Often included in these files are copies of important correspondence regarding the individual and more complete documentation of the major events, including both honors and disciplinary actions, if any, in his or her career. In many cases there is also a copy of the individual's obituary, which often provides information not available elsewhere in the archives. Finally, substantially all the incoming communication to the Mission House from the overseas field stations was preserved, and copies were made of the outgoing correspondence that left Basel for those outstations. These files (called *Gebietsakten*) are assembled by region; they are the principal source of primary corroborating information for the materials discussed and summarized in the Committee minutes. They contain personal and official letters as well as the missionaries' field notes and quarterly and annual reports. For Ghana the archival reference for incoming correspondence is series D-1. In my references I have provided writers' names, volume numbers (e.g., D-1,3), dates, specific station from which the letter originated (e.g., Akropong, Christiansborg, Ossu), document number, and where appropriate, page numbers. Archive series D-12,2 is a collection of English abstracts, translated and compiled by Hans Debrunner and Paul Jenkins, of many of these letters from Ghana.

Other important primary sources for the study include the regional organizational charters for the areas (such as Africa, China, and India) in which the Mission was active; diaries of some missionaries and their wives; a compilation of the rules and regulations *(Verordnungen und Mitteilungen)* that were issued between the periodic revisions of the more enduring documents such as the *Hausordnung* and the regional charters; publications of the terms of admission to the seminary and contractual obligations that bound missionaries to the organization; an extensive collection of messages and pamphlets circulated among the field stations to inform agents in the field about Mission activities and policies; and the detailed individual instructions *(Instruktionen)* that were given to each person when posted to his or her field assignment. For all these primary archival resources, the footnotes for each chapter provide exact file references that make it possible to locate the specific documents that are cited.

Caught somewhere between the "primary" and "secondary" categories of information are three "in-house" histories, upon which I have drawn extensively, if cautiously. The first of these, *Entstehungsgeschichte der Evangelischen Missionsgesellschaft zu Basel,* is by Albert Ostertag. The second, *Geschichte der Basler Mission, 1815-1899,* is by Paul Eppler. The third and most extensive is *Geschichte der Basler Mission, 1815-1940,* volumes 1-5, begun by Wilhelm Schlatter and finished by Hermann Witschi. Also in this category are a series of didactic biographies of luminary missionaries *(Missionshelden)* and two periodicals published by the Mission for its interested publics and support groups, one called *Message to the Heathen (Der Evangelische Heidenbote)* and the other called *Evangelical Mission Magazine (Evangelische Missionsmagazin).* All are useful sources of information, often drawing on extensive field reports written by missionaries abroad, but because they were compiled and edited in Basel, for the most part for the edification of the larger Mission audience in Europe, they should also be seen as "glosses" that were never disinterested in their point of view.

In this second edition of the book, I have been able to include a number of photographs from the Mission's extensive pictorial archive. The missionaries were encouraged to use photography in their work from very early on, and the result is an extraordinary collection that numbers some 40,000 images. Most of these have been sorted and catalogued and preserved on laser disk in the Mission archive. I have included two dozen of these, taken between 1860 and 1917. Although such a small sampling of this large resource is necessarily somewhat arbitrary, I believe the ones chosen nicely illustrate some of the themes I have stressed in the narrative. I am indebted to Paul Jenkins for his assistance with the descriptions of the pictures.

A Note on Research Strategy

As with many case histories (see the introduction in *A Case for the Case Study,* edited by Joe Feagin, Anthony Orum, and Gideon Sjoberg), this one began with simple curiosity about an intriguing mystery. The disciplined questions entered later. The first time I was shown the Basel Mission Archive I was immediately reminded of Max Weber's preoccupation with the importance of literacy, information, and record keeping in modern organizations. The impulse in the Mission, which came remarkably close to fulfillment, was to note everything of any substance that happened, to record every important deliberation and decision that took place, and to preserve every bit of official and unofficial communication that moved up and down the hierarchy and between Basel and the remote field stations around the world. The mere possibility of reconstructing parts of the organization's past was sufficient to start a growing list of sociological questions. It takes only a very short exposure to the archival repository for certain key facts to become apparent: the emphasis on conformity; the dependency on the faith, zeal, and loyalty of individuals; the intrinsic difficulty, or ambition, of the evangelical enterprise; the troubles and the distinctive personalities that are revealed in the correspondence and in the records of the high-level discussions they provoked; and the persistence for the better part of two centuries of a collective undertaking for which nothing was easy or routine. The coherence of the study emerged from the attempt to stitch these facts together. How can emotional religious commitment be successfully turned into disciplined action? How can hierarchical control be projected over such great distances? Where does creativity come from when conformity is among the highest virtues? Where does cohesiveness come from when participants are expected to keep each other under surveillance in the interest of discipline? How can an organization in which conflict is endemic come to have a history longer than that of most nations? Even more basically, how did the missionaries dare to do what they did, and how did they survive? Once these questions were asked, an exercise in simple sociological nosiness became a study of the "institutional control of religious zeal" and a "case history of organizational contradictions."

These remarks explain my research strategy in a general way, but it is also important to describe my actual ingress into and path of movement through the archival materials. As anyone who has done historical research on organizations can attest, an unfamiliar repository does not at once represent "data" that can be neatly fitted to previously formulated research inquiries. There is no file in the Mission archive labeled "Organizational Contradictions" or "Control of Zeal." It is only with increasing familiarity with the record that heaps of raw material resolve into categories of interpretable information, and the choice of an entry point into such a mass can have an important effect on the way a study subsequently develops. Very early in my research, my attention was drawn to an intriguing set of entries in the Mission's personnel record, the *Brüderverzeichnis*. This document is organized as a grid spreading across the facing pages of a large, folio-sized, bound volume. Rows in the grid represent missionaries, listed in the order of their acceptance into the Mission, and columns represent vital facts about their social origins and careers in the Mission. The very last column is headed "Remarks" *(Bemerkungen)*. As information was added to this amorphous column over the years, the handwritten entries often became crowded and spilled over into the margin. The informality of this information in an otherwise orderly and rather formal document attracted my interest. I found myself scanning it (with a reading glass) to get a sense of the kinds of mundane events that were preserved there.

This casual interest in the "social construction of the record" soon attached itself to the broader questions about organizational control with which I originally approached the investigation. As a case in point, usually found among the miscellany under "Remarks" was the date that each person left the Mission. Words such as *gestorben* (died), *pensioniert* (retired), *ausgetreten* (resigned), and, in a small but noticeable minority of cases, *entlassen* (dismissed) were used to record the manner of leaving. Unpacking the record revealed that to be "entlassen" usually meant departure under less than ideal circumstances, in the sense of being "defrocked" or "cashiered." Considering the investment of scarce resources that each missionary represented, I was curious to know what kinds of offenses would move the leadership to take such a drastic step, and this linked itself to the broader issue of how offenses against the rules were dealt with in general. Rather than beginning with the minutiae of the rules themselves and looking for instances of violations and sanctions, this process works backward from the sanction to the sequence of action that provoked it, and most important, to the private reasoning behind it and the public explanations given out for it. The assumption was that the way sanctions are used by the power structure of an organization is the best clue to the priorities that are actually being pursued "on the ground." Given a dense historical record to work with, doing this kind of interpretive analysis is a major advantage of the case approach.

As if anticipating my initial curiosity about this matter, most of the

Brüderverzeichnis entries indicating dismissal included cross-references to more detailed documentation in other parts of the archives, especially the minutes of the governing Committee, the personal files of the individual missionaries, and the regional correspondence files. By following those references case by case, I was able to reconstruct with remarkable clarity even the dismissals and the collateral troubles to which they were almost inevitably linked. The stories of Riis, Süss, and Schiedt, for example, discussed at length in chapter 4, took shape in just this way. I gradually learned how personal troubles and interpersonal tensions traced a melancholy vein right through the Mission's history. The problems never seemed to go away, yet they never brought the programs of the Mission to a halt. Some of the early conflicts, including cases that resulted in dismissal, involved individuals whose actions violated Mission policy, undermined interpersonal relations, and in the end compromised the organization's ability to address the challenges it had set for itself. The underlying causes of these problems could often be traced to policies the leadership itself had determined to enforce, despite their costs to internal peace and external effectiveness. This discovery in turn led to the question I have raised about organizational contradictions and organizational persistence in the face of those contradictions. How could a group that could not resolve its recurrent internal troubles continue to survive those troubles for so long?

In short, the discovery of specific cases of individual trouble, motivated in part by simple inquisitiveness, converged with and gradually gave shape to more basic sociological questions about organizational discipline, legitimation, and survival. I have explained this component of my research strategy here in order to acknowledge the shifting interplay of data, personal curiosity, and theoretical interest that took place in my thinking. The research did not follow a steady deductive track from opening questions to closing answers, and because of this, no other investigator would be likely to replicate exactly what I have done. A researcher who pursued questions similar to the ones I have raised, however, would not reach conclusions about the Mission that contradict those offered here. In any event, the Mission's archives, while extensive, are a finite, unmoving, and open resource for scholars with the time and energy to make use of them. In the text and notes I have provided sufficient detail about my sources and research procedures to make my tracks through that body of data visible. Those tracks could be followed by anyone with the requisite German skill who wanted to compare his or her reconstructions or interpretations of events with mine.

Bibliography

Addo, Ebenezer Obiri. *Kwame Nkrumah: A Case Study of Religion and Politics in Ghana.* Lanham, Md.: University Press of America, 1997.

Agyemang, Fred. *We Presbyterians: The 150th Anniversary of the Presbyterian Church of Ghana.* Accra: Presbyterian Church of Ghana, Select Publications and Promotions, 1978.

———. *Amu the African: A Study in Vision and Courage.* Accra: Asempa, 1988.

Ajayi, J. F. Ade. *Christian Missions in Nigeria, 1841-1891: The Making of a New Elite.* Evanston, Ill.: Northwestern University Press, 1969.

Amu, Ephraim. *Twenty-Five African Songs in the Twi Language.* London: Sheldon Press, 1932.

Antonio, Robert J. "The Contradiction of Domination and Production in Bureaucracy: The Contribution of Organizational Efficiency to the Decline of the Roman Empire." *American Sociological Review* 44 (December 1977): 95-112.

Archive of the Basel Mission, series D-1, D-4, and D-10.

Archive of the Church Missionary Society, series G/AC, 18/1:476ff. London, 1820-34.

Arends, Siegfried. "'One Piece of Firewood . . .': Life and Work of C. G. Baëta." Ph.D. diss., University of Amsterdam, 1991.

Baëta, C. G., ed. *Christianity in Tropical Africa.* London: Oxford University Press, 1968.

Bainbridge, William Folwell. *Around the World Tour of Christian Missions: A Universal Survey.* 3rd ed. New York: C. R. Blackall and Company, 1882.

Baltzell, E. Digby. *Philadelphia Gentlemen: The Making of a National Upper Class.* New York: Free Press, 1958.

———. *The Protestant Establishment: Aristocracy and Caste in America.* New York: Random House, 1964.

————. *Puritan Boston and Quaker Philadelphia*. New York: Free Press, 1979.

Barnard, Chester I. "Cooperation." In *The Sociology of Organizations: Basic Studies*, edited by Oscar Grusky and George A. Miller, pp. 84-97. New York: Free Press, 1981.

Bartels, F. L. *The Roots of Ghana Methodism*. Cambridge: Cambridge University Press, 1965.

Basel Mission. *175. Jahresbericht der Basler Mission*. 1989.

Bearth, Thomas. "J. G. Christaller: A Holistic View of Language and Culture." In *The Recovery of the West African Past: African Pastors and African History in the Nineteenth Century*, edited by Paul Jenkins, pp. 83-101. Basel: C. C. Reindorf and Samuel Johnson, Basler Afrika Bibliographien, 1998.

Becker, George. "Pietism and Science: A Critique of Robert K. Merton's Hypothesis." *American Journal of Sociology* 89 (March 1984): 1065-90.

————. "The Fallacy of the Received Word: A Reexamination of Merton's Pietism-Science Thesis." *American Journal of Sociology* 90 (March 1986): 1203-18.

————. "Pietism's Confrontation with Enlightenment Rationalism: An Examination of the Relation between Ascetic Protestantism and Science." *Journal for the Scientific Study of Religion* 30 (June 1991): 139-58.

Beidelman, T. O. *Colonial Evangelism: A Socio-historical Study of an East African Mission at the Grassroots*. Bloomington: Indiana University Press, 1982.

Bendix, Reinhard. *Max Weber: An Intellectual Portrait*. Garden City, N.Y.: Doubleday, 1962.

Benson, J. Kenneth. "Organizations: A Dialectical View." *Administrative Science Quarterly* 22 (March 1977): 1-21.

Berinyuu, Abraham A., ed. *History of the Presbyterian Church in Northern Ghana*. Accra: Asempa, 1997.

Beyreuther, Erich. *Geschichte des Pietismus*. Stuttgart: J. F. Steinkopf, 1978.

Blau, Peter. *The Dynamics of Bureaucracy*. Chicago: University of Chicago Press, 1955.

————. *Exchange and Power in Social Life*. New York: Wiley, 1964.

Blumhardt, Christian G. *Hausordnung*. Basel: Basel Mission, 1816.

Boer, Harry R. *A Short History of the Early Church*. Grand Rapids: Eerdmans, 1976.

Borscheid, Peter. "Unternehmer, Arbeiter, Industriekultur." In *Wege in die Welt: Die Industrie im Deutschen Südwesten Seit Ausgang des 18. Jahrhunderts*, edited by Otto Borst, pp. 175-95. Stuttgart: Deutsche Verlags-Anstalt, 1989.

Bottomore, Tom, Laurence Harris, V. G. Kiernan, and Ralph Milliband. *A Dictionary of Marxist Thought*. Cambridge: Harvard University Press, 1983.

Bourdieu, Pierre. *Reproduction in Education, Society, and Culture*. London and Beverly Hills, Calif.: Sage, 1977.

Bourdieu, Pierre, and Jean-Claude Passeron. *Outline of a Theory of Practice*. Cambridge: Cambridge University Press, 1977.

Bowie, Fiona, Deborah Kirkwood, and Shirley Ardener, eds. *Women and Missions: Past and Present.* Providence and Oxford: Berg Publishers, 1993.

Brokensha, David. *Social Change at Larteh, Ghana.* London: Oxford University Press, 1966.

Brouwer, Ruth. *New Women for God: Canadian Presbyterian Women and India Missions, 1876-1914.* Toronto: Toronto University Press, 1990.

Burawoy, Michael. *Manufacturing Consent.* Chicago: University of Chicago Press, 1979.

Burns, Robert I., S.J. "The Missionary Syndrome: Crusader and Pacific Northwest Religious Expansionism." *Comparative Studies in Society and History* 30 (April 1988): 271-85.

Calhoun, Craig. *The Question of Class Struggle.* Chicago: University of Chicago Press, 1982.

Cassirer, Ernst. *The Philosophy of the Enlightenment.* Princeton: Princeton University Press, 1979.

Cecil, Lamar. *The German Diplomatic Service.* Princeton: Princeton University Press, 1976.

Christensen, Torben, and William R. Hutchinson, eds. *Missionary Ideologies in the Imperialist Era: 1880-1920.* Copenhagen: Aros, 1982.

Clarke, Peter B. *West Africa and Christianity.* London: Edward Arnold, 1986.

Cohen, Robin. "From Peasants to Workers in Africa." In *The Political Economy of Contemporary Africa,* edited by Peter C. W. Gutkind and Immanuel Wallerstein, pp. 155-68. Beverly Hills, Calif.: Sage, 1976.

Coleman, Michael C. *Presbyterian Missionary Attitudes toward American Indians, 1837-1893.* Jackson: University Press of Mississippi, 1985.

Collins, Randall. *The Credential Society.* New York: Academic Press, 1979.

————. *Max Weber: A Skeleton Key.* Newbury Park, Calif.: Sage, 1986.

Comaroff, Jean, and John Comaroff. *Of Revelation and Revolution.* Vol. 1: *Christianity, Colonialism, and Consciousness in South Africa.* Chicago: University of Chicago Press, 1991.

Comaroff, John, and Jean Comaroff. *Of Revelation and Revolution.* Vol. 2: *The Dialectics of Modernity on a South African Frontier.* Chicago: University of Chicago Press, 1997.

Dah, Jonas. "The Basel Mission in Cameroon." In *Missionary Ideologies in the Imperialist Era: 1880-1920,* edited by Torben Christensen and William R. Hutchinson, pp. 208-20. Copenhagen: Aros, 1982.

Dahrendorf, Ralf. *Class and Class Conflict in Industrial Society.* Stanford: Stanford University Press, 1959.

Davis, Nanette J., and Bo Anderson. *Social Control: The Production of Deviance in the Modern State.* New York: Irvington, 1983.

Dawe, Alan. "Theories of Social Action." Chapter 10 in *A History of Sociological Analysis,* edited by Tom Bottomore and Robert Nisbet. New York: Basic Books, 1978.

Debrunner, Hans. "The Moses of the Ghana Presbyterian Church." *Ghana Bulletin of Theology* 1, no. 4 (June 1958): 12-18.

Dillenberger, John. *Martin Luther: Selections from His Writings.* Garden City, N.Y.: Anchor Books, 1961.

DiMaggio, Paul, and Walter W. Powell. "The Iron Cage Revisited: Institutional Isomorphism and Collective Rationality in Organizational Fields." *American Sociological Review* 48 (April 1983): 147-60.

Domhoff, G. William. *Who Rules America Now?* Englewood Cliffs, N.J.: Prentice-Hall, 1984.

Dornbusch, Sanford M. "The Military Academy as an Assimilating Institution." *Social Forces* 33 (May 1955): 316-21.

Dubach-Vischer, Marianne. *Mit Boot und Stethoskop: Das Ehepaaar Dr.med. M. & B. Vischer-Mylius in Borneo von 1928 bis 1943.* Basel: Friedrich Reinhardt Verlag, 1998.

du Plessis, J. *The Evangelisation of Pagan Africa.* Cape Town: J. C. Juta and Company, 1929.

Durkheim, Emile. *Suicide.* New York: Free Press, 1951.

———. *The Rules of Sociological Method.* Edited by George E. G. Catlin. 8th ed. Glencoe, Ill.: Free Press, 1964.

Ebaugh, Helen Rose Fuchs. *Out of the Cloister: A Study of Organizational Dilemmas.* Austin: University of Texas Press, 1977.

———. "The Growth and Decline of Catholic Religious Orders of Women Worldwide: The Impact of Women's Opportunity Structures." *Journal for the Scientific Study of Religion* 32 (March 1993): 68-75.

Eberl, Immo. "Die Klosterschüler in Blaubeuren, 1708-1751." In *Blätter für Württembergische Kirchengeschichte* 1977, edited by Gerhard Schäfer and Martin Brecht, pp. 25-101. Stuttgart: Verlag Christian Scheufele, 1977.

———. "Die Klosterschüler in Blaubeuren, 1751-1810." In *Blätter für Württembergische Kirchengeschichte* 1980/81, edited by Gerhard Schäfer and Martin Brecht, pp. 38-142. Stuttgart: Verlag Christian Scheufele, 1980/81.

Eiselin, Tobias. "'Zur Erziehung einer zuverlässigen, Wohl-disziplinierten Streiterschar für den Missionskrieg.' Basler Missionar-ausbildung im 19. Jahrhundert." In *Mission im Kontext,* edited by Werner Ustorf, pp. 47-120. Bremen: Übersee Museum, 1986.

Eppler, Paul. *Geschichte der Basler Mission, 1815-1899.* Basel: Verlag der Missionsbuchhandlung, 1900.

Erikson, Kai. *Wayward Puritans: A Study in the Sociology of Deviance.* New York: Wiley, 1966.

Etzioni, Amitai. *A Comparative Analysis of Complex Organizations.* Rev. ed. New York: Free Press of Glencoe, 1975.

Evangelische Missionsgesellschaft. *175. Jahresbericht der Basler Mission.* Basel: Basel Mission, 1989.

Falk, Peter. *The Growth of the Church in Africa.* Grand Rapids: Zondervan, 1979.

Fanon, Frantz. *The Wretched of the Earth.* New York: Grove Press, 1966.

Faunce, William Herbert Perry. *The Social Aspects of Foreign Missions.* New York: Missionary Education Movement of the United States and Canada, 1914.

Feagin, Joe, Anthony Orum, and Gideon Sjoberg, eds. *A Case for the Case Study.* Chapel Hill: University of North Carolina Press, 1991.

Fischer, Friedrich Hermann. *Der Missionsarzt Rudolf Fisch und die Anfange Medizinischer Arbeit der Basler Mission an der Goldküste (Ghana).* Herzogenrath: Verlag Murken-Altrogge, 1991.

Fischer, Rudolf. *Die Basler Missionsindustrie in Indien, 1850-1923.* Zürich: Verlag Reihe W., 1978.

Fischer, Wolfram. "Staat und Wirtschart im 19. Jahrhundert." In *Wege in die Welt: Die Industrie im Deutschen Südwesten Seit Ausgang des 18. Jahrhunderts,* edited by Otto Borst, pp. 58-106. Stuttgart: Deutsche Verlags-Anstalt, 1989.

Forell, George W. *Christian Social Teachings: A Reader in Christian Social Ethics from the Bible to the Present.* Minneapolis: Augsburg, 1971.

Frenz, Albrecht. *Herman Gundert: Quellen zu Seinem Leben und Werk.* Ulm: Süddeutsche Verlagsgesellschaft, 1991.

Fulbrook, Mary. *Piety and Politics: Religion and the Rise of Absolutism in England, Württemberg, and Prussia.* Cambridge: Cambridge University Press, 1984.

Gewecke, Helga, et al. *Women Carry More Than Half the Burden: Texts from a Workshop on the History of the Basel Mission and Its Partner-Churches in the Twentieth Century.* Basel: Basel Mission, 1996.

Giddens, Anthony. *The Constitution of Society: Outline of the Theory of Structuration.* Cambridge: Polity, 1984.

Gifford, Paul. *African Christianity: Its Public Role.* London: Hurst, 1998.

Gilbert, Michelle. "The Cimmerian Darkness of Intrigue, Queen Mothers, Christianity and Truth in Akuapem History." *Journal of Religion in Africa* 23, no. 1 (1993): 2-43.

———. "The Christian Executioner: Christianity and Chieftaincy as Rivals." *Journal of Religion in Africa* 25, no. 4 (1995): 347-86.

Gminder, Ernst. *Arzt im Busch und Steppe.* Stuttgart: Hippokrates, 1941.

Gouldner, Alvin W. *Patterns of Industrial Bureaucracy.* Glencoe, Ill.: Free Press, 1954.

Gove, Walter. "The Labelling Perspective: An Overview." In *The Labelling of Deviance: Evaluating a Perspective,* edited by Walter Gove, pp. 3-20. Beverly Hills, Calif.: Sage, 1975.

Graham, W. Fred. *The Constructive Revolutionary: John Calvin and His Socioeconomic Impact.* Atlanta: John Knox, 1978.

Gramsci, Antonio. *Selections from the Prison Notebooks.* Edited by Quintin Hoare and Geoffrey Nowell Smith. London: Laurence and Wishart, 1971.

Gray, Richard. *Black Christians and White Missionaries.* New Haven: Yale University Press, 1990.

Groves, C. P. *The Planting of Christianity in Africa.* Vol. 1, 1948; vol. 2, 1954; vol. 3, 1955; vol. 4, 1958. London: Lutterworth, 1948-58.

Gründer, Horst. *Christliche Mission und Deutscher Imperialismus, 1884-1914.* Paderborn: Ferdinand Schöningh, 1982.

————. "Die Basler Mission und die Land- und Arbeiterfrage am Kamerunberg." *Texte und Dockumente* (herausgegeben durch die Basler Mission) 7 (November 1986): 11-25.

Haas-Lill, Waltraud. "Missionsgeschichte aus der Sicht der Frau: Die Missionarin in der Geschichte der Basler Mission." *Texte und Dokumente* (herausgegeben durch die Basler Mission) 12 (May 1989): 11-30.

————. *Erlitten und Erstritten: Der Befreiungsweg von Frauen in der Basler Mission 1816-1966.* Basel: Basileia Verlag, 1994.

Habermas, Jürgen. *Legitimation Crisis.* Boston: Beacon Press, 1975.

Haenger, Peter. *Slaves and Slave-holders on the Gold Coast.* Basel: P. Schlettwein Publishing, 2000.

Hahn, Joachim, and Hans Mayer. *Das Evangelische Stift in Tübingen: Geschichte und Gegenwart-Zwischen Weltgeist und Frömmigkeit.* Stuttgart: Konrad Theiss Verlag, 1985.

Hallden, Erik. *The Culture Policy of the Basel Mission in the Cameroons, 1886-1905.* Lund: Berlingska Boktryckeriet, 1968.

Hannan, Michael T., and John H. Freeman. "The Population Ecology of Organizations." *American Journal of Sociology* 82 (March 1977): 929-64.

Hartenstein, Karl. *Anibue, die 'Neue Zeit' auf der Goldküste und unsere Missionsaufgabe.* Basel: Evang. Missionsverlag, 1932.

Heinecken, Friedli. "When Grandfather Was a Young Man; or, A Missionary in the Making." Manuscript. 1938.

Heise, David R. "Prefatory Findings in the Sociology of Missions." *Journal for the Scientific Study of Religion* 65, no. 1 (April 1967): 49-58.

Hesse, Johannes. *Joseph Josenhans: Ein Lebensbild.* Calw and Stuttgart: Verlag der Vereinsbuchhandlung, 1895.

Hill, Patricia R. *The World Their Household: The American Woman's Foreign Mission Movement and Cultural Transformation, 1870-1920.* Ann Arbor: University of Michigan Press, 1985.

Hirschmann, Albert O. *Exit, Voice, and Loyalty.* Cambridge: Harvard University Press, 1970.

Hobsbawm, E. J. *The Age of Revolution: Europe, 1789-1848.* London: ABACUS (Sphere Books Ltd.), 1977.

Hoffmann, Robert. "Die Neupietistische Missionsbewegung Vor dem Hintergrund des Sozialen Wandels um 1800." *Archiv für Kulturgeschichte* 59, no. 2 (1977): 445-70.

Hoffmann, Wilhelm. *Eilf Jahre in der Mission.* Stuttgart: J. F. Steinkopf, 1853.

Hollister, C. Warren. *Medieval Europe: A Short History.* New York: Knopf, 1982.

Höpfl, Harro, ed. *Luther and Calvin on Secular Authority*. Cambridge: Cambridge University Press, 1991.

Hopkins, Anthony C. *An Economic History of West Africa*. New York: Columbia University Press, 1973.

Huber, Mary, and Nancy Lutkehaus, eds. *Gendered Missions: Women and Men in Missionary Discourse and Practice*. Ann Arbor: University of Michigan Press, 1999.

Hunter, Floyd. *Community Power Structure*. Chapel Hill: University of North Carolina Press, 1953.

Hunter, Jane. T*he Gospel of Gentility: American Women Missionaries in Turn-of-the-Century China*. New Haven: Yale University Press, 1984.

————. "The Home and the World: The Missionary Message of U.S. Domesticity." In *Women's Work for Women: Missionaries and Social Change in Asia*, edited by Leslie A. Flemming, pp. 159-66. Boulder, Colo.: Westview, 1989.

Jenkins, Paul. "A Comment on M. P. Frempong's History of the Presbyterian Church at Bompata." *Ghana Notes and Queries* 12 (1972): 23-27.

————. "The Anglican Church in Ghana 1905-1924." *Transactions of the Historical Society of Ghana* 15 (1974): 23-39, 177-200.

————. "Villagers as Missionaries: Wuerttemberg Pietism as a Nineteenth-Century Missionary Movement." *Missiology: An International Review* 8 (October 1980): 425-32.

————. "Class Analysis and the Role of the Basel Mission Committee in the Nineteenth Century." *Nachrichten der Basler Afrika Bibliographien* 5 (1981): 51-55.

————. "Sozialer Hintergrund und Mission: Pietismus im Schwaebischen Dorf und die Wirkung der Basler Mission in Afrika im 19. Jh." Paper presented to the Vereinigung von Afrikanisten in Deutschland Conference, Hannover, June 1984.

————. "Die Basler Mission im kolonialen Spannungsfeld Indien." *Traverse* (1998): 41-55.

————. "The Church Missionary Society and the Basel Mission: An Early Experiment in Inter-European Cooperation." In *The Church Mission Society and World Christianity, 1799-1999*, edited by Kevin Ward and Brian Stanley, pp. 43-65. Studies in the History of Christian Missions. Grand Rapids: Eerdmans, 2000.

————, ed. *The Recovery of the West African Past: African Pastors and African History in the Nineteenth Century*. Basel: C. C. Reindorf and Samuel Johnson, Basler Afrika Bibliographien, 1998.

Johnson, Doyle Paul. "Dilemmas of Charismatic Leadership: The Case of the People's Temple." *Sociological Analysis* 40 (winter 1979): 315-23.

Jones, Raymond A. *The British Diplomatic Service, 1815-1914*. Gerrards Cross: Colin Smythe, 1983.

Kanter, Rosabeth Moss. *Communes: Creating and Managing the Collective Life.* New York: Harper, 1973.

Katz, Jack. "Deviance, Charisma, and Rule-Defined Behavior." *Social Problems* 20 (fall 1972): 186-202.

Kieser, Alfred. "Organizational, Institutional, and Societal Evolution: Medieval Craft Guilds and the Genesis of Formal Organizations." *Administrative Science Quarterly* 34 (December 1989): 540-64.

Klandermans, Bert. "Mobilization and Participation: Social-Psychological Expansions of Resource Mobilization Theory." *American Sociological Review* 49 (October 1984): 583-600.

Koelle, Sigismund W. *African Native Literature, or Proverbs, Tales, Fables, and Historical Fragments in the Kanuri or Bornu Language.* London: Church Missionary House, Salisbury Square, 1854.

————. *Grammar of the Bornu or Kanuri Language.* London: Church Missionary House, Salisbury Square, 1854.

Konrad, Dagmar. *Missionsbräute: Pietistinnen des 19. Jahrhunderts in der Basler Mission.* Inauguraldissertation zur Erlangung des Grades eines Doktors der Philosophie, Phipps-Universität Marburg, 1999.

Krüdener, Barbara Juliane, Freifrau von. *Valérie.* Introduction, notes, and commentary by Michel Mercier. Paris: Klincksieck, 1974.

Langer, Eric D., and Robert H. Jackson. "Colonial and Republican Missions Compared: The Cases of Alta California and Southeastern Bolivia." *Comparative Studies in Society and History* 30 (April 1988): 286-311.

Latourette, Kenneth Scott. *A History of Christian Missions in China.* New York: Macmillan, 1929.

Lehmann, Hartmut. *Pietismus und Weltliche Ordnung in Württemberg von 17. bis zum 20. Jahrhundert.* Stuttgart: W. Kohlhammer Verlag, 1969.

Lichtheim, George. *Marxism: An Historical and Critical Study.* New York: Columbia University Press, 1982.

Maduro, Otto. "New Marxist Approaches to the Relative Autonomy of Religion." *Sociological Analysis* 38, no. 4 (1977): 359-67.

Magubane, Bernard. "The Evolution of the Class Structure in Africa." In *The Political Economy of Contemporary Africa,* edited by Peter C. W. Gutkind and Immanuel Wallerstein, pp. 169-97. Beverly Hills, Calif.: Sage, 1976.

Marx, Karl. "The Class Struggles in France." In *Karl Marx: Selected Writings,* edited by David McLellan, pp. 286-97. Oxford: Oxford University Press, 1977.

————. "The Eighteenth Brumaire of Louis Bonaparte." In *Karl Marx: Selected Writings,* edited by David McLellan, pp. 300-325. Oxford: Oxford University Press, 1977.

McAdam, Doug, John D. McCarthy, and Mayer N. Zald. "Social Movements." In *Handbook of Sociology,* edited by Neil J. Smelser, pp. 695-738. Newbury Park, Calif.: Sage, 1989.

McCaskie, T. C. "Social Rebellion and the Inchoate Rejection of History — Some

Reflections on the Career of Opon Asibe Tutu." *Asante Seminar* 4 (1976): 34-38.

———. "Asante and Ga: The History of a Relationship." In *The Recovery of the West African Past: African Pastors and African History in the Nineteenth Century,* edited by Paul Jenkins, pp. 135-53. Basel: C. C. Reindorf and Samuel Johnson, Basler Afrika Bibliographien, 1998.

McGuire, Meredith B. *Religion: The Social Context.* 2nd ed. Belmont, Calif.: Wadsworth, 1987.

McLoughlin, William. *Champions of the Cherokees.* Princeton: Princeton University Press, 1990.

Mechanic, David. "Sources of Power of Lower Participants in Complex Organizations." *Administrative Science Quarterly* 7 (December 1962): 349-62.

Meier, Fritz. *Basler Heimatgeschichte.* Basel: Buchdruckerei und Verlagsbuchhandlung AG, 1974.

Merton, Robert K. "Puritanism, Pietism, and Science." Chapter 23 in *Social Theory and Social Structure,* by Robert K. Merton. New York: Free Press, 1968.

———. *Social Theory and Social Structure.* New York: Free Press, 1968.

———. "The Fallacy of the Latest Word: The Case of 'Pietism and Science.'" *American Journal of Sociology* 89 (March 1984): 1091-1121.

Meyer, John W., and Brian Rowan. "Institutionalized Organizations: Formal Structure as Myth and Ceremony." *American Journal of Sociology* 83 (November 1977): 340-63.

Meyer, John W., and W. Richard Scott, eds. *Organizational Environments: Ritual and Rationality.* Beverly Hills, Calif.: Sage, 1983.

Meyer, Marshall, and Lynne Zucker. *Permanently Failing Organizations.* Beverly Hills, Calif.: Sage, 1988.

Middleton, John. "One Hundred and Fifty Years of Christianity in a Ghanaian Town." *Africa* 53, no. 3 (1983): 2-18.

Miller, Jon. "Class Collaboration for the Sake of Religion: Elite Control and Social Mobility in a Nineteenth-Century Colonial Mission." *Journal for the Scientific Study of Religion* 29 (March 1990): 35-51.

———. "Institutionalized Contradictions: Trouble in a Colonial Mission." *Organization Studies* 12, no. 3 (1991): 337-64.

———. "Missions, Social Change, and Resistance to Authority: Notes toward an Understanding of the Relative Autonomy of Religion." *Journal for the Scientific Study of Religion* 32 (March 1993): 29-50.

———. "Politics, Economics, and the International Missionary Movement." In *The Encylopedia of Politics and Religion,* edited by Robert Wuthnow. Washington, D.C.: Congressional Quarterly Books Division, 1998.

Mills, C. Wright. *The Power Elite.* New York: Oxford University Press, 1956.

———. *The Sociological Imagination.* New York: Oxford University Press, 1959.

Mitchison, Wendy. "Canadian Women and Church Missionary Societies in the

Nineteenth Century: A Step towards Independence." *Atlantis: A Women's Studies Journal* 2, no. 2 (spring 1977): 57-75.

Mobley, Harris W. *The Ghanaian's Image of the Missionary: An Analysis of the Published Critiques of Christian Missionaries by Ghanaians, 1897-1965*. Leiden: E. J. Brill, 1970.

Moorhouse, Geoffrey. *The Missionaries*. Philadelphia: Lippincott, 1973.

Morgan, Gareth. *Images of Organization*. Beverly Hills, Calif.: Sage, 1997.

Murray, Jocelyn. *Proclaim the Good News: A Short History of the Church Missionary Society*. London: Hodder and Stoughton, 1985.

Neill, Stephen. *A History of Christian Missions*. 1st ed. London: Penguin Books, 1964.

————. *A History of Christian Missions*. 2nd ed. Revised by Owen Chadwick. London: Penguin Books, 1986.

Neitz, Mary Jo. *Charisma and Community: A Study of Religious Commitment within the Charismatic Renewal*. New Brunswick, N.J.: Transaction Books, 1987.

Newcomb, Rev. Harvey. *Cyclopedia of Missions*. New York: Scribner, 1854.

Odamtten, S. K. *The Missionary Factor in Ghana's Development up to the 1880s*. Accra: Waterville Publishing House, 1978.

Oliver, Roland. *The Missionary Factor in East Africa*. 2nd ed. London: Longmans, 1965.

Osafo, Ernest A. "Der Beitrag der Basler Mission zur Wirtschaftlichen Entwicklung Ghanas von 1828 bis zum Ersten Weitkreig." Ph.D. diss., Economics and Social Science Faculty, University of Cologne, 1972.

Ostertag, Albert. *Entstehungsgeschichte der Evangelischen Missionsgesellschaft zu Basel*. Basel: Verlag des Missionshauses, 1865.

Parsons, Talcott. *Societies: Evolutionary and Comparative Perspectives*. Englewood Cliffs, N.J.: Prentice-Hall, 1966.

Parsons, Talcott, and Edward Shils, eds. *Toward a General Theory of Action*. New York: Harper Torchbooks, 1951.

Piggin, Stuart. "The Social Background, Motivation, and Training of British Protestant Missionaries to India, 1789-1858." Ph.D. diss., King's College, University of London, 1974.

————. *Making Evangelical Missionaries, 1789-1858*. London: Sutton Courtenay Press, 1984.

Portes, Alejandro, and Julia Sensenbrenner. "Embeddedness and Immigration: Notes on the Social Determinants of Economic Action." *American Journal of Sociology* 98, no. 6 (May 1993): 1320-50.

Powell, Walter W., and Paul DiMaggio, eds. *The New Institutionalism in Organizational Analysis*. Chicago: University of Chicago Press, 1991.

Predelli, Line Nyhagen. *Contested Patriarchy and Missionary Feminism: The Norwegian Missionary Society in Nineteenth Century Norway and Madagascar*. Lewiston, N.Y.: Edwin Mellen Press, forthcoming.

Bibliography

Predelli, Line Nyhagen, and Jon Miller. "Piety and Patriarchy: Contested Gender Regimes in Nineteenth-Century Colonial Missions." In *Gendered Missions: Women and Men in Missionary Discourse and Practice*, edited by Mary Huber and Nancy Lutkehaus, pp. 67-111. Ann Arbor: University of Michigan Press, 1999.

Prempeh, Samuel. "The Basel and Bremen Missions in the Gold Coast and Togoland, 1914-1926: A Study in Protestant Missions and the First World War." Ph.D. diss., University of Edinburgh, 1977.

Prodolliet, Simone. *Wider die Schamlosigkeit und das Elend der Heidnischen Weiber: Die Basler FrauenMission und der Export des Europäischen Frauenideals in die Kolonien.* Zürich: Limmat Verlag, 1987.

Ragin, Charles C. *The Comparative Method: Moving beyond Qualitative and Quantitative Strategies.* Berkeley: University of California Press, 1987.

Reed, Michael I. "The Problem of Human Agency in Organizational Analysis." *Organization Studies* 9, no. 1 (1988): 33-47.

Reindorf, Rev. Carl Christian. *History of the Gold Coast and Asante: Based on Traditions and Historical Facts, Comprising a Period of More than Three Centuries, from about 1500 to 1860.* Basel: Missionsbuchhandlung, 1895.

Ritschl, Albrecht. *Three Essays.* Philadelphia: Fortress, 1972.

Robert, Dana L. *American Women in Mission: A Social History of Their Thought and Practice.* Macon, Ga.: Mercer University Press, 1997.

Roof, Wade Clark, ed. *World Order and Religion.* Albany: State University of New York Press, 1991.

Rose, Susan D. "Women Warriors: The Negotiation of Gender in a Charismatic Community." *Sociological Analysis* 48, no. 3 (fall 1987): 245-58.

Rothschild, Joyce, and J. Allen Whitt. *The Cooperative Workplace: Potentials and Dilemmas of Organizational Democracy and Participation.* Cambridge: Cambridge University Press, 1986.

Saayman, Willem. "Christian Keysser Revisited." In *Perspectives in Theology and Mission from South Africa: Signs of the Times,* edited by Daryl M. Balia. Lewiston, N.Y.: Edwin Mellen Press, 1993.

Sanneh, Lamin. "The Yogi and the Commissar: Christian Missions and the New World Order in Africa." In *World Order and Religion,* edited by Wade Clark Roof, pp. 173-92. Albany: State University of New York Press, 1991.

Sarasin, Phillip. *Stadt der Bürger: Struktureller Wandel und Bürgerliche Lebenswelt, Basel 1870-1900.* Basel and Frankfurt am Main: Helbing und Lichtenhahn, 1990.

Scharfe, Martin. *Die Religion des Volkes: Kleine Kultur- und Sozialgeschichte des Pietismus.* Gütersloh: Gütersloher Verlagshaus Gerd Mohn, 1980.

Scherer, Ross P. "A New Typology for Organizations: Market, Bureaucracy, Clan, and Mission, with Application to American Denominations." *Journal for the Scientific Study of Religion* 27 (December 1988): 475-98.

Schlatter, Wilhelm. *Geschichte der Basler Mission, 1815-1915*. Vols. 1-3. Basel: Verlag der Basler Missionsbuchhandlung, 1916.

———. *Geschichte der Basler Mission, 1915-1919*. Vol. 4. Revised by Hermann Witschi from a manuscript by Wilhelm Schlatter. Basel: Verlag der Basler Missionsbuchhandlung, 1965.

Schluchter, Wolfgang. *The Rise of Western Rationalism: Max Weber's Developmental History*. Berkeley: University of California Press, 1981.

Schmid, Carol L. *Conflict and Consensus in Switzerland*. Berkeley: University of California Press, 1981.

Schrenk, Elias. "What Is to Become of the Gold Coast?" Unpublished pamphlet in English, dated January 26, 1865.

Schumacher, E. F. *Small Is Beautiful*. London: Blond and Briggs, 1973.

Schweizer, Peter. *Survivors on the Gold Coast, the Basel Missionaries in Colonial Ghana, with a Foreword by His Majesty Otumfuo Osei Tutu II, the Asantehene*. Accra: Smartline Publishing, 2000.

Scott, W. Richard. "Introduction: From Technology to Environment." In *Organizational Environments: Ritual and Rationality*, edited by John W. Meyer and W. Richard Scott, pp. 13-20. Beverly Hills, Calif.: Sage, 1983.

———. *Organizations: Rational, Natural, and Open Systems*. 4th ed. Englewood Cliffs, N.J.: Prentice-Hall, 1998.

Selznick, Philip. *TVA and the Grass Roots*. Berkeley: University of California Press, 1949.

———. "Institutional Vulnerability in Mass Society." *American Journal of Sociology* 56 (January 1951): 320-31.

Simensen, Jarle, ed. *Norwegian Missions in African History*. Vol. 1. Oxford: Oxford University Press, 1986.

Simensen, Jarle, with Vidar Gynnild. "Norwegian Missionaries in the Nineteenth Century: Organizational Background, Social Profile and World View." In *Norwegian Missions in African History*, edited by Jarle Simensen, 1:11-57. Oxford: Oxford University Press, 1986.

Skocpol, Theda, ed. *Vision and Method in Historical Sociology*. Cambridge: Cambridge University Press, 1984.

Smelser, Neil J., ed. *Handbook of Sociology*. Newbury Park, Calif.: Sage, 1989.

Smith, Noel. *The Presbyterian Church of Ghana, 1835-1960 — a Younger Church in a Changing Society*. Accra: Ghana Universities Press, 1966.

Snow, David A., E. Burke Rocheford, Jr., Stephen K. Wordon, and Robert D. Benford. "Frame Alignment Processes, Micromobilization, and Movement Participation." *American Sociological Review* 51 (August 1986): 464-81.

Stähelin, Ernst. *Die Christentumsgesellschaft in der Zeit von der Erweckung bis zur Gegenwart*. Basel: Friedrich Reinhardt Verlag, 1974.

Staw, Barry M., and Jerry Ross. "Understanding Behavior in Escalation Situations." *Science* 246 (October 1989): 216-20.

Steiner, P. *Auf Einsamen Pfaden.* Missionshelden IV. Basel: Basel Missionsbuchhandlung, 1906.

Stinchcombe, Arthur. "Bureaucratic and Craft Administration of Production: A Comparative Study." *Administrative Science Quarterly* 4 (September 1959): 168-87.

————. "Social Structure and Organizations." In *Handbook of Organizations*, edited by James G. March, pp. 142-93. Chicago: Rand McNally, 1965.

Thorne, Susan. *Congregational Missions and the Making of an Imperial Culture in Nineteenth-Century England.* Stanford: Stanford University Press, 1999.

————. "Missionary-Imperial Feminism." In *Gendered Missions: Women and Men in Missionary Discourse and Practice*, edited by Mary Huber and Nancy Lutkehaus, pp. 39-65. Ann Arbor: University of Michigan Press, 1999.

Tilly, Charles. *As Sociology Meets History.* New York: Academic Press, 1981.

Troeltsch, Ernst. *The Social Teaching of the Christian Churches.* Vol. 2. New York: Macmillan, 1981.

Tschudi-Barbatti, Beatrice. "Die Halbbatzen-Kollekte: Ein Kapitel aus der Finanzgeschichte der Basler Mission." Lizentiatsarbeit, Philosophische Fakultät 1, University of Zürich, 1991.

Tufuoh, I. "Relations between Christian Missions, European Administrations, and Traders in the Gold Coast, 1828-1874." In *Christianity in Tropical Africa*, edited by C. G. Baëta, pp. 34-60. London: Oxford University Press, 1968.

Türler, Heinrich, Marcel Godet, and Victor Attinger. *Historisch-biographisches Lexikon der Schweiz.* Herausgegeben mit der Empfehlung der Allgemeinen Geschichtsforschenden Gesellschaft der Schweiz. 8 vols. Neuenburg: Administration des Historisch-Biographischen Lexikons der Schweiz, Verlagsanstalt Victor Attinger, 1921-34.

Ustorf, Werner. *Mission im Kontext.* Bremen: Obersee Museum, 1986.

van den Broek, Atze. *Simon Süss: A Difficult Visionary.* Pamphlet. Accra: Presbyterian Church of Ghana, 1984.

Vogelsanger, Cornelia M. R. *Pietismus und Afrikanische Kultur an der GoldKüste: Die Einstellung der Basler Mission zur Haussklaverei.* Zürich: A. Wohlgemuth Druck, 1977.

Waldburger, Andreas. *Missionare und Moslem.* Basel: Basileja Verlag, 1982.

Walker, Williston, Richard A. Norris, David W. Lotz, and Robert T. Handy. *A History of the Christian Church.* 4th ed. New York: Scribner, 1985.

Wallerstein, Immanuel. *The Road to Independence.* Paris: Mouton and Company, 1964.

Wanner, Gustav Adolf. *Die Basler Handels-Gesellschaft 1859-1959.* Basel: privately printed, 1959.

Ward, Kevin, and Brian Stanley, eds. *The Church Mission Society and World Christianity, 1799-1999.* Studies in the History of Christian Missions. Grand Rapids: Eerdmans, 2000.

Warner, R. Stephen. *New Wine in Old Wineskins: Evangelicals and Liberals in a Small-Town Church.* Berkeley: University of California Press, 1988.

Weber, Max. *From Max Weber: Essays in Sociology.* Edited by Hans Gerth and C. Wright Mills. New York: Oxford University Press, 1946.

———. *The Methodology of the Social Sciences.* New York: Free Press, 1949.

———. *The Protestant Ethic and the Spirit of Capitalism.* New York: Scribner, 1958.

———. *The Sociology of Religion.* Boston: Beacon Press, 1963.

———. *Economy and Society.* Berkeley: University of California Press, 1978.

Werking, Richard H. *The Master Architects: Building the United States Foreign Service.* Lexington: University of Kentucky Press, 1977.

Wesleyan Methodist Missionary Society. *WMMS Reports. Vol. 7, 1838-1840.* London: P. P. Thoms, 1840.

———. *WMMS Reports. Vol. 33, 1913-1914.* London: P. P. Thoms, 1914.

Wilke, A. W. "An Attempt to Conserve the Work of the Basel Mission on the Gold Coast." *International Review of Mission* 9 (January 1920): 86-94.

Willer, David. "Max Weber's Missing Authority Type." *Sociological Inquiry* 37 (1967): 231-39.

Williams, Cecil Peter. "The Recruitment and Training of Overseas Missionaries in England between 1850 and 1900: With Special Reference to the Records of the Church Missionary Society, the Wesleyan Methodist Missionary Society, the London Missionary Society, and the China Inland Mission." Master's thesis, University of Bristol, 1976.

Willis, Paul. *Learning to Labor.* New York: Columbia University Press, 1981.

Witschi, Hermann. *Geschichte der Basler Mission, 1920-1940.* Vol. 5. Basel: Basileia Verlag, 1970.

Wolf, Eric, ed. *Religious Regimes and State-Formation: Perspectives from European Ethnology.* Albany: State University of New York Press, 1991.

Wood, James R. *Leadership in Voluntary Organizations: The Controversy over Social Action in Protestant Churches.* New Brunswick, N.J.: Rutgers University Press, 1981.

Wuthnow, Robert. "International Realities: Bringing the Global Picture into Focus." In *World Order and Religion,* edited by Wade Clark Roof, pp. 19-37. Albany: State University of New York Press, 1991.

Wyss, Edmund. *Die Soziale Politik des Konservativen Bürgertums in Basel (1833-1875).* Weinfelden: Buchdruckerei Neuenschwander, 1948.

Yates, Timothy. *Christian Mission in the Twentieth Century.* Cambridge: Cambridge University Press, 1994.

Young, Ed. "On the Naming of the Rose: Interests and Multiple Meanings as Elements of Organizational Culture." *Organization Studies* 10, no. 2 (1989): 187-206.

Zablocki, Benjamin. *Alienation and Charisma: A Study of Contemporary American Communes.* New York: Free Press, 1980.

Bibliography

————. *The Joyful Community: An Account of the Bruderhof.* Chicago: University of Chicago Press, 1980.

Zald, Mayer N., and John D. McCarthy, eds. *The Dynamics of Social Movements: Resource Mobilization, Social Control, and Tactics.* Cambridge: Winthrop, 1979.

Zaret, David. *The Heavenly Contract: Ideology and Organization in Pre-revolutionary Puritanism.* Chicago: University of Chicago Press, 1985.

Zucker, Lynne G. "Institutional Theories of Organization." *Annual Review of Sociology* 13 (1987): 443-64.

Index

Accra, Ghana, 195n, 196n

Addo, Ebenezer Obiri, 215n

Adjayi, J. F. A., 80

Adjei, Ako, 29

Admission criteria, 59n, 59-60, 83, 93-94, 123

Africa, West: and colonialism, 16-17, 18-20, 19n, 20n, 192; culture of, 16, 17-18; divisions of labor and class, 7-8; and domestic slavery, 147-49; elective affinities and European beliefs, 185; European racism and assumed superiority, 58n, 124n, 124-25, 141-51, 147n, 181; history of missions in, 14-15, 18n, 18-21, 19n, 80; Mission strategies aimed at, 15-16, 52; and religion of missionaries, 20-21, 22-23; and World War I, 15, 19n, 199. *See also* Converts; Gold Coast (Ghana); Impact of Mission; Relationships between missionaries and natives

Agogo, Ghana, 202, 203

Agrarian ideal: of Lutheranism, 89, 99-100, 144; social ideal and authority, 99-100, 189; and traditional way of life, xiv, 52-53, 89, 99-100; and village communities patterned on, xiv, 16-17, 80, 100

Agyemang, Fred, 26, 29

Akropong (Akuropon) community, 80, 130, 136, 197n, 198, 202, 204, 213-14, 217

Akwapim, Ghana, 214, 214n

American missionary movement, x, xi, 50

American Women in Mission (Roberts), 188

Amu, Ephraim, 204, 213, 214n, 214-15, 215n

Anderson, Bo, 6

Anibue (Hartenstein), 203, 219

Antonio, Robert, 109n

Archives of Basel Mission: and author's sociological study, xv-xvi, 2, 33, 223-26, 228; and children, 66-67; Committee members in, 39; deaths, 21; and *Hausordnung* (charter), 105-8, 225; and *Komiteeprotokolle* (Committee Minutes), 224-25; and marriages, 63; number of agents, 25; origins of recruits, 47-48; personnel records (the *Brüderverzeichnis*), 21, 25, 47-48, 50, 63, 224, 225; women, 53; and Zimmermann, 150

Arlt, Veit, 201n, 216n, 217n

Asante, 198, 202, 203, 222

Auf Einsamen Pfaden (On Lonely Pathways) (Süss), 140

Authority. *See* Discipline and authority

247

tive affinities, xvi, 3-4; on "enthusiastic" movements, 35, 36; on evolution of organizational authority, 189; on forms of imperative control, 8-9, 85-88; and "historical accidents," 4, 180; "instrumental rationality" and "value rationality," 169; on interaction among elites, 73; methodological strategy of, 2-4; portrait of early capitalists, 40; and Protestant ethic, xv, 3, 8, 76; and social architecture of institutions, 84-85; as theorist of class dynamics, 185-86; on those vulnerable to missionary endeavors, 49

Werking, Richard H., 126n

Wesleyan Methodist Missionary Society, 46-47, 66n

Wesleyans, 20n, 22n, 27n, 91n

West Indian Mission volunteers, 197; Mulgrave, 23, 145; and Riis, 130n, 130-31, 132-33, 133n, 134, 135

Whitt, Alan, 6

Widmann, Johann, 133n, 142

Wilkie, A. W., 200, 219n

Williams, Peter, 46-47, 57

Willis, Paul, 121

Women: Committee policies for contact with, 61; deaths of, 22n; experiences in missions, 187-89; female children of early missionaries, 68-69; importance of Mission work of, 25n, 25-26; as indispensable to Christian communities, 62; marriage of missionaries and, 62-63; ordained missionaries, 25; and Pietist worldview, 62; post-War Mission initiatives regarding, 203, 203n; scholarship on missionary movements of, 188; social gains as missionaries, 71, 71n, 188; social origins of, 53, 63-64, 64n, 188; wives, 22n, 25n, 25-26, 62-63, 71, 71n, 197n

Women and Missions (Bowie), 188

Women's Teacher Training College (Agogo), 203

Wood, James, 6, 8, 150n, 174

World War I: and British control of West African territories, 15, 19n, 199; and interruption of Mission efforts, xiii, 15,

26, 34, 70-71, 199-200, 210, 218; as pivotal episode in history of Mission, 196, 199-200, 218

World War I, post, 199-205, 209-21; and changes in Mission, 200, 218-21; impact of Mission in Ghana, 209-17; Mission changes in Europe, 218-21; Mission leadership policies, 220-21; Mission's return to Gold Coast, 28, 199-200, 201n, 201-4, 202n; and Presbyterian Church of Ghana, 200-205; tensions and conflicts, 203-4

World War II and post-War, 205-7, 220-21

Wuhrmann, Anna, 46n

Württemberg, Germany, xii, 13, 41-42, 48, 64, 77-78, 98, 99, 105; recruits from, 48; and upward mobility, 64, 77-78

Wuthnow, Robert, 104

Yates, Timothy, xi

Young, Ed, 37

Zablocki, Benjamin, 6

Zald, Mayer, 6

Zeal, 1-2, 6, 183

Ziegenbalg, Bartholomäus, x

Zimmermann, Johannes: admission autobiography, 59, 77; appreciation of African culture, 143-45, 148; challenges to interracial marriages, 150-51; as challenge to Mission authority, 149-50; charismatic traits of, 153; and domestic slavery, 147-49, 150; on liberal European thinking, 96-97; life changes as result of joining Mission, 77-78; marriage appeals to Committee, 101, 146n, 146-47; marriage to Mulgrave, 145-47, 150, 187; and Mission's "official" ideas about African culture, 141-51; on personal freedom, 116; on race relations and hierarchical distance, 143-44; and Riis and Süss, 138n, 141, 150, 153; as strategic deviant, 128-29, 141-51, 153, 163, 170, 172

Zucker, Lynne, 184

Zürcher, A. W., 200